Genital Cutting and
Transnational Sisterhood

Genital Cutting and Transnational Sisterhood

Disputing U.S. Polemics

EDITED BY STANLIE M. JAMES
AND CLAIRE C. ROBERTSON

University of Illinois Press

URBANA AND CHICAGO

Library of Congress Cataloging-in-Publication Data
Genital cutting and transnational sisterhood : disputing U.S. polemics /
edited by Stanlie M. James and Claire C. Robertson.
p.   cm.
Includes bibliographical references and index.
ISBN 0-252-02741-8 (cloth : alk. paper)
1. Female circumcision. 2. Infibulation. 3. Clitoridectomy.
4. Feminist theory—Africa. 5. Feminist theory—United States.
I. James, Stanlie M. (Stanlie Myrise) II. Robertson, Claire C., 1944– .
GN484.G46   2002
392.1'4—dc21   2001005763

Contents

Prologue: Position Paper on Clitoridectomy and Infibulation, Women's Caucus of the African Studies Association *1*

Introduction: Reimaging Transnational Sisterhood *5*
Stanlie M. James and Claire C. Robertson

1. Searching for "Voices": Feminism, Anthropology, and the Global Debate over Female Genital Operations *17*
   Christine J. Walley

2. Getting beyond the Ew! Factor: Rethinking U.S. Approaches to African Female Genital Cutting *54*
   Claire C. Robertson

3. Listening to Other(ed) Voices: Reflections around Female Genital Cutting *87*
   Stanlie M. James

4. Female Genital Surgeries: Eradication Measures at the Western Local Level—A Cautionary Tale *114*
   Isabelle R. Gunning

5. "Cultural Practice" or "Reconstructive Surgery"? U.S. Genital Cutting, the Intersex Movement, and Medical Double Standards *126*
   Cheryl Chase

Appendix: Advocacy Organizations Opposed to Female
Genital Cutting   *153*

Suggested Reading and Films   *159*

Contributors   *163*

Index   *165*

Prologue:
Position Paper on Clitoridectomy
and Infibulation, Women's Caucus
of the African Studies Association

Editors' Note: Although this position paper first appeared in 1983, it remains relevant. Unfortunately, in the intervening time the lamentable tendency of the Western media and some Western feminists to sensationalize the issues of clitoridectomy and infibulation has only gotten worse. Thus it is important to continue to stress the rational approach that was advocated so cogently in the early 1980s.

* * *

During the past year there has been much discussion in the United States about the custom of performing clitoridectomy and infibulation on young girls which is practiced in many African countries. The operations vary in extent and severity from a nicking of the clitoris to draw blood to its complete removal, and from the sewing together of the labia minora to the complete removal of the labia minora and the inner surfaces of the labia majora with the stitching together of the remaining tissue so that the genital area heals to form a solid wall of flesh over all but a small portion of the vaginal opening. The opinions about this practice range from an extreme cultural-relativist position (if it's part of a group's tradition, it's all right) to a position that would forbid all U.S. aid to a country where the custom is still practiced.

Not many people espouse the cultural-relativist position. Few would consider themselves in favor of the genital mutilation of young women, any more than they would consider themselves in favor of female infanticide, footbinding, rape, slavery, or genocide. Thus the extreme relativist position can be discounted. Given that the elimination of clitoridectomy and infibulation is the desired goal, the task then is to find appropriate and effective means of achieving that goal.

Fran Hosken, the publisher of a newsletter called *Women's International Network News* and the author of *The Hosken Report on Genital Mutilation* as well as several articles in medical and other journals on clitoridectomy and infibulation, has urged the cessation of all aid to one country where clitoridectomy and infibulation are practiced as means to the desired end. It is the opinion of the Women's Caucus of the African Studies Association that such an approach by outsiders is not helpful. All activity takes place in a geopolitical context of race relations and national identity, and it is very important for Westerners to be sensitive to the complexities involved. Surely no one residing in a nation in which newborn males are routinely circumcised without benefit of anesthesia and in which other operations such as Caesarian sections, tubal ligations, hysterectomies, and radical mastectomies are sometimes performed on women for questionable medical reasons ought to single out any other group's customs for special attention. Western cultures have in the recent past practiced clitoridectomy on young women as a cure for masturbation and nymphomania and certainly do not regard the sexuality of women as a benign or positive force.

The Women's Caucus of the African Studies Association feels that changes in the practice of clitoridectomy and infibulation in Africa must be initiated and carried out by members of those African cultures in which the custom exists, and that outsiders' contributions to this effort can be most effective in the areas of collaborative research, discussion and dissemination of information about the progress of efforts elsewhere, and technical support. There is a great need for work in these areas with significant opportunities for genuine collaboration. The Women's Caucus also feels that clitoridectomy and infibulation should not be addressed as phenomena isolated from the larger context of women's general needs. Many African women need food for themselves and their children, greater control over the means of food production, access to clean water, a secure fuel supply, access to health care, including family planning, and ways to acquire cash income. Concern about clitoridectomy and infibulation as the sole issue affecting the status of women may be a luxury that only the West can afford.

. . . We urge all members of the ASA to become as informed as possible about the subject . . . and to that end we are appending a short bibliography.

Abdalla, Raqiya Haji Dualeh. *Sisters in Affliction: Circumcision and Infibulation of Women in Africa.* London: Zed Press, 1982.

Assad, Marie B. "Female Circumcision in Egypt: Social Implications, Current Research, and Prospects for Change." *Studies in Family Planning* 2, no. 1 (1980): 3–16.

Barker-Benfield, G. J. *The Horrors of the Half-Known Life: Male Attitudes towards Women and Sexuality in Nineteenth-Century America.* New York: Harper and Row, 1997.

El Dareer, Asma. *Woman, Why do You Weep?* London: Zed Press, 1982.

El Saadawi, Nawal. *The Hidden Face of Eve: Women in the Arab World.* Trans. and ed. by Sherif Hetata. London: Zed Press, 1980.

Female Circumcision, Excision, and Infibulation: The Facts and Proposals for Change. Report 47, rev. ed. London: Minority Rights Group, 1983.

Hosken, Fran P. *The Hosken Report: Genital and Sexual Mutilation of Females.* 3d rev. ed. Lexington, Mass.: Women's International Network News, 1982.

Introduction:
Reimaging Transnational Sisterhood

STANLIE M. JAMES AND

CLAIRE C. ROBERTSON

POPULAR WESTERN PERCEPTIONS reduce Africa and African women in three distinct ways that could be called the "three Rs." First, they reduce Africa's fifty-four countries and hundreds of cultures to one uncivilized, "traditional" place outside of history to be compared with the "modern" "West." Second, they reduce Africans, and African women in particular, to the status of their genitals, to being malicious torturers or hapless victims. Finally, uniform depictions reduce all cutting of female genitals to the most severe practice—infibulation. The cumulative effect of these reductions is that all African women are represented as having been infibulated due to unreasoned adherence to tradition and/or malicious ignorance.

As feminist scholars from diverse backgrounds and activists committed to eliminating harmful genital cutting, we are distressed by these perceptions and by media misrepresentations of those practices often referred to as female genital mutilation (FGM) or sometimes female genital surgeries (FGS). Whether through exaggeration, overgeneralization, stereotyping, inaccuracy, voyeurism, or misplaced militance, the U.S. media has succeeded in portraying African women as victims of sensationalized FGM in a manner that has eclipsed any reasoned consideration of historical contexts, contemporary experiences, and the agency of African women themselves.

Positions on this issue range from cultural relativism to a militant stance that would forbid all U.S. aid to countries where these customs continue to be practiced by any of their citizens. Recognizing that neither of these approaches appeared to be effective in struggles to eradicate such practices, in 1983 the Women's Caucus of the African Studies Association (ASA) advocated a different approach in the "Position Paper of the Women's Caucus of the

African Studies Association on Clitoridectomy and Infibulation," which is included as the prologue to this volume. The caucus concluded that "changes in the practice of clitoridectomy and infibulation in Africa must be initiated and carried out by members of those African cultures in which the custom exists." The paper also observed that "many African women need food for themselves and their children, greater control over the means of food production, access to clean water, a secure fuel supply, access to health care including family planning and ways to acquire cash income. *Concern about clitoridectomy and infibulation as the sole issue affecting the status of women may be a luxury that only the West can afford*" (emphasis added).

A decade later in 1993, Lynda Dey attended the New York City opening of the "documentary" *Warrior Marks* by Alice Walker and Pratibha Parmar. Dey reported to the Women's Caucus that she was appalled by the film's implications for those engaged in efforts to eradicate the practices. She urged caucus members to see it (it was available for viewing at the annual meeting of the African Studies Association that year) and argued that members should take a stand against such simplistic constructions. It was decided that the keynote speaker for the caucus's annual luncheon the following year would address this issue and that the caucus would sponsor at least one roundtable on the subject. Although invitations were issued to both Alice Walker and Pratibha Parmar to attend the annual meeting and participate in the roundtable, we received no response from Walker and an oblique refusal from Parmar. Seble Dawit, an attorney who specializes in international human rights and is an activist engaged in the struggle to eradicate the practices, did accept the invitation, however. Her moving address, "African Women in the Diaspora and the Problem of Female Mutilation," provided the inspiration for this volume, as did years of Women's Caucus discussions.

The editors of this volume eventually began to work independently on papers, excerpts of which were presented on panels at later ASA meetings and were subsequently published in *Signs*.[1] Despite those efforts, we still felt an obligation as Western women to respond in a more consistent manner to the admonition found in the Women's Caucus's Position Paper "that outsiders' contributions to this [eradication] effort can be most effective in the areas of collaborative research, discussion and dissemination of information about the progress of efforts elsewhere, and technical support." Although the caucus recognized the great need for work in this area, with "significant opportunities for genuine collaboration" the paper had also insisted that the practices must be contextualized rather than be addressed as isolated phenomena.

Genital Cutting and Transnational Sisterhood: Disputing U.S. Polemics represents our efforts to respond to the challenge of the position paper. It problematizes the often simplistic, sensationalized, and inaccurate portrayals of female genital cutting (FGC, the term we will use) in U.S. media and legal discourses. It plots a third course between the relativistic and the militant approaches that appear to have been ineffective in eradicating these harmful practices. We suggest that these approaches have sometimes demonized and/or victimized African women in a manner that has been detrimental to fragile endeavors to construct the bonds of transnational sisterhood. There may be elements, however, within these approaches that, when combined, could provide new ways to push beyond polarization and the immediate, visceral feelings of revulsion the topic provokes in the United States. If, as Parker Palmer suggests, "opposites do not negate each other [but] . . . cohere in mysterious unity at the heart of reality," then those of us committed to eradicating FGC must intentionally engage in the creative synthesis of paradox through scholarship that carefully examines the specificities of history and culture.[2]

* * *

Challenging Western perceptions and misrepresentations around the cutting of women's genitalia requires careful examination of overgeneralizations. One critical, and frequent, area of overgeneralization concerns terminology, where both the terms *female circumcision* and *female genital mutilation* have currency. Each contributor to this volume has her own critique of these terms, which are loaded with theoretical and political implications. Suffice it to say that "female circumcision" as a blanket term to cover FGC is misleading because it makes a false analogy to the much more minor operation performed on men and then places all FGC in this category, minimizing the impact of sometimes drastic and harmful cutting. Meanwhile, "female genital mutilation" as a term errs in the other direction, assuming that all FGC is mutilating. The contributors have therefore chosen to use several more precise terms to describe the cutting of women's and girls' genitalia. Stanlie James and Claire Robertson use "female genital cutting," while Isabelle Gunning uses "female genital surgeries" and Christine Walley uses "female genital operations." Cheryl Chase uses "clitoridectomy" to refer to the particular operation that is the chief subject of her essay and "pediatric genital surgeries" for the general category.

In Africa the widespread practices of FGC are as differentiated as the people themselves. In general, there are two different bundles of characteristics that have often been uncritically lumped together in the literature as "female circumcision" or "female genital mutilation." They differ according to what is done, the cultural significance of the practices, where they occur, and the pattern of spread or diminution. The following description and analysis is a summation of more extensive material available elsewhere.[3]

The first and most drastic type of female genital cutting is often called pharaonic circumcision or infibulation in the literature. Here we will call it infibulation, which includes the excision of the clitoris. It is an ancient practice, recorded as far back as pharaonic Egypt, which Westerners have found to be most repulsive. The practice involves removing a woman's entire external genital area, the labia majora and minora and the clitoris, and sewing the wound together to leave a single opening the size of a pencil to allow for evacuation of urine and menses. Infibulation is often performed privately on young girls, or even infants, by older women relatives or hired operators of either gender in various locations and often without ritual. The drastic nature of the cutting and the usually unsanitary conditions in which it occurs often bring massive complications. Even if the initial wound heals properly without infection, the inelasticity of the resultant scar tissue and the smallness of the opening may require routine defibulation using a knife or other instrument at the time of marriage and childbirth.[4] In some cases, women are reinfibulated after childbirth.

The psychological effects of such mutilation may also be drastic, all the more so because it is often done to small children with no preparation or warning, with force used to restrain the unanesthetized girls. Because female relatives are usually those who forcibly restrain the girls it seems likely that the resultant feelings of mistrust might well militate against female solidarity, while sexual intercourse would be strongly associated with pain.[5]

What are the reasons behind what could easily be termed an unprovoked attack on young girls by their female or male relatives, who if they do not do it themselves will at least make the arrangements to have it done? Understanding the reasons for infibulation invites us to venture beyond simplistic statements of "it's a ritual" or a "tradition." According to the literature on infibulation, the goal is to make the girl into a desirable bride, meaning that she will be chaste and virginal until marriage and faithful after marriage. Many are convinced that a girl who has not been infibulated will not find a husband. Their duty to the child then requires that infibulation be done. Female genitalia in their unaltered state may be regarded as dirty and ugly. Thus some people believe that the aesthetics of beauty, fertility, and health are enhanced by removal of the external genitalia.[6]

Infibulation occurs chiefly in the Horn of Africa: Ethiopia, Sudan, Egypt (including among Egyptian Coptic Christian communities), Eritrea, and Somalia, and sporadically in West African countries like Chad (fig. 1).[7] The practice is almost universal in some countries of the Horn (an exception is

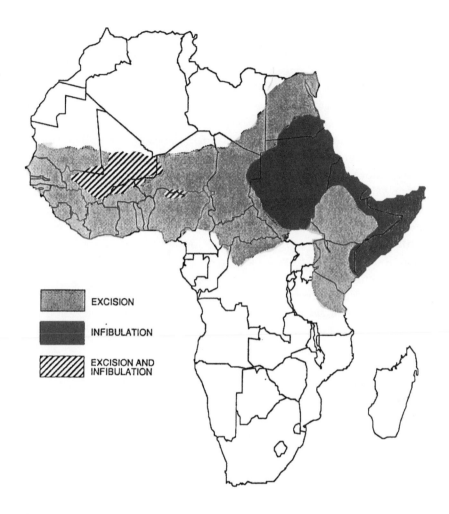

EXCISION

INFIBULATION

EXCISION AND
INFIBULATION

Fig. 1. Africa.
From Hanny Lightfoot-Klein, *Prisoners of Ritual: An Odyssey into Female Genital Circumcision in Africa* (New York: Haworth Press, 1989), 32. Map by Daniel V. Klein. Reprinted by permission of The Haworth Press, Inc.

Eritrea, where it largely stopped during the long war of independence from Ethiopia) and has even spread into new areas along with Islam. Despite the lack of justification for it within the Koran itself, scholars acknowledge that Islam has incorporated and accommodated practices of genital cutting into its religious and worldviews.[8] Its persistence and spread are also associated with lesser economic opportunities for women that encourage economic dependency on a husband, with the misery caused by the longstanding civil war in Sudan, and with the neocolonial economies of these countries, in which well-paying jobs are scarce. The rise of fundamentalist Islam has also promoted the practice.

Clitoridectomy or excision of the clitoris, the other form of female genital cutting that is widely practiced, varies according to the portion of the clitoris removed and whether or not the labia majora or minora are also removed.[9] There is, as well, more minor cutting that may be mislabeled as clitoridectomy, but that involves only pricking or nicking the clitoris or removing the prepuce of the clitoris, as described by Emmanuel Babatunde with the Yoruba.[10] This practice, which is most analogous to male circumcision, will be referred to as female circumcision, or *sunna,* in this volume. Clitoridectomy also has a history of being practiced in Western countries as well as in parts of Africa.[11] In France, it began to be promoted as a cure for female homoeroticism as early as the late sixteenth and seventeenth centuries.[12] It is now practiced in the United States as one of the pediatric genital surgeries discussed by Cheryl Chase in this volume.

Less drastic procedures, ranging from merely pricking the clitoris to removing most but not all of the external genitalia, extend over a larger area of Africa than infibulation but are more discontinuous. The southernmost extent is usually accounted to be northern Tanzania, while people who most engage in clitoridectomy live in a belt that crosses Africa's mid-section from Senegal to Kenya and Tanzania, although there have been reports that certain women in southern Africa also practice clitoridectomy. The practices seem not to occur north of the Sahara. There are many people in countries where clitoridectomy exists who have never engaged in any of its variations, such as the Akan people in Ghana and Ivory Coast who compose the dominant portion of the population of both of those countries. Some Igbo in Nigeria continue to practice clitoridectomy, whereas some stopped doing it during the 1920s. In West Africa, clitoridectomy is more common upcountry, away from the coast in less urbanized areas; in Kenya it is not practiced on the predominantly Islamic coast. One of the chief areas where it was practiced extensively was around Nairobi, the largest city, where there has now been a substantial diminution in clitoridectomy among the largest ethnic group, the Kikuyu. The reasons for that decline are connected to the meanings people invest in clitoridectomy, which differ sharply from those accompanying infibulation.

In many societies, clitoridectomy was often performed as a part of puberty rites for girls, preceding or at the time of the first menses. The reason that clitoridectomy was frequently referred to as "female circumcision" in the anthropological literature was because it was viewed as being analogous to male circumcision and was often performed at the same time. Most people who practice clitoridectomy in the context of puberty rites also practice male circumcision. Excising the clitoris or its prepuce only was thought to remove the male principle from females, and many believed that male circumcision removed the female principle from males. Elders, who deemed these rites necessary to establish gender identity and induct the youth into adulthood, also believed the rites to be critical to the survival of the society. Senior males or senior females usually performed the procedures in sex-segregated settings, sometimes accompanied by isolation of the participants from the rest of the village for some period of time. Their elders prepared boys and girls for the ceremonies by instructing them in proper behavior and the significance of the rites. Those being excised were supposed to demonstrate bravery by keeping silent during their surgeries, which were usually performed without anesthetic. Other tests of courage and sometimes of athletic skills for both sexes also accompanied the rites. Groups of boys and girls experienced these procedures alongside rites that included education on how to be a successful adult.[13] Often initiates became an age-set pledged to each other for life; male and female solidarity was fostered, and healing together became one of the factors solidifying the group.[14]

In Sierra Leone, women initiated girls into Sande, a powerful women's secret society, and gave extensive instruction over several years in housewifery, beauty culture, arts and crafts, fishing, farming, childrearing, hygiene and sanitation, care of the sick, singing, drumming, dancing and drama, herbal lore, and respect for the elders.[15] The new initiates reentered society with great celebration, showered with gifts and acclaimed as newly fledged adults. Many women in societies where clitoridectomy was practiced recalled their experiences during and after initiation with pleasure as the most carefree time of their lives.[16]

The past tense here reflects changes that seem to be pervasive in many societies that still practice clitoridectomy. Although fostering sexual control among initiates was one motive for clitoridectomy, in some places that has assumed primary motivation for the practices, which are now done when girls are younger so they will not protest. Securing a husband has also become more important in a few areas. As more girls attend school, the seclusion and education period has diminished.[17] Many people have simply stopped doing initiation rites at all. Paradoxically, where women's groups that use puberty rites as induction rituals remain powerful, clitoridectomy may continue along with the substantial power of such groups. But where women's groups have been weakened or have transformed themselves, the practices may be disappearing. Their disappearance thus has ambivalent implications, for some women signaling an overall lessening of women's power. Yet the disappearance may also symbolize a transformation toward more democratic forms of women's power.[18] Thus, the chief declines in the cutting of women's and girls' genitals have occurred in areas where clitoridectomy or circumcision rather than infibulation have been prevalent.

It is this kind of specific context that is critical to our attempts to diminish the practices. The best knowledge about the practices is local. That knowledge must be respected and learned by those who work to eradicate female genital cutting, including Africans from other cultures. Thus, neither criminalization in the United States and Africa nor U.S. media condemnations that distort the complicated situations in Africa are very helpful. To avoid overgeneralization and set these practices within the complex contexts from which they emerge, we have tried to use terminology as precisely as possible for the specific practice that is under discussion.

Exploding the Binaries: Rethinking Gender in the United States

Claude Lévi-Strauss suggested that the human brain tended to establish binaries as a way of knowing due to its binary structure, but it is not clear that this form of biological determinism must govern our practice.[19] The terminological issue is only one of several problems of binaries that this volume hopes to address. The range of terms for varied FGC practices in Africa reflect colonialist perspectives and polarize cultural relativist and militant feminist positions (see Christine J. Walley, "Searching for 'Voices': Feminism, Anthropology, and the Global Debate over Female Genital Operations" and Claire C. Robertson, "Getting beyond the Ew! Factor: Rethinking U.S. Approaches to African Female Genital Cutting," both in this volume). There are as well rigid concepts of gender established by sex in the United States that have had a detrimental impact on society's responses to intersexed individuals (those with ambiguous genitalia) and in far too many instances resulted in pediatric genital surgeries intended to established definitive gender/sex (see Cheryl

Chase, "'Cultural Practice' or 'Reconstructive Surgery'? U.S. Genital Cutting, the Intersex Movement, and Medical Double Standards" in this volume). Although second-wave feminists have been at the forefront of critiquing binary gender definitions, neither second- nor third-wave feminists have often dealt well with the issues of FGC and pediatric genital surgeries.

Problematic feminist approaches to issues of FGC and pediatric genital surgeries are frequently connected to what one might call the colonial flaw. In the African case, these are heavily inflected by race, whereas the U.S. case may be affected by the analogue to the African case. That is, although many feminists by now are aware that clitoridectomy was practiced at different times and places in the United States, most confine it to the past. Routine pediatric genital surgeries continue in the United States, which suggests that the distance between some African cultures and U.S. society is not as great as many would like to imagine; these surgeries are regularly categorized as different from African practices and necessary, medically not culturally ordained. In some African societies, "ugly" female genitalia are made "beautiful" by infibulation; in the United States, nonconforming genitalia are regarded with aesthetic distaste, theoretical puzzlement, and possibly even fear. In both contexts, questions arise as to how conventional gender analysis can be applied to such individuals. Are we as feminists actually covertly, and perhaps even unconsciously, committed to the very categories of sex/gender that we deconstruct? What if a society developed in which all sex/gender categories were fluid, recognized, and accepted? Why are definitive categories necessary anyway? Why is it necessary to claim biological sex and/or sexual orientation as identity to achieve at least a modicum of acceptance and comfort within society? If we can move beyond our preoccupation with reconstructing binary gender by deconstructing it as the preeminent feminist project, and beyond colonial othering in terms of race and gender, perhaps we can begin to think through the paradox of a multicultural, multigendered world that may, in turn, be more hospitable to difference.

Notes

1. Claire C. Robertson, "Grassroots in Kenya: Women, Genital Mutilation and Collective Action, 1920–1990," *Signs: Journal of Women in Culture and Society* 21, no. 2 (1996): 615–42; Stanlie M. James, "Shades of Othering: Reflections on Female Circumcision/Genital Mutilations," *Signs: Journal of Women in Culture and Society* 23, no. 4 (1998): 1031–48.

2. Parker Palmer, *Let Your Life Speak: Listening for the Voice of Vocation* (San Francisco: Jossey Bass, 2000), 99.

3. Short texts that give excellent overview of the female genital surgeries issue are those by Efua Dorkenoo, *Cutting the Rose: Female Genital Mutilation* (London: Minority Rights

Group, 1994), and Lillian Passmore Sanderson, *Against the Mutilation of Women: The Struggle to End Unnecessary Suffering* (London: Ithaca Press, 1981).

4. Aamina Warsame, Sadiya Ahmed, and Aud Talle, *Social and Cultural Aspects of Female Circumcision and Infibulation* (Mogadishu/Stockholm: Somali Academy of Sciences and Arts and Swedish Agency for Research Cooperation, 1985), 10–11, have noted that women see the prospect of defibulation as the second trauma in their sexual lives; many try to postpone consummation of a marriage by running away. The prevalence of routine episiotomies in the United States is also worth noting in this regard; see Robbie E. Davis-Floyd, "Gender and Ritual: Giving Birth the American Way," in *Gender in Cross-Cultural Perspective*, ed. Caroline B. Brettell and Carolyn F. Sargent (Upper Saddle River, N.J.: Prentice-Hall, 1997).

5. The psychological impacts of FGC seem to be analyzed very sparsely in the literature, which looks only at infibulation and notes a decline in self-confidence. Ahmed Ibrahim Ballal's *Psychological Effects of Female Circumcision* (New York: Vantage Press, 1992) falls into this category in looking only at women in Khartoum. He goes further, however, to exculpate men entirely by noting that men, whatever they say, "are puppets in the hands of mothers and grandmothers" (33), and women can enjoy sex (not defined) after infibulation. See also Mahdi Ali Dirie, *Female Circumcision in Somalia: Medical and Social Implications* (Collaborative Report between SOMAC and SAREC, 1985), 9.

6. As Dirie aptly stated, "[T]radition as a reason does not explain the underlying motives, which first made the practice necessary and later allowed it to continue, hereby becoming 'traditional'" (*Female Circumcision*, 91). The best summations of justifications for FGC can be found in Olayinka Koso-Thomas, *The Circumcision of Women: A Strategy for Eradication* (London: Zed Press, 1987), 2–12; Sanderson, *Against the Mutilation of Women*, 46–52; and Dorkenoo, *Cutting the Rose*, 46.

7. Esther Hicks, *Infibulation: Female Mutilation in Islamic Northeastern Africa* (New Brunswick: Transaction Publishers, 1996), 8.

8. Jonathan P. Berkey, "Circumcision Circumscribed: Female Excision and Cultural Accommodation in the Medieval Near East," *International Journal of Middle East Studies* 28 (1996): 19–38. See also Dorkenoo, *Cutting the Rose*, 37, for an excellent discussion of arguments by Muslim scholars for and against FGC.

9. Dorkenoo's discussion of the different procedures belies the singularity that her title implies (*Cutting the Rose*, 5–6).

10. Emmanuel D. Babatunde, *Women's Rights versus Women's Rites: A Study of Circumcision among the Ketu Yoruba of South Western Nigeria* (Trenton: Africa World Press, 1998).

11. In Great Britain and the United States, the reasons for the practices were also various, whether as a cure for epilepsy, frigidity, masturbation, or nymphomania. In Russia it was part of a sectarian religious rite. Sanderson, *Against the Mutilation of Women*, 28–29; Raqiya Abdalla, *Sisters in Affliction: Circumcision and Infibulation of Women in Africa* (London: Zed Press, 1982), 60.

12. Katharine Park, "The Rediscovery of the Clitoris: French Medicine and the *Tribades*, 1570–1620," in *The Body in Parts: Fantasies of Corporeality in Early Modern Europe*, ed. David Hillman and Carla Mazzio (New York: Routledge, 1997), 186–87.

13. There is a long history of human societies using pain as a social mechanism to manipulate or transform identity or to induce spiritual revelations.

14. One of the key misrepresentations of clitoridectomy in Alice Walker's novel *Possessing the Secret of Joy* (New York: Harcourt Brace, 1992) is the solitary confinement of the chief character undergoing the rite. When performed properly, initiation rites were and are normatively collective in nature, which makes them easier to modify than to eradicate. It may be that clitoridectomy, in some areas where initiation is disappearing, is left without its original context and collective aspects but has new meaning as an individual procedure, but we have no evidence to that effect.

15. Koso-Thomas, *The Circumcision of Women*, 21.

16. Christine J. Walley, "Searching for 'Voices': Feminism, Anthropology, and the Global Debate over Female Genital Operations," chapter 1 in this volume. Claire Robertson found that older women among traders in Nairobi in 1987–88 invariably cited this time as the happiest in their lives and the most free.

17. Koso-Thomas, *The Circumcision of Women*, 23; Dorkenoo, *Cutting the Rose*, 40.

18. Robertson, "Grassroots in Kenya."

19. Claude Lévi-Strauss, *The Raw and the Cooked* (New York: Harper Torchbooks, 1969).

1. Searching for "Voices": Feminism, Anthropology, and the Global Debate over Female Genital Operations

CHRISTINE J. WALLEY

THE ISSUE OF "female circumcision" has generated heated public debate in Europe and the United States over the last several years. The controversy has centered not only on the North African and sub-Saharan African countries where most clitoridectomies and infibulations have historically been performed, but increasingly on those Euro-American countries where immigrants who perform such practices now reside. Several legal cases in France in the early 1990s generated widespread publicity when African immigrant parents and a circumcisor were charged with child abuse and assault for performing clitoridectomies.[1] In 1994, a Nigerian woman residing in the United States, Lydia Oluloro, successfully contested her deportation by arguing that if she returned to Nigeria her daughters would be forced to undergo "circumcision."[2] The case of Fauziya Kassindja, a young Togolese woman who came to the United States seeking political asylum in an effort to escape a forced clitoridectomy and a forced marriage, has generated even greater media attention; a public outcry emerged when it was revealed that Kassindja had been incarcerated in a Pennsylvania prison for sixteen months along with other asylum-seekers.[3] In a more literary vein, Alice Walker's widely publicized novel *Possessing the Secret of Joy* has strongly condemned the practice of female genital mutilation. She then collaborated with Pratibha Parmar to produce a documentary film and companion volume on the subject, both of which are entitled *Warrior Marks,* garnering still more media attention in Western countries.[4] Media accounts have included articles and op-ed pieces in the *New York Times,* the *Washington Post,* and *Time* magazine, and segments have aired on TV and radio news programs, including

ABC World News Tonight, Dateline NBC, ABC-TV's *Nightline,* CNN's *News-night,* and National Public Radio's *All Things Considered.*[5]

Despite, or perhaps because of, the explosiveness of the topic, feminist anthropologists have paid relatively little attention to female genital operations in the past (although this has begun to change rapidly in recent years).[6] Yet clearly, there is a need for analysis. The issue strikes numerous nerves, as it challenges fundamental understandings of body, self, sexuality, family, and morality and plays upon tensions relating to cultural difference, the relationship between women and "tradition," and the legacy of colonial-era depictions of gender relations in non-Western countries. The public debates over female genital operations also raise pertinent questions about our contemporary social world. While an earlier international debate about female genital mutilation reflected the growing influence of feminist movements in the 1970s, the recent controversy bears a distinctly 1990s cast. As is now commonly acknowledged, the exponential growth of global communications and multinational corporations has been accompanied by increasingly migratory habits, as immigrants, refugees, and tourists, among others, crisscross the globe. These transformations are breaking down what has been a pervasive, if always problematic, assumption—namely that internally homogeneous first and third worlds exist as radically separate "worlds."[7] The centrality of African immigrants in Europe and the United States to recent Western media accounts of female genital operations, as well as the role Africans have played on both sides of the debate, suggests the growing permeability of national and social boundaries in an increasingly "globalized" era. In short, the current controversy surrounding female genital operations is inextricably linked to other contemporary debates that include the nature of universal human rights and the way such rights include, or exclude, women; the cultural rights of minorities as immigration increases in Euro-American countries; and, ultimately, the meaning and viability of "multicultural" societies.

The issue of female genital operations poses particular challenges for feminist anthropologists in that the topic viscerally encapsulates the potential tension between feminism and anthropology. Marilyn Strathern once accurately characterized the relationship between the two as "awkward."[8] Part of that awkwardness stems from a perennial conflict: When feminist political concerns challenge anthropology's trademark emphasis on cultural understanding, where should the allegiance of feminist anthropologists lie? This apparent awkwardness, however, may instead prove useful by challenging us to grapple with a central assumption underlying the debate. Namely, why is there a tendency to understand female genital operations in either/or terms, in other words, *either* in terms of cultural relativism *or* politically informed outrage?

In this essay, I attempt to address this issue by offering a dual perspective that looks at the practices of, and discourses surrounding, female genital operations. I will ground an analysis of the discursive politics surrounding genital operations by offering an ethnographic account of clitoridectomy within the context of daily life for a rural population in western Kenya's Kikhome village in 1988.[9] In doing so, I question whether either of the seemingly polar viewpoints commonly expressed toward female genital operations in Europe and the United States—that of moral opprobrium or relativistic tolerance— is sufficient to construct an adequate feminist or humanist political response to this issue.[10] I instead suggest that within the Euro-American debates both sides—critics and relativists—often share an unacknowledged common thread. This commonality is a hardened view of "culture" based on a rigid, essentialist notion of difference that can be historically linked to the colonial era.[11] By addressing these issues, I hope to help lay the groundwork for a more productive feminist and anthropological debate capable of transcending the binary terms in which female genital operations are commonly discussed— binary terms that falsely suggest an insurmountable chasm between "us" and "them."

Circumcision, Mutilation, or Torture? The Politics of Naming

Female genital operations are known by a variety of names. In addition to the names found in the languages of those conducting the practices, there is an extensive terminology in English that includes "female circumcision," "clitoridectomy," "excision," "infibulation," "genital mutilation," and, in the perspective of some Anglo-American observers, "torture." The practices, like the names, are not monolithic; the severity of the procedure varies, as do the people and geographical regions involved. Female genital operations occur in a variety of places, from Indonesia to the Middle East to Europe and the United States; however, the vast majority of female genital operations occur on the African continent in countries as diverse as Sudan, Somalia, Ethiopia, Egypt, Kenya, Tanzania, Nigeria, Togo, Senegal, and Mali. Practitioners include Muslims, Christians, Falasha Jews, and followers of indigenous African religions. Although the reliability of such statistics is unclear, estimates suggest that up to one hundred million women have presently undergone some form of genital operation.[12] The physical operation ranges from removal of the tip of the clitoris (a procedure known as *sunna*), to the excision of the clitoris itself and potentially portions of the labia minora and majora (clitoridectomy or excision), to the most radical form, which includes clitoridectomy as well as the removal of the labia minora and majora and the sewing together of the remaining tissues (infibulation). These practices also have a history in Europe and the United States. Ancient Romans pierced the genitalia of their female slaves with pins or fibula, hence the term *infibulation,* while some turn-of-the-century European and American doctors used clitoridectomy as a cure for masturbation and so-called nymphomania.[13]

The act of naming these practices is controversial in and of itself. The generic use of the term *circumcision* in English treats the removal of the foreskin in males as equivalent to the removal of the clitoris in females, obscuring the permanent loss of sexual sensation in girls.[14] Similar usages often exist in the languages of those people engaging in such practices, suggesting the social and symbolic links that many practitioners make between "circumcision" for boys and girls. In this essay, I have sought to avoid this mystifying usage while I have also avoided the terms *female genital mutilation* and *female genital torture,* which carry the implicit assumption that parents and relatives deliberately intend to harm children. When referring to the full range of such practices, I have instead adopted the term *female genital operations.* My goal in doing so is not to coin a new phrase that purports to escape the problematic power relationships surrounding this topic, for clearly that is impossible. Nevertheless, existing usages are deeply embedded in the "either/ or" perspectives characteristic of discussions of female genital operations, with "circumcision" signaling relativistic tolerance, and "mutilation" implying moral outrage. Although I find the term *female genital operations* preferable to existing terminology, whenever possible I have preferred the more historically and geographically specific terms *clitoridectomy* and *infibulation.*

Contextualizing Clitoridectomy: Excision as Initiation in Western Kenya

By sketching the social context of clitoridectomies as performed by the people living around the village of Kikhome in western Kenya in 1988, I hope to encourage a reinfusion of humanity into a debate that has often been reduced to dehumanizing abstractions. By drawing on my own observations and experiences in the Kikhome region, however, I also run certain risks. In Kikhome I was an outsider, a young, white, female North American living in the community while on a teaching stint, and my knowledge of the practice of excision was limited.[15] My goal, however, is not to offer a generically applicable social scientific analysis of female genital operations—an impossible task given the diversity of practices and the plethora of meanings attributed to them. Nor is my intention to offer a definitive ethnographic account of clitoridectomies as performed in the Kikhome region. Instead, my purpose is to describe the quest to know, the desire to understand these practices as an outsider, someone inevitably forced (as we all are) to draw upon her or his own resources for understanding the world. In Kikhome, I felt compelled to try to understand the ritual clitoridectomies performed there both because the practice deeply troubled me and because I sought some way of thinking about the issue that I could reconcile with my sense of myself as a feminist, as a student of anthropology, and as a friend of many in the community where I was staying.

Although my account is written by someone on the cultural margins of life in Kikhome, such a location is perhaps ironically appropriate. The international controversy over female genital operations has largely occurred in human rights reports, health bulletins, international conferences, and media accounts across a variety of countries. In this international debate, I, along with many Euro-Americans, have been a privileged "insider" with greater access to the international flow of representations concerning female genital operations than most women in Kikhome, whose bodies carry such intimate knowledge of these practices. We are all, to various degrees, both insiders and outsiders, and these statuses are deeply embedded in the power dynamics that structure our relationships with each other. In writing this, I hope to blur our sense of where the problem with female genital operations lies, at the same time blurring distinctions over who has the right to speak about such issues. To suggest that only those who have experienced a practice, or those who can lay claim to it on the basis of race or ethnicity, have the right to speak essentializes both practitioners and nonpractitioners by locating them in bounded groups assumed to share common beliefs—a reductionist view that ignores a far messier reality. In choosing to write on this topic, however, I do not justify the ways in which Euro-Americans have dominated international debates over female genital operations, both historically and at present. Instead, by locating this controversy "interculturally," I intend to draw attention to the responsibility that Westerners hold for the terms of these debates—for interest in Europe and the United States stems not only from feminist or humanist concern but also from the desire to sensationalize, to titillate, and to call attention to differences between "us" and "them" in ways that reaffirm notions of Western cultural superiority.

"Circumcision": The Ceremonies

Kikhome, a village that consists of a few small storefronts, is located amid the dispersed mud-and-thatch homes and the subsistence farm plots that checker the foothills of Mount Elgon near the Ugandan border. For town- and city-dwellers in the heavily populated western province of Kenya, the village of Kikhome in 1988 was seen as a remote backwater, difficult to reach by transportation and almost inaccessible when the rainy season turned the dirt roads and paths into slippery, viscous mud. The high school compound where I stayed as an English teacher was located in the flat valley at the base of the foothills. Although the Bukusu, a Bantu-speaking group, formed the majority of the people living in the valley, the Sabaots, a group of Kalenjin Nilotic ancestry who had historically been pastoralists, now farmed the hills overshadowing Kikhome. Although the majority of students at Kikhome were Bukusu, there was a sizable minority of Sabaots. Immediately after I arrived, my high school students, both male and female, began telling me with a boisterous pride about their circumcision ceremonies. They informed me that while the Bukusu circumcised only boys, the Sabaots initiated both girls and boys. Unfortunately, they lamented, I had missed the Bukusu ceremonies, but assuredly I would be invited to Sabaot circumcisions over the December school holidays.

True to their word, and to my unacknowledged discomfort, several of my teenage students did invite me, months later, to their initiations. On the evening before one of the initiations I attended was to take place, Beatrice, a teenage student at Kikhome, led me and a fellow U.S. teacher along the wind- ing paths crisscrossing the foothills of Mount Elgon to the family compound of her cousins. It was just before dusk when we entered the compound, which encompassed a series of round, mud houses neatly roofed with thatch, and where we encountered a festive atmosphere that reminded me of graduation parties at home in the midwestern United States. The compound was crowd- ed with people of all ages, and many of the older guests were sitting on the ground, drinking homemade grain beer, or *buzaa*, brewed especially for the occasion. Near the main house, both male and female initiates "danced," or rather paced strenuously back and forth, swinging their arms and loudly blowing whistles. The teenage girls wore skirts, and the boys wore shorts of bright-red fabric decorated with colored strips of cloth and white T-shirts emblazoned with "Datsun" or "Free Mandela" logos. Their arms and faces were painted with white, chalky designs; the girls wore colored, knitted caps, and the boys, colobus monkey headdresses. Beatrice explained that when young people felt they were ready (generally between the ages of fourteen and sixteen for the Sabaot) they would request their parents' permission to be initiated. After training for several months to learn the necessary songs and dances under the guidance of their sponsors, the initiates would go around inviting friends and relatives to the ceremonies.[16]

As darkness fell, the increasingly drunken crowd surrounded the candidates and encouraged them by joining in the dancing and singing. The bright glow of pressure lamps cast a flickering light on the raucous, gyrating crowd as well as on the wooden faces of the initiates, which were masked with the expressionlessness expected of those awaiting circumcision. The dancing continued throughout the night; we were told it would tire the novices and numb them for the pain to come. At dawn, the initiates were led by circuitous routes to a stream, and before being bathed in its water (a restricted part of the ceremony witnessed only by the initiated) they were harangued by their mothers and warned not to disgrace their relatives, living or dead, by showing cowardice. After being led back to the family compound, they were immediately circumcised. The cutting was public and demonstrated to the community the bravery of the initiated. The boys were cut by a male circumcisor while standing; the girls were excised by a woman as they sat, legs spread on the ground and their backs supported by their sponsors. The crucial test was for the initiate to show no pain, to neither change expression nor even blink, during the cutting. Remarkably enough to my friend and I, the initiates remained utterly stoic and expressionless throughout. We were told it is this ability to withstand the ordeal that confers adulthood, that allows one to marry and have children, and that binds one to one's age-mates.[17]

Mary, one of the students whose ceremony I had witnessed, later told me that she and her fellow initiates had recuperated for a month, boys and girls separately, in special huts. After both male and female initiates judged themselves sufficiently healed, they informed the adults, and then the boys and girls rejoined and ceremonially climbed up into the lower hills of Mount Elgon to a large cave behind a small waterfall. After a ceremony at the cave, during which the ancestors were invoked, the celebrating initiates were allowed to raid local gardens on their return, mischievously stealing bananas and pelting the houses of their owners without fear of punishment. In a final ceremony at the family compound, they were given new clothes and gifts, and they then reentered daily life as adults.

The Search for Voices

After witnessing these ceremonies, I had a better idea of what Sabaot initiation entailed.[18] Yet I had not come any closer to relieving my inner distress about excision. I decided that if I could ascertain what these young people "really" thought about the practice, it would help me formulate a position of my own. But the question remained—how could I discover their "real" thoughts? Obviously, there was a great deal of public support for initiation. For them to criticize circumcision publicly or to reject it would have led to accusations of cowardice, to social ostracism, and perhaps physical violence, as Beatrice acknowledged had happened in the past. Thus, pondering the relationship between the public voices of these young people and their "real" voices, I embarked on a search for an "authentic" perspective on female genital operations.

In my capacity as an English teacher at the secondary school where I taught, I gave the Form III students—the equivalent of U.S. high school juniors—the option of writing an essay about "female circumcision," and some of the Sabaot students did so. Although clitoridectomies have been illegal in Kenya since 1982 and were denounced in the social education classes at the secondary school where I taught, the students who responded argued that the continuation of the practice was important on the grounds that it was, as they described it, "our custom." They stated that the primary purpose of the practice was to keep unmarried girls from getting "hot," that is, from having sexual relations and getting pregnant before marriage or having extramarital affairs later. Yet while the one essay written by a boy contained no objections to the practice, the essays by girls (who had already had clitoridectomies) did. These students argued that the practice was "bad" because it was forbidden by President Moi and by Christianity (most people in the area were syncretic in their religious beliefs, espousing both Christianity and indigenous African religions). One female student, who had enthusiastically invited me to her sister's initiation, stated that the practice was simply another way of "destroying" women's bodies, a use of language that seemed to mirror the social education curriculum more than the usual voices of my teenage students.

At the time, I was perplexed. Were the objections raised by these young women what they really thought, or were they merely parroting what they had learned in school or in the sermons of local Christian leaders, who had a long history of deploring the practice? Were objections based on Christian teaching "authentic," or was this simply another way their voices had been colonized? What "authentic" voice might these young women use to object to the practice? Certainly, they would not use the language of individual rights prominent in Euro-American feminism but which seemed selfish and anti-family to many East Africans. Perhaps these young women were strategically merging their voices with those of more powerful others, such as the Christian church or President Moi, and hence circuitously expressing their "real" thoughts?

I attempted to address these issues when several young female Sabaot students stopped by my house on the school compound one afternoon to see the pictures I had taken during their initiation. Trying to summon a neutral tone, I explained that I wanted to know more about the practice. I pleaded ignorance, stating that although baby boys were often circumcised in hospitals in the United States, we do not have public circumcision ceremonies.[19] The four young women assured me that their "custom," as they called it in English, was good. Lydia, who had recently been initiated and who had a look of religious ecstasy on her face that startled me, argued that it was something a person had to accept with her "whole being," and when one did so one did not feel the pain. Laughing at my skepticism, they told me that the pain at the time of the ceremony was not very bad (due presumably to shock and fatigue) and that it was only later that the pain became intense. But, I asked carefully, women in my country would worry that they would regret the ceremony later. My innuendoes to the sexual consequences of excision met with boisterous laughter, and the young women replied in a light yet serious tone, "But we are already regretting it!" In other words, there was no delusion among these adolescent girls, some of whose married and unmarried peers were already pregnant, about how it would affect their sexual pleasure. I asked whether they wanted their daughters to be "circumcised." One said she would because it was an important custom to continue; a second, after some thought, said she would not; and Mary, whose initiation photos we were perusing, looked uncomfortable and declined to comment.

The interactions that I have narrated, a few among many, were complex and full of nuances. I began to recognize the naiveté of my search for "real" voices, for clearly the girls' voices shifted according to context, depending on whether they were at the ceremonies, with adults or peers, in mixed-sex settings, among female friends, or, I surmised, alone. Given the legacy of both Freud and Erving Goffman, it seems evident that each self has a public as well as a private side and many more layers within it, from the conscious to the deeply unconscious. What happens, however, when these apparent layers of the self contradict each other? Do these young women, and indeed all of us, have straightforward best interests, or are our interests, on the contrary, multiple and contradictory? And where would one locate the "authentic" self? In Western thought, we tend to privilege that which is most interior or private. Yet obviously, as critics of Freud's universalism would emphasize, our unconscious is also a product of the times and places in which we exist, thus challenging the idea of a layered self that possesses an inner core untouched by our contemporary surroundings.

Another incident in Kikhome supported my later interpretation that the "best interests" of these young women were indeed contradictory. My responsibilities at the secondary school included organizing schoolwide debates. Before the main debate, students were allowed to publicly raise issues in front of their classmates. On one occasion, a young Sabaot woman who had recently been initiated demanded to know why Sabaot girls were forced into circumcision. In a mirror image of this challenge, a female Bukusu student at a later debate asked why Bukusu girls were not allowed to be initiated like Bukusu boys. Here, the Bukusu young men jeered, saying derisively that Bukusu girls were not allowed to be circumcised because circumcision of girls did not happen "in the Bible." The irony that at least some of the girls of both ethnic groups envied the position of the other reconfirmed for me that excision was both in *and* against the interests of the Sabaot young women. By undergoing the painful public ordeal of initiation, not only did they develop a personal sense of self-confidence and pride that made them feel like adults but they also were awarded considerable public respect. But this respect came at a price—the price of decreased pleasure and the containment of their sexuality, even if in ways widely considered appropriate by both women and men.

Kikhome through the Anthropological Looking-Glass

Later during the course of graduate studies, I combed the anthropological literature for help in understanding the clitoridectomies I had witnessed in Kikhome, hoping that other scholars could assist in untangling the complex questions these practices raised. As I searched for deeper insight into why Sabaot women and girls in Kikhome supported excision, I wanted to know how the significance of these practices extended beyond their ritual and psychological meanings and related to other forms of social life such as kinship groups, ethnic identity, and economic practices. Furthermore, I wondered how women's support for excision in Kikhome could be reconciled with the Western assumption that female genital operations are an expression of male dominance and, in a different vein, how women who have experienced these practices conceived of their sexuality.

There was, however, little in the anthropological literature at the time that focused on excision in sub-Saharan Africa.[20] Anthropologists and social theorists, from Arnold van Gennep to Victor Turner, offered context for excision as a social ritual by discussing the meanings of rites of passage and adolescent initiation; none, however, focused specifically on clitoridectomies.[21] Goldschmidt's fieldwork during the 1960s among the "Sebei," a Ugandan subgroup of the Mount Elgon Sabaot, proved more pertinent, although his account of initiation rites was largely descriptive and touched upon differences between male and female circumcision only in passing.[22] He did, however, briefly speculate that excision was less about controlling women's sexual desire than about offering Sebei women a source of collective strength as a counterweight to male dominance. Goldschmidt suggested that excision enhanced women's status by binding them together as a group in possession of ritual secrets revealed through initiation; men respected and feared these secrets, thereby offering women greater leverage in male/female interactions. Although this insight was suggestive, his assumption that the practice was not about sexuality gave me pause; not only did it seem counter-intuitive, but it also did not accord with the accounts of people I knew in Kikhome.

I later turned to the work of Rose Oldfield Hayes and Janice Boddy, who each had conducted research in the northern Sudan during the 1970s and examined another type of female genital operation—the more severe infibulation, which involves both excision and the sewing together of the remaining tissues. This procedure was usually performed on small girls, often four to five years of age, and was not the test of endurance leading to adulthood that it was among the Sabaot. Many people in the area felt the practice to be an Islamic religious duty, although most Muslim people do not engage in this practice, and it is not required by the Koran, as some contend. Despite the physical and social differences between infibulation and clitoridectomy, Hayes's and Boddy's analyses were relevant to Kikhome in that they further explored social settings in which it was widely considered desirable to "socialize" female sexuality or fertility through genital operations. In addition, both analyses focused on the motivations of women as participants in these practices, not simply as victims.

In her 1975 article, Hayes argued that in order to understand why women, particularly older women, were the most vocal supporters of infibulation, it was necessary to consider their positioning within family groups. In the northern Sudan, families were organized around lineages that traced descent solely through men, while women moved to join their husbands' lineages upon marriage. The importance of maintaining the integrity of patrilineages was paramount and served to determine the social status of individuals. As in many other Muslim societies (as well as in many Christian, circum-Mediterranean regions), strict sex-segregation prevailed, and the honor of families was intrinsically linked to the sexual purity of their female members and of the in-marrying women under its protection. According to Hayes, proof of virginity remained a prerequisite for marriage, and infibulation was taken to index both physical and "social" virginity, as evidenced by the practice of reinfibu-lating women after childbirth or upon later marriages. If not properly chan-neled, female sexuality was considered to be the greatest possible source of disgrace to the patrilineage. As a consequence, women infibulated their daugh-ters to protect them from the supposedly wanton sexuality believed intrinsic to women and which, if uncontrolled, could lead to rape, illegitimate children, social disgrace, and, potentially, retributive death. Given that family and so-cial organization in this area was clearly male-dominant, the women who vig-orously adhered to such practices were responding pragmatically to the exi-gencies of everyday life.

Hayes's analysis also helped illuminate the Sabaot context. Although the Sabaot are not preoccupied with chastity and virginity as are the northern Sudanese, kinship organization in both places is similar. Sabaot women ex-perience the characteristic ambiguity of women in patrilineal and patrilocal social orders. Although each Sabaot woman is a member of her father's patri-lineage and thus an outsider in her husband's kin group, her hopes of increas-ing her social status are linked to producing offspring for the husband's patri-lineage.[23] As is true in other parts of the world, kinship arrangements have strong economic dimensions, and for the Sabaot, as largely sedentary former pastoralists, cattle remain symbolically and economically important. It is cattle that an excised, and thus marriageable, young woman's family receive from the groom and his family, thereby transferring rights in her reproduc-tive potential; it is cattle (perhaps the very same cattle) that are used to pay the bridewealth for women's brothers' marriages, thus permitting those brothers to perpetuate the lineage for both living and the dead relatives; and it is the reluctance to return cattle that may make a woman's father and broth-ers fail to support her claim for a divorce.[24]

Janice Boddy's work has contributed a symbolic interpretation to the so-cial structural explanation of infibulation offered by Hayes. Unlike the situa-tion in Kikhome, Boddy noted that in the northern Sudanese village of Hof-riyat, the ritual infibulation of little girls was only mildly celebrated compared to the elaborate festivities associated with boys' circumcisions. Nevertheless, infibulation held meaning for Hofriyatis as a source of purification. Boddy offered a richly detailed analysis linking infibulation, purification, and clean-liness to the symbolic properties of birds, ostrich eggs, warmth, moisture, en-closures, and wombs. She concluded that infibulation is actually an assertive symbolic act for Hofriyati women that serves to emphasize a type of femi-ninity that focuses on fertility while deemphasizing their sexuality. She wrote, "By insisting on circumcision for their daughters, women assert their social indispensability, an importance that is not as the sexual partners of their husbands, nor, in this highly segregated male-authoritative society, as their servants, sexual or otherwise, but as the mothers of men."[25] The ability of women to reproduce or found lineages was the stuff on which the social careers of women were based, and it was older women, as mothers and grandmothers, who emerged as powerful forces within patrilineages through control over their offspring.

Boddy also noted that in this strictly sex-segregated society, women achieved social recognition not by becoming like men but by emphasizing their differences. By removing that part of the external genitalia thought to most resemble that of the opposite sex, circumcision was believed to enhance the masculinity of boys and the femininity of girls. In an interesting parallel, this belief mirrors that of the Dogon of Mali, who also practice female genital operations, as well as that of some West African immigrants in France who have argued that not to excise a girl would leave her "not only 'unclean' but 'masculine,' in that she retains a vestige of a male sex organ."[26] A Kenyan teacher from a village neighboring Kikhome offered an argument about excision that echoed Boddy's interpretation that female genital operations served to emphasize differences between women and men. The female teacher argued that clitoridectomies were positive for women in that while men were enslaved to their sexuality, women who had undergone excision were better able to resist their desires, thus affording them more control than men. This argument recalls the strategy of Victorian feminists in the United States who based claims to public authority on their alleged moral and sexual superiority to men.[27] However there is an important difference. In Sudan, although women's sexuality might be harshly "socialized," it was not repressed in the sense of encouraging prudishness, as was common among the European and North American Victorian middle classes. Hanny Lightfoot-Klein, an opponent of genital operations, noted the lustiness and bawdiness of older North African village women.[28] To her surprise, some village women who had been infibulated gave detailed descriptions of orgasms, presumably because other areas of the body had become intensified erogenous zones. Lightfoot-Klein's account was confirmed by a Sudanese doctor, Nahid Toubia, who cautioned that little is known to medical practitioners about the sexual functioning of infibulated women or the processes by which women might compensate for loss of the clitoris through other sensory areas, emotion, or fantasy.[29]

Among the Sebei Sabaots, Goldschmidt recorded an open interest in sexual matters and a concern with sexual prowess. He noted that a culturally sanctioned form of sexual petting in which orgasms were allowed but penetration prohibited had historically been permitted to both boys and girls prior to marriage and even excision.[30] Drawing on fieldwork observations from the

1960s, he expressed doubt as to whether "any normal boy or girl reaches circumcision a virgin," although, he noted, it was still strongly disapproved of for an uncircumcised girl to be pregnant.[31] He also described the initiation festivity itself as a time for open sexual license and noted that extramarital affairs were relatively common for both men and women, although women could be beaten on this account whereas wives held no sanctions over their husbands' behavior. On the basis of this apparent openness, Goldschmidt deemed implausible the view that clitoridectomies were intended to decrease women's sexual desire. He did, however, stress that sexual activity between men and women was tension-filled and that relationships between the sexes were generally characterized by hostility and mistrust. Thus, in this context, clitoridectomies might be best understood not as a simple attempt to eradicate the sexual desires of women but as attempts to control, and appropriately channel, women's sexuality and fertility in a patrilineal and patrilocal context. The reality that most forms of clitoridectomies and infibulations originated and continue to be performed in patrilineal and patrilocal societies suggests the importance of such contexts.

After exploring these anthropological accounts of female genital operations, illuminating as the accounts were, I was frustrated by the numerous questions that remained unanswered. One crucial question concerned how these practices had changed over time. How, I wondered, had the ritual initiation of girls in Kikhome been transformed from the pre-colonial to the colonial and, ultimately, to the post-colonial era? Furthermore, was there room in existing anthropological accounts of female genital operations for the agency of individuals and for resistance to social norms? Goldschmidt noted that the refusal of girls or boys to be circumcised was called "crying the knife." Had those who cried the knife always shared the dominant viewpoint that their actions were shameful? Did such actions ever take on connotations of active resistance, and were such actions ever more than individual? While social structural and symbolic interpretations of genital operations provided insight into the practice of female genital operations at a given moment in time, such interpretations also had their limitations. The theoretical legacy of functionalist and symbolic schools within anthropology has meant that many accounts have focused too narrowly on the present, on bounded social groups, and on cultural consensus.

What alternative understandings might historically based accounts of female genital operations suggest? Historian Claire Robertson, who looked at the relationship between clitoridectomies and collective social organization for Kikuyu women in Kenya, offers one attempt to consider female genital operations as historically malleable practices.[32] Robertson argues that women's age-sets, a form of social organization originating in the pre-colonial era and characterized by gerontocracy and an emphasis on the ritual practices of initiation and excision, also historically served the little-known function of organizing women into collective work groups on farms. With the increased stratification of Kenyan society in the colonial and post-colonial periods, the importance of women's collective efforts to organize their labor have, according to Robertson, not died out but been transformed. She argues that age-sets have metamorphosized in the contemporary period into relatively egalitarian grass-roots saving associations, environmental groups, and other cooperative labor and financial ventures that are being strategically used by Kikuyu women in their battle against poverty. Robertson writes, "From the 1920s to 1990 women's collective efforts moved from a more specific form of patriarchally sanctioned organization concerned with controlling sexuality and fertility to a more class-based women's solidarity involved with promoting women's economic activities."[33] As a result of this transformation, Robertson suggests that the importance and incidence of initiation and clitoridectomy have decreased, which she supports with statistics derived from her small sample and from a Kenyan source. Theoretically, this account focuses on the agency of Kikuyu women and in doing so allows space for these women to either agree with or resist the valorization of excision and thereby, potentially, to transform such practices. The possibility of resistance, for example, is suggested by colonial-era accounts in which some Kikuyu women are reported to have run away to mission stations in apparent attempts to escape forced marriages and possibly clitoridectomies.[34]

Presumably, female genital operations also play an important role as markers of social, ethnic, religious, and other forms of identity, an interpretation that has thus far gone largely unexplored in anthropological accounts. Even a brief consideration of the practice of male circumcision, which has historically been and at present remains a potent marker of group identity in European countries, would suggest the need to explore such a possibility.[35] Although, according to Robertson, excision appears to be on the wane among the Kikuyu, Goldschmidt's earlier account noted that the importance of the practice appeared to be on the rise among the Sabaot. Given the considerable violence that erupted between the Bukusu and the Sabaot in the years after I left Kikhome, one productive avenue for future research would be to explore the potential relationship between ethnic identity and this increased support for clitoridectomies. In other words, how and to what extent do clitoridectomies serve as symbols of ethnic identity and tradition within the volatile politics of the Kenyan nation-state?[36]

Despite the insights provided by the literature on these practices, stumbling blocks remain for anthropologists in developing a politically engaged, feminist position on female genital operations. Anthropological accounts that focus on how such practices either function or provide meaning, without attendant focus on how practices are transformed and given new meaning, discourage activism by implying that if such practices ceased, a social "need," symbolic or material, would be left unfulfilled. The transformation of the role of female genital operations in initiation and age-sets for Kikuyu women challenges any such rigid link between social needs and particular practices. If our analyses do not similarly emphasize the potential for transformation, the result can be a dangerous perceived dichotomy between cultural others for whom cultural practices function (and thus should be respected) and Europe and the United States, where traditions are open to challenge. Alternatively, attempts to provide historically based, non-essentialized accounts of such practices may offer one route to overcoming the widespread Euro-American tendency to view female genital operations solely in terms of either cultural relativism or moral outrage.

Beyond the Village: The International Controversy Surrounding Female Genital Operations

Clearly, the questions raised by female genital operations extend beyond Kikhome or Hofriyat in Sudan and even beyond the boundaries of Kenya, Sudan, and other African nation-states. Even before arriving in western Kenya, my perceptions of "female circumcision" had already been shaped by the vocal international controversy surrounding the issue. I had first learned of the practice from an article by Robin Morgan and Gloria Steinem that I read in a women's studies class as an undergraduate.[37] Obviously, I was operating in a particular social and cultural context as much as the villagers of Kikhome, and media accounts of female genital operations in places like Africa formed part of the background noise of the cultural world in which I was an insider. As I followed the written and televised reports on female genital operations in the United States, I became increasingly intrigued by the cultural dynamics of the debate itself. After living in Kenya, the "commonsense" terms operative in Western accounts of such practices seemed increasingly peculiar and deserving of explanation in their own right. Consequently, I will now leave Kikhome to begin addressing the discourse of this international debate, its historical roots, and its relationship to preexisting Euro-American understandings of Africa and Africans.

Although opposition to female genital operations by Westerners has a long history, extending back at least to the colonial era, it became an issue of concern to second-wave feminists in the United States and Europe during the 1970s.[38] Influential articles and books by Gloria Steinem, Mary Daly, and others, including third-world activists such as Nawal El Saadawi, condemned the practices, and international health organizations also took up the cause.[39] In this depiction of female genital operations for an international audience, the practices became largely severed from their sociocultural context (with the exception of El Saadawi's volume). While in Kikhome male and female initiations were performed side by side (albeit with very different consequences), in the Western-oriented literature opposing such practices there was an exclusive focus on the tormenting of girls, if not solely by men, then by a monolithic patriarchy.

During the United Nations Decade for Women (1975–85), female genital operations became a prominent and controversial issue. However, the response to the ensuing publicity was not what many first-world feminists might have expected. Instead of being congratulated for their opposition to female circumcision, they were called to task by some African and third-world women, including a group that threatened to walk out of the mid-decade international women's conference in Copenhagen in 1980. Although some of these women themselves opposed female genital operations, they objected to the way the issue was being handled and called attention to the troubling power dynamics that exist between first and third worlds as well as between first- and third-world women.[40] This confrontation led by African women formed merely one segment of a broader challenge to mainstream Euro-American feminism by women of color, working-class women, lesbians, and many third-world women who felt that their experiences and understandings had been excluded by white, middle-class formulations of feminism.[41] This challenge to Euro-American feminism also resulted in a shift of attention toward issues of difference among women as well as toward a reformulation of feminist politics that focused on coalition-building and the recognition of diversity rather than an assumption of homogeneous interests.[42]

Despite criticisms of the way third-world women have been represented, Alice Walker's novel, the film *Warrior Marks* and its companion volume, and essays published by the National Organization for Women have provoked a replay of debates over female genital operations in terms remarkably like those of the 1970s.[43] This frustrating sense of déjà vu might be dismissed as Walker's and NOW's refusal to engage the productive aspects of earlier debates.

More pertinent to understanding why these accounts have generated such a barrage of media attention, however, is the way that Walker's and NOW's presentation of female genital operations has fed into powerful and value-laden understandings of differences between Africans and Euro-Americans—understandings that are being reemphasized with increased immigration from the third world to the first. Such understandings presume a radical difference, a binary opposition between first and third worlds that is itself built upon the historical belief in a chasm between "modern" Euro-Americans and "native," colonized others. Reading through much of the Western-based literature opposing female genital operations, the degree to which many of the arguments work to reproduce such beliefs is striking.

One common trope in much of the Euro-American–oriented literature opposing female genital operations has been the tendency to characterize African women as thoroughly oppressed victims of patriarchy and ignorance or both, not as social actors in their own right. Sub-Saharan and North African women are alternately seen as not being allowed to express their voices or as having defective or confused understandings if they speak in favor of genital operations. For example, Mary Daly wrote that in relation to genital operations "the apparently 'active' role of the women, themselves mutilated, is in fact a passive instrumental role. . . . Mentally castrated, these women participate in the destruction of their own kind."[44] Here women are blamed for their false consciousness and are seen as the mere pawns of men. More recently, in the case of African immigrants in France, Bronywn Winter similarly argued that "one of the greatest problems facing feminists campaigning against excision is, in fact, women's complicity in their own oppression and in that of their children."[45] Hosken had attributed the apparent complicity of African women to their isolation from the "outside" world, stating, "Local women—who it is said should speak for themselves (the majority of whom are illiterate . . .)—have no connection with the outside world and have no way to organize against the practice."[46] This position is particularly belied by the current organizing of African women's groups, both on and off the continent, in relation to female genital operations. Feminist scholars, particularly those from non-Western countries, are increasingly critiquing portrayals that presume third-world women to be dominated by an ahistorical, patriarchal tradition that is assumed to be more severe than that in Europe or the United States. The anthropological literature does support the view that gender inequality is widespread; nevertheless, the cultural and historical particulars of how gender relations are constructed differently in different places, and the alternate sources of power and authority that women often hold, are ignored in these generalized assumptions about the oppression of third-world women.[47]

Much of the Western-oriented literature opposing female genital operations also constructs culture and tradition in problematic ways. Rather than focusing on "culture" as historically changeable and broadly encompassing beliefs and practices characteristic of a social group, the discourse on genital operations understands culture as ahistorical "customs" or "traditions." Such traditions are simultaneously depicted as the meaningless hangovers of a pre-modern era and as the defining characteristic of the third world. In this scenario, traditions in the third world are hardened essences that can only be shed by modernization, whereas in the West, "backward" cultural traditions are conceived of as being steadily replaced by "rational" ways of life. To quote Hosken once again, "The myth about the importance of 'cultural traditions' must be laid to rest, considering that 'development'—the introduction of imported Western technology and living patterns—is the goal of every country where the operations are practiced today."[48] Development, assumed to be the intrinsic property of Europe and the United States rather than a cultural construct in its own right, emerges in this discourse as the antithesis of cultural traditions.

Culture and traditions are often coded as harmful, coercive, and superfluous. Pratibha Parmar proclaims that women who have undergone genital operations have "been irrevocably wounded by traditions," and she and Walker adopt the slogan "Culture is not Torture" in *Warrior Marks*.[49] Linda Weil-Curiel, a lawyer prominent in legal battles against female genital operations in France, criticized the suspended sentences given to some African immigrant parents, stating, "The parents are the real culprits. They know they are going to hurt the child, and they nonetheless take the child to the excisors, to the knife . . . there is no excuse, ever, for such a deed."[50] Here, immigrant parents are condemned for not being able to think outside culture, implying that the author feels herself capable of doing so. Forrest Sawyer, the anchor of ABC-TV's *Day One*, emphasized the presumed weight of culture: "This is a brutal, disabling ritual so tied to culture and tradition that for thousands of years women have been powerless to stop it. In fact, the taboos are so strong that the women subjected to it will rarely talk about it at all."[51]

A front-page article in the *New York Times* concerning Fauziya Kassindja highlights this assumption of the oppressive nature of tradition.[52] Despite information in the article suggesting Kassindja's elite and "modern" background (for example, Kassindja's father owned a successful trucking business in Togo, and she attended boarding school in Ghana), the language of the article stresses the exotic, relying on such terms as *tribal law, bloody rite, banish[ment]*, and *family patriarchs in their tribe*. Rhetorically, the article suggests the ironic parallels between the alleged fetters of "tribal customs" and actual fetters in a Pennsylvania prison where Kassindja was detained while seeking political asylum. The irony emerges as journalist Celia Dugger challenges the assumption of "freedom" in the United States by suggesting parallels with the (unquestioned) oppression of "tradition" in African countries. Kassindja's televised answer to a surprised Ted Koppel, informing him that most young women in Togo are happy to have the procedure done and that they "think it is something very great," could not dislodge the program's implicit assumption that all young women are coerced and would gladly flee their own countries to escape such practices.[53] Thus, rather than acknowledging Kassindja as a young woman who had dared to resist the social norms of which she disapproved (in part because she was raised in a liberal household that offered alternative life choices), media accounts instead emphasized the allegedly coercive and oppressive nature of African cultures and societies as a whole.

In other accounts, collective "culture" is judged to be less relevant than rights premised on the individual. As Tilman Hasche, the lawyer for Lydia Oluloro, the Nigerian woman who legally petitioned to remain in the United States to prevent the excision of her daughters, stated in a *New York Times* article, "Frankly, I don't give a damn if opposing this is a violation of someone's culture. To me, female genital mutilation is a violation of the physical and spiritual integrity of a person."[54] In some accounts, cultural beliefs are recognized only as "insanity." For example, A. M. Rosenthal of the *New York Times* called on the people and governments of the countries where genital operations are practiced "to revolt against the sexual and social insanities that allow the mutilation of half their population."[55]

In contrast to this image of sub-Saharan and North African societies as tradition-bound and oppressed by culture, Euro-American institutions and values are depicted as exemplars of culture-free reason and rationality, as represented in particular by Western medicine. This binary distinction between a rational West and an overly traditional and cultured "rest" has been underscored in the oppositional literature by emphatic attention to the health problems associated with such practices. Health consequences *are* real and disturbing. For clitoridectomies, these include the possibility of hemorrhage and infection. In the case of infibulation they include difficulties with urination, intercourse, and childbirth; fluid retention; and cyst formation.[56] Yet as a position statement issued by the Women's Caucus of the African Studies Association noted, these health consequences must be located within a larger context in which women's health may also be severely affected by malnutrition, lack of clean water, and inadequate health care.[57] Henry Louis Gates asks, "Is it, after all, unreasonable to be suspicious of Westerners who are exercised over female circumcision, but whose eyes glaze over when the same women are merely facing starvation?"[58] The question of why these particular health issues generate such a barrage of interest deserves closer examination.

Clearly, popular interest in female genital operations stems in part from their sensational aspects, practices that simultaneously horrify and titillate Euro-American audiences. This tendency toward sensationalism draws on a long history in which sub-Saharan and North African women's bodies have been simultaneously exoticized and eroticized, as evidenced in the pickling of a San ("Bushman") woman's vulva and its display in France in the nineteenth century and erotic French colonial postcards that draw on sexually charged ideas about veiling and the alleged languorous harems of imprisoned Muslim women.[59] Concerning the recent interest in female genital operations, Dawit noted the voyeurism implicit in a CNN newscast that spent nearly ten minutes graphically depicting the infibulation of an Egyptian girl.[60] Modern medical discourse may, in fact, perform the dual role of using the "objective" language of science to construct the issue as outside of culture while simultaneously offering a sanitized way of continuing the historical preoccupation with the genitalia and sexuality of African women.

The privileging of Euro-American experience in the medical discourse surrounding genital operations is also apparent in the discussion of pain. Most of the literature lists pain at the forefront of the medical consequences or problems associated with genital operations.[61] And it is pain that leads to accusations that genital operations are "torture." For the adolescent initiation rituals that I described for Kikhome, however, pain is an intrinsic part of the ritual and is socially meaningful—although it is not for infibulation and *sunna* operations, for which an anesthetic is sometimes used or which are done in the hospital. Although all humans presumably have the same range of physiological responses, barring individual differences and learned techniques for controlling pain, the meanings associated with pain and ideas about how one should respond to it vary situationally as well as cross-culturally. Within the context of sub-Saharan African initiation rituals (or, for that matter, U.S. military boot camps or Indian ascetic rites), pain may be viewed not simply as something to be avoided but as something to be endured and that can result in the positive transformation of the individual.

To summarize, much of the Western-oriented literature by Euro-Americans that opposes female genital operations invokes a series of binary oppositions:

First World	Third World
modernity	tradition
science	superstition
civilized	barbarous
freedom	torture/repression
women as actors	women as oppressed
medical knowledge	ignorance/disease

The cumulative effect of these binary oppositions is to perpetuate a dichotomous understanding of first and third worlds, an enduring division between "us" and "them." This opposition is apparent in Walker's novel *Possessing the Secret of Joy*, where the dysfunctional sex life, intensely painful childbirth, deformed child, troubled marriage, and tortured soul of the main character, Tashi, are all attributed to "circumcision." Tashi is then contrasted with her U.S. husband's French lover, who emerges as the embodiment of female liberation and for whom birth is orgasmic. Perhaps the sense of a radical separation between first and third worlds, however, is most forcefully reproduced in the accusations of "torture." Because clitoridectomies or infibulation are usually performed at the request of parents and relatives, those whom Weil-Curiel classifies as "the real culprits," this discourse implicitly assumes that even family members in such societies are callous or barbaric enough to torture their own.

Colonial History and the Debate over the Status of Women

A perusal of the Western-oriented literature opposing genital operations, much of which reproduces such disturbing power hierarchies, makes starkly apparent why gender is a fraught issue between so-called first and third worlds. It is also clear that understanding the tenacity of the discourse discussed above requires understanding its history, and, in fact, much recent scholarship has focused on colonial discourses of gender and the uses to which such discourses were put. This scholarship has argued that the alleged overwhelming oppression of "native" women by "native" men was consistently used to justify colonial domination and that Euro-American feminism was itself used toward those ends.

The colonial discourse on female genital operations in Africa resembles that on other practices, such as *sati* (widow-burning) in India, foot-binding in China, and veiling in Muslim societies. Numerous scholars have documented how representations of the domination of non-Western women by non-Western men were used to justify British and French imperialism.[62] Colonial representations that reified male domination as "traditional" throughout the third world ignored the ways in which colonialism, and the economic transformations that accompanied it, systematically oppressed both colonized women and men. It also ignored the ways that colonialism hurt women in particular by economically undermining what was an already vulnerable group and by subverting women's historical sources of power and autonomy. The symbolic importance of Algerian women's "oppression" in underpinning French colonialism was given physical form in a staged ceremony in which Algerian women were unveiled by French women in a symbolic enactment of the "enlightenment" of French rule. This ceremony was staged during the 1950s in response to the growing resistance to French rule by the Algerian nationalist party, the National Liberation Front (FLN), which itself included many women.[63] The reality of gender inequality in France—for instance, French women were not allowed to vote until after World War II—did not stop French women from being held up as the liberated ideal for Algerians.

Leila Ahmed argues that budding Euro-American feminist ideals were co-opted into the service of justifying colonial domination. She writes: "Even as the Victorian male establishment devised theories to contest the claims of feminism, and derided and rejected the ideas of feminism and the notion of men's oppressing women with respect to itself, it captured the language of feminism and redirected it, in the service of colonialism, toward Other men and the cultures of Other men."[64] Ahmed addresses the ironies of this situation. She notes that Lord Cromer, the British consul-general in Egypt at the turn of the century, wrote at length about the degraded status of Muslim women as epitomized by the veil and by sex segregation. It was this degradation that symbolized for him the cultural inferiority of Egyptian men and underscored the importance of the Western "civilizing" mission that could help Egyptians "develop."[65] Ahmed notes, however, that in England Cromer was a founding member and even president of the Men's League for Opposing Women's Suffrage and that in Egypt he did little to implement educational policies that would help Egyptian women. Liddle and Joshi and Mani make similar arguments for colonial India.[66] Mani argues that the debate over *sati* was less about women than about evaluating the worth of Hindu tradition in terms that would cast colonialism as a civilizing mission. Liddle and Joshi note that Katherine Mayo's 1927 book *Mother India,* which documented in detail male abuses of women, was used in England to justify the denial of self-rule to India.[67]

What Ahmed labels "colonial feminism" was often replaced in the postcolonial era by "state feminism" in which many women's organizations were co-opted by national governments and staffed by female relatives of male politicians. For example, in Kenya the colonial government's women's orga-

nization, Maendeleo ya Wanawake, was later taken over by the national government.[68] Despite the centrality of women in many nationalist movements
in the 1950s and 1960s (and earlier in India), male nationalists were often
ambivalent towards gender reform. In some cases, legal reforms affecting
women were extremely limited, as in Algeria and Egypt, or they were gestures
offered by male politicians to demonstrate their countries' "modernity."[69] In
the case of India, although male nationalists supported a women's movement
that provided support for the nationalist cause, men were often hostile toward reform of personal law that challenged the status quo within families.[70]
As Deniz Kandiyoti suggests, in order to understand reactions to feminism
in many third-world countries, it is necessary to understand the ways in
which feminism has been co-opted and monopolized by ruling interests and
elites in these countries.[71] Furthermore, focusing solely on formal "feminist"
organizations obscures indigenous forms of feminism that do not necessarily accord with the middle-class, Euro-American model.[72] For example, the
activism of peasant, working-class, and minority women may be downplayed
when evaluated solely in terms of gender interests rather than the intersec-
tion of gender with ethnic and class issues. The reality that first- and third-
world women have different needs, concerns, and power bases, combined
with the particular histories of feminism in former colonies, has contributed to tensions in the midst of efforts to create an international women's
movement.[73] Female genital operations have proven to be one of the most
powerful fault lines along which such tensions erupt.

Gender and the Hardening of "Tradition"

Attention to colonial history reveals that cultural arguments can be a dou-
ble-edged sword. Although such arguments may be used to argue for tolerance in the face of difference, they may also be used to stifle change and
impose or buttress particular culturally defined power relationships. The
conceptual fusing of women with culture and tradition has particular implications for women, who may become symbols in a battle to construct
particular versions of "modern" or "traditional" society. This tendency is
clear in the case of female genital operations. In Kenya in the late 1920s and
early 1930s, missionaries of the Church of Scotland waged a campaign to stop
the practice of clitoridectomy among the Kikuyu who lived in the area surrounding Nairobi. Clitoridectomy, which appeared to be on the wane despite
its importance to the age-grade system, was revitalized and given new meaning not by traditionalists but by the young nationalists of the Kikuyu Central Association.[74] As Pedersen notes, "As a defense of clitoridectomy became

entangled with long-standing Kikuyu grievances about mission influence and access to land, clitoridectomy, always the sign of the 'true Kikuyu,' also came to be seen as a mark of loyalty to the incipient, as yet imaginary, nation."[75] Although women's voices were largely unrecorded in this debate, Robertson suggests that the fight against the missionary ban on clitoridectomies was also related to the desire of Kikuyu elders and young militant men to control women's trading in Nairobi because it threatened male sexual and economic dominance.[76] Jomo Kenyatta, leader of the Kikuyu Central Association and later the powerful first president of an independent Kenya, was himself a prominent cultural nationalist proponent of clitoridectomies. Kenyatta, who had been a student of the famous anthropologist Bronislaw Malinowski in England, positively portrayed and defended the practice in *Facing Mount Kenya,* an ethnographic study of his Kikuyu ethnic group.[77]

According to both Leila Ahmed and Lata Mani, the association between women and tradition was in large part the result of the colonial legacy. Underlying much colonial thought (and much anthropology) has been the assumption that cultures are bounded, discrete units defined by ahistorical "traditions" or "customs."[78] Ahmed argues that colonialist isolation of the veil as not simply the symbol but the enactment par excellence of Muslim cultural inferiority and degradation positioned women as the ahistorical embodiment of that "tradition." She maintains that this link between women and "tradition" was perpetuated by nationalists, who, in their fight for independence, simply inverted the equation and instead championed the veil as the embodiment of religious and national identity.[79] Partha Chatterjee contends that Indian nationalists, operating under colonial control in public arenas, conceded Euro-American superiority in technological terms but came to view the inner world of domesticity and tradition associated with women as the sphere in which Indians could demonstrate their superiority, spiritually and culturally, over the West.[80] Thus, while "tradition," codified in its most rigid and hierarchical form under British colonial law, was understood by the colonizers as both intrinsic to the character of the colonized and the embodiment of their inferiority, it was often inverted in its essentialist form by the colonized themselves to epitomize a cultural integrity and worth that was defined in highly gendered ways.

This association between women and culture-tradition has also meant that attempts to increase or maintain control over women are often argued in cultural terms, as demonstrated by a Kenyan legal case that attracted international attention in the 1980s.[81] This case pitted a socially prominent Kikuyu widow, Wambui Otieno, against her deceased husband's Luo patrilineage for the right to bury his body. The battle tapped deep tensions within Kenyan society, including the relations between Luo and Kikuyu ethnic groups, nuclear families versus patrilineages, and urban elites versus the rural poor. Nevertheless, the case was argued through an intertwined discourse of gender and reified tradition. The Otieno lawsuit encapsulated the same potentially contradictory meanings associated with tradition as have female genital operations, and it similarly pricked national pride as the controversy circulated in the international media. Particularly when portrayed for international audiences, female genital operations have often been a symbol of "backwardness" and a source of shame to those in third-world countries who are concerned that their nations live up to Western-defined standards of "modernity."[82] At the same time, in a cultural nationalist tradition, defense of these practices has also served as a symbol of cultural integrity or resistance to Euro-American domination—ironically, a thoroughly "modern" position. What is disturbing to feminists, however, are the ways that attempts to create particular versions of cultural tradition may be translated into attempts to create, and thus control, particular kinds of women.

This association between women and hardened notions of culture and tradition is not limited to the so-called third world. Kristin Koptiuch, for example, explores its implications in the use of "cultural defense" arguments in legal cases dealing with immigrants in the United States.[83] She cites a case in which a Chinese man living in Brooklyn murdered his wife for allegedly having an extramarital affair. His lawyers defended him on the grounds that his actions were dictated by his rural Chinese background in which adultery brings great shame to a man and his ancestors—a position defended by an anthropologist brought in to offer expert testimony. The judge downgraded the charge from murder to manslaughter and gave him the lightest sentence possible—five years of probation, even though, as Koptiuch notes, he would have been sentenced for murder had he been living in China.[84] Unfortunately, this case is not unusual; in the United States, many cases that make use of cultural defense arguments do so on behalf of men in instances of violence against women. To extrapolate from Koptiuch's argument, if cultural defense arguments are allowed to stand, the specter is also raised of a potential dismantling of protective legislation through the creation of innumerable exceptions. Such an escalation is possible because "cultural" arguments can be made not only for non-nationals but also for numerous other racial, ethnic, religious, and other identity-based groups.

Koptiuch's argument carries implications for international debates over female genital operations. It suggests that the common responses to such practices—both the relativist argument, which privileges cultural tolerance, and the blatantly ethnocentric argument, which assumes the backwardness of African traditions and the inferiority of immigrants—carry male-dominant and colonial legacies based on hardened notions of tradition and culture. This raises difficult questions for feminist anthropologists. If we resort to cultural-relativist arguments in the attempt to divert the racism embedded in much of the international outcry over female genital operations, do we end up undermining those African women who are themselves working to change these practices? Are we participating in leaving them exposed to charges that they are denigrating their own "traditions" and being culturally "inauthentic"? In using an uncritical notion of culture, do we in fact create the same sense of difference, of estrangement from each other's lives and worlds, that is also generated in the flagrantly ethnocentric literature that opposes female genital operations?

Conclusion: Who Speaks?

Soon after the opening of the film *Warrior Marks,* an op-ed piece appeared in the *New York Times* written by two African professional women, Seble Dawit and Salem Mekuria, with the named support of six others, all of whom oppose and have been working to abolish female genital operations. They wrote:

> We take great exception to the recent Western focus on female genital mutilation in Africa, most notably by the author Alice Walker.
>
> Ms. Walker's new film *Warrior Marks* portrays an African village where women and children are without personality, dancing and gazing blankly through some stranger's script of their lives. The respected elder women of the village's Secret Society turn into slit-eyed murderers wielding rusted weapons with which to butcher children.
>
> As is common in Western depictions of Africa, Ms. Walker and her collaborator, Pratibha Parmar, portray the continent as a monolith, African women and children are the props, and the village the background against which Alice Walker, heroine-savior, comes to articulate their pain and condemn those who inflict it.
>
> Like Ms. Walker's novel *Possessing the Secret of Joy,* this film is emblematic of the Western feminist tendency to see female genital mutilation as the gender oppression to end all oppressions. Instead of being an issue worthy of attention in itself, it has become a powerfully emotive lens through which to view personal pain—a gauge by which to measure distance between the West and the rest of humanity.

They concluded by noting: "Neither Alice Walker nor any of us here can speak for them [African women on the continent]; but if we have the power and the resources, we can create the room for them to speak, and to speak with us as well."[85]

Efua Dorkenoo, a woman of West African descent living in England, responded to Dawit and Mekuria's op-ed piece in an article that was signed as well by a number of other African professional women living in the West. The article was printed in a special section of a 1994 NOW newsletter under the heading "African Women Speak Out on FGM [female genital mutilation]." Dorkenoo wrote:

> The authors of . . . [the op-ed piece in the *New York Times*] made the mistake of presenting themselves as speaking on behalf of all African women. African women working on this problem come from different perspectives and different experiences. . . . If we Africans sincerely wish to see an end to this harmful practice, both in Africa and the West, we cannot rule out media coverage irrespective of how painful the memories of FGM might be. It is time that we stop blaming others and being hysterical whenever this subject is raised; rather we should focus on how to tap into international goodwill to stop this suffering of our girls. . . . Many may not care for Alice Walker's perspective on raising awareness of FGM, but at least we should be honest enough to acknowledge that her recent work is bringing the subject to the attention of a wider international audience.[86]

That Dorkenoo and her supporters see Dawit and Mekuria as attempting to speak for *all* African women—despite their stated intention to the contrary—alerts us to the ongoing importance attached to "authentic voices" and the presumed ability of such voices to speak for others. This preoccupation with authentic voices stems from the recognition that such voices are widely considered persuasive in an Euro-American political discourse that focuses heavily on identity. At the same time, this exchange provides a graphic demonstration of the inadequacy of such a model. Obviously, there is no unified voice for African women, even among such a relatively distinct category of women as African professionals who oppose genital operations and live in Europe or the United States.

Post-structuralist feminist scholars like Judith Butler have criticized this preoccupation with identity politics.[87] In a challenge similar to that posed against hardened understandings of culture, Butler criticizes identity politics for building on and encouraging essentialism—that is, the reduction of complex human experiences and competing identities to static essences presumed to emanate from the unambiguous facts of gender, race, or nationality.[88] While historically the concept of culture provided a space that allowed for respect and understanding of differences, identity politics has similarly provided dominated groups with an arena for organizing and demanding rights. If not problematized, however, the terms in which such claims are made can work to create new forms of oppression rather than greater liberation. Hardened conceptions of culture can suggest both insurmountable barriers between "us" and "them" and a predetermined "authenticity" to which individuals are pressured to conform. Similarly, a feminist politics based on identity can be reduced to a preoccupation with ever-finer distinctions between categories of women, each presumed to be internally homogeneous. These questions are not theoretical niceties but reflect serious political concerns, particularly in this ever-globalizing era. In the United States, where politics are often organized around identity and pleas for tolerance are made in the name of "multiculturalism," we need to know which understandings of identity and culture are at work. How, for example, do we interpret the calls being made for cultural asylum in cases like those of Oluloro and Kassindja? How can universalized conceptions of human rights be made to include culture and the particular situations in which women find themselves without creating new cages for ourselves by reducing culture to coercion and identity to hardened essences?

In the effort to transcend "either/or" reactions to female genital operations that are limited to either moral outrage or cultural relativism, one initial step is to recognize that "female genital operations"—despite my use of the phrase—do not exist as a category. To lump together the diverse forms of the practice into a single term known as *female genital mutilation, female circumcision,* or *female genital operations* obscures the diverse geographic locations, meanings, and politics in which such practices are embedded and rhetorically constructs a generic "they" who conduct such practices and a generic "we" who do not. In offering an account of a particular place, Kikhome, my goal was not to provide a neatly argued social-scientific account of the practice. Instead, my goal was to use this particular place at a particular point in time, as well as my encounters with some of the young women I knew there, as a means to explore the myriad issues surrounding female genital operations and to begin to phrase the kinds of questions that might help to elucidate these practices. Such questions range from symbolic meaning and individual psychology to the gendered politics of family organization, ethnic identity, and colonial and post-colonial states to the presumed links between women and culture/tradition.

The questions suggested by the situation in Kikhome, however, can just as productively illuminate the international controversies surrounding female genital operations. Just as we might explore the historical and political contexts in which clitoridectomies are embedded in Kikhome and how such practices are both in and against the interests of young women there, we might ask related questions about the contexts in which international struggles around such practices occur. When and why do we exhibit relativistic tolerance to female genital operations? In what contexts do we express moral outrage? How might our responses hurt, as well as help, African women? How does the global politics of relationships between first- and third-world countries, from the legacy of colonialism to contemporary global economic and population flows, shape our participation in these controversies? And just as the young women in Kikhome might have strategically merged their voices with more powerful others like the church and state, so, too, can we ask how those of us participating in these international controversies are strategically merging our voices with one or more of the powerful discourses of feminism, cultural nationalism, relativism, humanism, and, in some cases, to be blunt, racism. What are the histories of such discourses, and to what ends are we using them?

Ultimately, however, the theoretical separation between clitoridectomy in Kikhome as ritual practice and the international controversy surrounding female genital operations as discourse is untenable. Discourse is also practice. It is not simply a way of understanding or thinking about the world, it is also a way of acting in it. Given that our discourse also signals a form of intervention, I would like to encourage feminists of whatever national origins, race, or gender to work against those assumptions being made in Western-oriented media accounts of female genital operations that reproduce colonial and neo-colonial ideologies. Feminist anthropologists can also make a productive contribution by examining the social contexts of both ritual practices and international controversies and by exploring the power dynamics surrounding support and opposition to such practices, whether in rural African villages or urban France. For those interested in more hands-on styles of activism, critics of identity politics and hardened notions of culture are also pointing us in the direction of a feminist politics based on alliances and coalitions.[89] Hopefully, this brand of feminist politics will also be capable of critiquing practices such as clitoridectomy and infibulation without resorting to neo-colonial ideologies of gender and without denigrating women who support such practices. At the same time, the Kenyan anthropologist Achola Pala-Okeyo cautions that "the role of [Western] feminists is not to be in front, leading the way for other women, but to be in back *supporting* the other women's struggles to bring about change."[90] Here Pala-Okeyo forces us to recognize that all of us, along with the debates in which we are engaged, are the products of tenacious power relationships with long histories. The hope is that we can bring this recognition to bear at the same time that we form alliances based on shared politics across boundaries of race, nationality, and gender.

Notes

An earlier version of this essay appeared in *Cultural Anthropology* 12, no. 3 and is reproduced by permission of the American Anthropological Association. Not for sale or further reproduction. I would like to thank Lila Abu-Lughod for her insight, encouragement, and advice during the course of endless drafts of this essay, and Connie Sutton for her insistence that I finally finish it. Thanks also to Daniel Segal and the anonymous reviewers at *Cultural Anthropology* for their perceptive comments on the originally published version of this article as well as to Claire Robertson and Stanlie James for including it in this volume. Finally, I would like to thank Chris Boebel for moral as well as intellectual support and for pushing me to the final conclusion.

1. Linda Weil-Curiel, "Mali Woman Challenges International Law," *National NOW Times Special Edition* (June 1994): 5; Bronwyn Winter, "Woman, the Law and Cultural Relativism in France: The Case of Excision," *Signs: Journal of Women in Culture and Society* 13, no. 4 (1994): 939–74.

2. Beth Corbin, "Deportation vs. Female Genital Mutilation," *National NOW Times Special Edition* (June 1994): 5; Sophfronia Scott Gregory, "At Risk of Mutilation," *Time*, March 21, 1994, 45–46.

3. Celia W. Dugger, "Women's Pleas for Asylum Puts Tribal Ritual on Trial," *New York Times*, April 15, 1996, A1, B4; Celia W. Dugger, "U.S. Frees African Fleeing Ritual Mutilation," *New York Times*, April 26, 1996, A1, B7.

4. Pratibha Parmar, "Pratibha's Journey," in *Warrior Marks: Female Genital Mutilation and the Sexual Blinding of Women*, ed. Alice Walker and Pratibha Parmar (New York: Harcourt Brace, 1993), 99–238.

5. Seble Dawit and Salem Mekuria, "The West Just Doesn't Get It," *New York Times*, Dec. 7, 1993, A27; Dugger, "Women's Pleas for Asylum"; Dugger, "U.S. Frees African"; William Raspberry, "Women and a Brutal Tradition," *Washington Post*, Nov. 8, 1993, A21; A. M. Rosenthal, "On My Mind: Female Genital Torture," *New York Times*, Dec. 29, 1992, A15; Gregory, "At Risk of Mutilation"; "Female Genital Mutilation and Political Asylum," ABC-TV *Nightline*, May 2, 1996; "African Woman Seeks Asylum from Genital Mutilation," ABC-TV *World News Tonight*, April 29, 1996; "Nigerian Says Daughter Faces Mutilation if Deported," CNN *Newsnight*, March 23, 1994; "Lydia's Choice," *Dateline NBC*, March 22, 1994; "Activists Denounce Female Genital Mutilation," National Public Radio *All Things Considered*, March 23, 1994. See also "Female Circumcision," and "Egypt's Hosni Mubarak," both on CNN Specials *Beyond the Numbers*, Sept. 7 and Sept. 9, 1994; "Scarred for Life," ABC-TV *Day One*, Sept. 20, 1993; and "New Book and Film Deals with Female Genital Mutilation," National Public Radio *Morning Edition*, Dec. 7, 1993.

6. See, however, Janice Boddy "Womb as Oasis: The Symbolic Context of Pharaonic Circumcision in Rural Northern Sudan," *American Ethnologist* 9, no. 4 (1982): 682–98; Janice Boddy, *Wombs and Alien Spirits: Women, Men and the Zar Cult in Northern Sudan* (Madison: University of Wisconsin, Press, 1989); Ellen Gruenbaum, "Women's Rights and Cultural Self-Determination in the Female Genital Mutilation Controversy," *American*

Anthropology Newsletter May 1995, 14–15; Rose Oldfield Hayes, "Female Genital Mutilation, Fertility Control, Women's Roles, and the Patrilineage in Modern Sudan: A Functional Analysis," *American Ethnologist* 62, no. 4 (1975): 617–33; Corrine Kratz, *Affecting Performance: Meaning, Movement, and Experience in Okiek Women's Initiation* (Washington: Smithsonian Institution Press, 1994); Henrietta Moore, *Space, Text and Gender* (New York: Cambridge University Press, 1986); and Carolyn Martin Shaw, *Colonial Inscriptions: Race, Sex and Class in Kenya* (Minneapolis: University of Minnesota Press, 1995). For more recent accounts see Ellen Gruenbaum, *The Female Circumcision Controversy* (Philadelphia: University of Pennsylvania Press, 2001); and Bettina Shell-Duncan and Ylva Hernlund, eds., *Female "Circumcision" in Africa: Culture, Controversy, and Change* (Boulder: Lynne Rienner, 2000).

7. Despite the problematic aspects of the terms *first* and *third worlds*, which include the assumption of hierarchy, the proclivity toward homogenization, and the attendant lack of specificity and historicity, I will nevertheless follow Chandra Talpade Mohanty, Ann Russo, and Lourdes Torres and retain this usage (*Third World Women and the Politics of Feminism* [Bloomington: Indiana University Press, 1991]). Because I seek to critique precisely these types of homogenizing and unhistorical tendencies, the continued use of the terms *first* and *third worlds* signals a desire to problematize rather than accept such assumptions.

8. Marilyn Strathern, "An Awkward Relationship: The Case of Feminism and Anthropology," *Signs: Journal of Women in Culture and Society* 12, no. 2 (1987): 276–92.

9. "Kikhome" and all names mentioned herein are pseudonyms.

10. As Lila Abu-Lughod has observed, although the universalist presumptions of "humanism" must be problematized, the concept continues to hold value for anthropologists as the "language of human equality with the most moral force." Abu-Lughod, "Writing against Culture," in *Recapturing Anthropology*, ed. Richard G. Fox (Santa Fe: School of American Research Press, 1991), 158.

11. See also Kristin Koptiuch, "'Cultural Defense' and Criminological Displacements: Gender, Race and (Trans)Nation in the Legal Surveillance of U.S. Diaspora Asians," in *Displacement, Diaspora and Geographies of Identity*, ed. Smadar Lavie and Ted Swedenburg (Durham: Duke University Press, 1996), 215–33.

12. Nahid Toubia, "Female Circumcision as a Public Health Issue," *New England Journal of Medicine* 331, no. 11 (1994): 712–16. Robertson notes that statistics may be based on the erroneous assumption that if some members of an ethnic group now practice genital operations or had in the past, then all members continue to do so today. Claire Robertson "Grassroots in Kenya: Women, Genital Mutilation, and Collective Action, 1920–1990," *Signs: Journal of Women in Culture and Society* 21, no 3 (1996): 61; Corbin, "Deportation vs. Female Genital Mutilation"; Gregory, "At Risk of Mutilation."

13. Seble Dawit, "African Women in the Diaspora and the Problem of Female Genital Mutilation," presented at the Women's Caucus of the African Studies Association, Nov. 1994; Wendy Harcourt, "Gender, Culture and Reproduction: North-South," *Development* 2, no. 3 (1988): 66–68; Hanny Lightfoot-Klein, *Prisoners of Ritual: An Odyssey into Female Genital Circumcision in Africa* (New York: Haworth Press, 1989). Natalie Angier has discussed U.S. women whose "abnormal" (often unusually large) clitorises were surgically altered at birth. The women are protesting that medical practice after encountering prob-

lems in sexual functioning (Angier, "New Debate over Surgery on Genitals," *New York Times,* May 13, 1997, C1, C6).

14. Although some opponents of male circumcision also argue that removal of the foreskin decreases male sexual pleasure, the removal of the clitoris would be more equivalent to the amputation of the penis (e.g., Toubia, "Female Circumcision," 712). What is not often discussed in the literature, however, is how women who have had such procedures experience their sexuality. The more radical procedure of infibulation, which includes not only removing the clitoris and labia but also sewing together the remaining tissues, commonly leads to painful sexual intercourse, and, Boddy notes ("Womb as Oasis"), some women she encountered in the Sudan avoided intercourse for that reason. Yet Nahid Toubia, a Sudanese doctor who opposes the practice, cautions, "The assumption that all circumcised women have sexual problems or are unable to achieve orgasm is not substantiated by research or anecdotal evidence" ("Female Circumcision," 714). She observes that the "ability of women to compensate for it [infibulation] through other sensory areas or emotions and fantasy is not well understood" (714; see also Lightfoot-Klein, *Prisoners of Ritual*).

Although there has been much concern by opponents of female genital operations with the psychological impact of genital operations (see, for example, Alice Walker, *Possessing the Secret of Joy* [New York: Harcourt Brace Jovanovich, 1992], and Walker and Parmar, *Warrier Marks*), this impact would obviously depend heavily on the social context and meanings that individuals attribute to such practices. Toubia does state that in her clinical experience in Sudan, many infibulated women seem to experience anxiety relating to their genitals. Presumably, the impact of such procedures would be different for women raised in Euro-American countries, where such practices are not prevalent and would be socially stigmatizing rather than valued. African women in France have organized against the practices and argue that "circumcised" adolescent girls living there experience "enormous psychosexual problems" (Mouvement pour la Défense des Droits de la Femme Noire [MODEFEN]), 1982, as cited in Winter, "Women, the Law, and Cultural Relativism in France," 956; Awa Thiam, *Speak Out, Black Sisters: Feminism and Oppression in Black Africa,* trans. Dorothy S. Blair (Dover, N.H.: Pluto Press, 1986).

15. I was teaching under the auspices of the World Teach Program, a nongovernmental, U.S.-based organization that helps college graduates find international teaching positions.

16. For a similar description among the Sebei, a subgroup of the Sabaot, see Walter Goldschmidt, *Culture and Behavior of the Sebei: A Study in Continuity and Adaptation* (Berkeley: University of California Press, 1976), and Goldschmidt, *The Sebei: A Study in Adaptation* (New York: Holt, Rinehart and Winston, 1986).

17. Goldschmidt, *The Sebei.*

18. There were, however, secret aspects of the initiation of which I would remain unaware. Goldschmidt describes a ceremony among the Sebei that parallels those of secret societies in other parts of Africa, all closely guarded from the uninitiated or from the opposite sex. Among the Sebei, at the end of the recuperation period and the night before the cave ceremony in the hills, initiates are taken out individually into the bush and frightened with a replica of an animal (a leopard for girls, a lion for boys). The encounter is accompanied by noise produced by twirling a stick, one end of which is attached to the head of a drum or

a bull-roarer. After receiving scratches from the animal, which mark one as initiated, they are "introduced" to the animal, learning its "secret" (*The Sebei*, 105–8).

19. A public circumcision ceremony, the bris, is performed on Jewish male babies in the United States.

20. However, in addition to the works discussed in this essay, see Henrietta L. Moore *Space, Text and Gender: An Anthropological Study of the Marakwet of Kenya* (New York: Cambridge University Press, 1986); Kratz, *Affecting Performance*; and Shaw, *Colonial Inscriptions*.

21. Max Gluckman, "The Role of the Sexes in Wiko Circumcision Ceremonies," in *Social Structure: Studies Presented to A. R. Radcliffe-Brown*, ed. Meyer Fortes (New York: Russell and Russell, 1963), 145–67; Audrey Richards, *Chisungu: A Girl's Initiation Ceremony in Zambia* (London: Tavistock, 1956); Victor Turner, *The Forest of Symbols: Aspects of Ndembu Ritual* (Ithaca: Cornell University Press, 1970); Arnold van Gennep, *The Rites of Passage* (London: Routledge and Kegan Paul, 1909).

22. Goldschmidt, *Culture and Behavior of the Sebei*; Goldschmidt, *The Sebei*.

23. Tellingly, Goldschmidt relates that women continue to hold the clan affiliation of their fathers, but Sebei men state that wives take the clan affiliation of their husband (Goldschmidt, *Culture and Behavior of the Sebei*, 87).

24. Goldschmidt, *Culture and Behavior of the Sebei*, 211, 235, 238.

25. Boddy, "Womb as Oasis."

26. Marcel Griaule *Conversations with Ogotomeli* (New York: Oxford University Press, 1965); Winter, "Women, the Law and Cultural Relativism in France," 941.

27. Barbara Epstein, *The Politics of Domesticity: Women, Evangelism, and Temperance in Nineteenth-Century America* (Middletown: Wesleyan University Press, 1981); Linda Gordon, *Woman's Body, Woman's Right: A Social History of Birth Control in America* (New York: Penguin, 1977).

28. Lightfoot-Klein, *Prisoners of Ritual*, 84.

29. Toubia, "Female Circumcision," 714. For further information see note 14.

30. Goldschmidt, *Culture and Behavior of the Sebei*, 203. This practices bears a striking resemblance to that described for the Kikuyu, among whom young women were also excised. Jomo Kenyatta *Facing Mount Kenya: The Tribal Life of the Gikuyu* (1938, repr. New York: Vintage, 1965); Shaw, *Colonial Inscriptions*.

31. Goldschmidt, *Culture and Behavior of the Sebei*, 204.

32. Robertson, "Grassroots in Kenya"; see also Lynn Thomas, "Imperial Concerns and 'Women's Affairs': State Efforts to Regulate Clitoridectomy and Eradicate Abortion in Meru, Kenya, c. 1910–1950," *Journal of African History* 39, no. 1 (1998): 121–45.

33. Robertson, "Grassroots in Kenya," 617.

34. Ibid., 624.

35. James A. Boon, "Circumscribing/Circumcision/Uncircumcision: An Essay amidst the History of Difficult Description," in *Implicit Understanding: Observing, Reporting, and Reflecting on the Encounters between Europeans and Other Peoples in the Early Modern Era*, ed. Stuart B. Schwartz (New York: Cambridge University Press, 1994), 556–85; Jonathan Boyarin, "Self-exposure as Theory: The Double Mark of the Male Jew," in Boyarin, *Thinking in Jewish* (Chicago: University of Chicago Press, 1996).

36. Also see Susan Pedersen, "National Bodies, Unspeakable Acts: The Sexual Politics of Colonial Policy-making," *Journal of Modern History* 63 (Dec. 1991): 647–80.

37. Robin Morgan and Gloria Steinem "The International Crime of Genital Mutilation," in Steinem, *Outrageous Acts and Everyday Rebellions* (New York: Holt, Rinehart and Winston, 1983), 330–40.

38. The first wave of feminism emerged in the United States at roughly the turn of the century.

39. Nawal El Saadawi, *The Hidden Face of Eve: Women in the Arab World,* trans. Sherif Hetata (London: Zed Press, 1980).

40. Author interview with Constance Sutton, New York University, May 10, 1995.

41. For example, Kumari Jayawardena, *Feminism and Nationalism in the Third World* (London: Zed Books, 1986); Mohanty, Russo, and Torres, *Third World Women and the Politics of Feminism;* Cherrie Moraga and Gloria Anzaldua, *This Bridge Called My Back: Writings by Radical Women of Color* (Watertown: Persephone Press, 1981); Michelle M. Tokarczyk and Elizabeth A. Fay, eds., *Working-Class Women in the Academy: Laborers in the Knowledge Factory* (Amherst: University of Massachusetts Press, 1993).

42. Judith Butler and Joan W. Scott, eds. *Feminists Theorize the Political* (New York: Routledge, 1992); Donna Haraway, "A Manifesto for Cyborgs," in *Coming to Terms: Feminism, Theory, Politics,* ed. Elizabeth Weed (New York: Routledge, 1989), 173–204; Caroline Ramazanoglu, *Feminism and the Contradictions of Oppression* (London: Routledge, 1989).

43. *National NOW Times Special Edition* (June 1994): 1–12.

44. Mary Daly, "African Genital Mutilation: The Unspeakable Atrocities," in Daly, *Gyn/Ecology: The Metaethics of Radical Feminism* (Boston: Beacon Press, 1978), 164.

45. Winter, "Women, the Law and Cultural Relativism in France," 964.

46. Fran Hosken, "Female Genital Mutilation and Human Rights," *Feminist Issues* 1, no. 3 (1981): 11.

47. Mohanty, Russo, and Torres, *Third World Women and the Politics of Feminism;* Aihwa Ong, "Feminism and the Critique of Colonial Discourse," *Inscriptions* 3, no. 4 (1988): 79–93; Gayatri Chakravorty Spivak, "Can the Subaltern Speak?" in *Marxism and the Interpretation of Culture,* ed. Cary Nelson and Lawrence Grossberg (Urbana: University of Illinois Press, 1988).

48. Hosken, "Female Genital Mutilation and Human Rights," 10.

49. Parmar, "Pratibha's Journey," 176.

50. Quoted in Walker and Parmar, *Warrior Marks,* 265.

51. "Scarred for Life," ABC-TV *Day One.*

52. Dugger, "U.S. Frees African."

53. "Female Genital Mutilation and Political Asylum," ABC-TV *Nightline,* May 2, 1996.

54. Timothy Egan, "An Ancient Ritual and a Mother's Asylum Plea," *New York Times,* March 4, 1994, A25.

55. Rosenthal, "On My Mind," A15.

56. Toubia, "Female Circumcision."

57. African Studies Association Position Paper of the Women's Caucus on Clitoridectomy and Infibulation, Oct. 30–Nov. 2, 1984, Los Angeles.

58. Henry Louis Gates, "A Liberalism of Heart and Spine," *New York Times*, March 27, 1994, 17.

59. Stephen Jay Gould, "The Hottentot Venus," in Gould, *The Flamingo's Smile: Reflections in Natural History* (New York: Norton, 1985); Malek Alloula, *The Colonial Harem*, trans. Myrna Godzich and Wlad Godzich (Minneapolis: University of Minnesota Press, 1986).

60. Dawit, "African Women in the Diaspora."

61. Daniel Gordon, "Female Circumcision and Genital Operations in Egypt and the Sudan: A Dilemma for Medical Anthropology," *Medical Anthropology Quarterly* 4, no. 1 (1991): 3–14; Leonard J. Kouba and Judith Muasher, "Female Circumcision in Africa: An Overview," *African Studies Review* 28, no. 1 (1985): 101.

62. Leila Ahmed, *Women and Gender in Islam: Roots of a Historical Debate* (New Haven: Yale University Press, 1992), 151; Marnia Lazreg, *The Eloquence of Silence: Algerian Women in Question* (New York: Routledge, 1994); Joanna Liddle and Rama Joshi, *Daughters of Independence: Gender, Caste and Class in India* (New Brunswick: Rutgers University Press, 1989); Lata Mani, "Contentious Traditions: The Debate on Sati in Colonial India," *Recasting Women: Essays in Indian Colonial History*, ed. Kumkum Sangari and Sudesh Vaid (New Brunswick: Rutgers University Press, 1990).

63. Peter R. Knauss, *The Persistence of Patriarchy: Class, Gender and Ideology in Twentieth-Century Algeria* (New York: Praeger, 1987); Lazreg, *The Eloquence of Silence.*

64. Ahmed, *Women and Gender in Islam*, 151.

65. Ibid., 153.

66. Liddle and Joshi, *Daughters of Independence*; Mani, "Contentious Traditions."

67. Liddle and Joshi, *Daughters of Independence*, 31; Katherine Mayo, *Mother India* (New York: Harcourt Brace, 1927).

68. Robertson, "Grassroots in Kenya," 633.

69. Mervat Hatem, "The Modernist Credentials of Egyptian Islamism," presented at a conference on "Women, Culture, Nation: Egyptian Moments," New York University, April 7, 1995; Deniz Kandiyoti, ed., *Women, Islam and the State* (Philadelphia: Temple University Press, 1991); Lazreg, *The Eloquence of Silence.*

70. Liddle and Joshi, *Daughters of Independence.*

71. Kandiyoti, ed., *Women, Islam and the State*, 1–47.

72. See also Leila Ahmed, "Feminism and Cross-Cultural Inquiry: The Terms of Discourse in Islam," in *Coming to Terms: Feminism, Theory, Poltics*, ed. Elizabeth Weed (New York: Routledge, 1989), 143–51; Jayawardena, *Feminism and Nationalism in the Third World.*

73. Kandiyoti, *Women, Islam and the State*; Caroline Moser, "Gender Planning in the Third World," in *Gender and International Relations*, ed. Rebecca Grant and Kathleen Newland (Bloomington: Indiana University Press, 1991), 83–121.

74. For additional accounts of this history, see Shaw, *Colonial Inscriptions*; and Thomas, "Ngaitana" and "Imperial Concerns and 'Women's Affairs.'"

75. Pedersen, "National Bodies, Unspeakable Acts," 651.

76. Robertson, "Grassroots in Kenya," 623.

77. Kenyatta, *Facing Mount Kenya*. The issue is further explored by the East African author Ngugi wa Thiong'o in *The River Between* (London: Heinemann, 1965).

78. See, for example, Richard Handler, *Nationalism and the Politics of Culture in Quebec* (Madison: University of Wisconsin Press, 1988).

79. Ahmed, *Women and Gender in Islam.*

80. Partha Chatterjee, "Colonialism, Nationalism, and Colonialized Women: The Contest in India," *American Ethnologist* 16, no. 4 (1989): 622–33; Partha Chatterjee, *The Nation and Its Fragments: Colonial and Postcolonial Histories* (Princeton: Princeton University Press, 1993); see also Kandiyoti, *Women, Islam and the State;* Knauss, *The Persistence of Patriarchy;* and Lazreg, *The Eloquence of Silence* for parallels in Middle Eastern and North African countries.

81. David William Cohen and E. S. Atieno Odhiambo, *Burying SM: The Politics of Knowledge and the Sociology of Power in Africa* (Portsmouth: Heinemann, 1992); Patricia Stamp, "Burying Otieno: the Politics of Gender and Ethnicity in Kenya," *Signs: Journal of Women in Culture and Society* 16, no. 4 (1991): 808–45.

82. For example, in a 1994 interview with CNN, Egyptian President Hosni Mubarek attempted to dismiss the topic by stating (inaccurately) that female "circumcision" was rarely performed in Egypt. Similarly, a top Nigerian official in the United States described Lydia Oluloro's plea for asylum in 1994 as calculated to "denigrate the image of Nigeria," arguing that female "circumcision," "in the very few cases where it is still practiced," was done with the consent of those involved (Jaya Dayal, "Nigerian Official Calls Mother's Plea Calculated," Inter Press Third World News Agency, listserv message, March 26, 1994). In "African Women in the Diaspora," Seble Dawit noted that the Nigerian Embassy had submitted a protest to the U.S. court, affirming that the practice of female genital mutilation was unheard of in Nigeria (although many Nigerian women undergo female genital operations) and that Oluloro was vilified and called a traitor by many Africans.

83. Koptiuch, "'Cultural Defense' and Criminological Displacements."

84. Ibid.

85. Dawit and Mekuria, "The West Just Doesn't Get It."

86. Efua Dorkenoo, "African Women Speak Out on FGM," *National NOW Times Special Edition* (June 1994): 11.

87. Judith Butler, *Gender Trouble: Feminism and the Subversion of Identity* (New York: Routledge, 1990); Judith Butler and Joan Scott, eds., *Feminists Theorize the Political* (New York: Routledge, 1992).

88. Butler, *Gender Trouble.*

89. Ibid.; Haraway, "A Manifesto for Cyborgs"; Mohanty, Russo, and Torres, *Third World Women and the Politics of Feminism.*

90. Achola Pala Okeyo, responding to media accounts of Euro-American feminist responses to female genital operations. Interview with Constance Sutton.

2. Getting beyond the Ew! Factor: Rethinking U.S. Approaches to African Female Genital Cutting

CLAIRE C. ROBERTSON

THIS ESSAY IS prompted not only by long-term involvement with research and teaching about African women but also by experiences in the United States. I am a white American feminist much concerned about effective means to diminish the female genital cutting (FGC) experienced by many African women, including hundreds of women with whom I have worked. Moreover, I am also interested in improving the situation of the many African women and their families who are in poverty. Poverty, especially for women, is an overwhelming and deadly phenomenon that affects everything in Africa, including FGC, yet it has increasingly been ignored in the furor over female genital surgeries in the United States and Europe. As a teacher of women's studies, African studies, and history, I am also concerned about the often biased and uninformed media representations of Africa in the United States and Europe and the tendencies toward sensationalism and polemics, even in academic circles at times. In addition, I am bemused by the phenomenon that the U.S. Congress and many state legislatures (see Isabelle R. Gunning, "Female Genital Surgeries," chapter 4 in this volume) have passed laws regarding FGC that seem to follow a militant feminist agenda. This unprecedented behavior demands explanation.

The reaction of many Westerners to news of female genital cutting performed in Africa has been very strong. Efua Dorkenoo noted, "the subject of genital mutilations provokes violent emotive reactions, both from those in the West, who are shocked and indignant, and from those in Africa and the Middle East who are shocked and hurt when these facts are mentioned."[1] I would add revulsion to this list, what I call the "Ew! factor" for the sound of disgust often made by Americans first learning about the practices. It is very difficult for students and others to get beyond these feelings to deal productively with practices they find revolting, especially female genital cutting.

These feelings have been very evident not only in class discussions but also when I have traveled around the country. I have been fortunate enough to have been asked to speak on topics concerning African women at various colleges and universities in this country and elsewhere. In this country by the mid-1980s it was obvious that whatever the topic I had addressed, the audience always wanted to know about female genital mutilation (FGM), as they usually called it. My cohorts and I began having discussions about how, whatever our own preferences concerning teaching about African women, we were being forced to begin by discussing FGC, a bit like beginning a discussion of women's work, religion, or health in the United States by addressing abortion as presented by the fundamentalist Christian right-to-life movement. All issues were being subsumed into this one and African women being reduced to their genital status.

Then there was the phenomenon that some of my colleagues in women's studies were teaching students in introductory or women's health courses about female genital cutting, usually in a section about violence against women, without providing any cultural context whatsoever. All of Africa was reduced to one place and all of the practices reduced to infibulation, called FGM, giving the impression that all African women are genitally mutilated. Finally, when five students in an introductory class I taught on the cross-cultural study of women were responsible for presenting information on the controversy surrounding female genital cutting, I advised them to differentiate among the practices and contextualize them culturally. Four out of five, because they had not coordinated their efforts, showed diagrams of the gruesome details of FGC, especially infibulation, thus reinforcing for the class the reduction of African women to their genitalia and producing the acute discomfort in our culture associated with contemplating such procedures. The students' presentations faithfully reflected a literature that often objectifies the bodies of African women and does little to contextualize the practices involved, a contextualization that is necessary if we are to take meaningful action to reduce the incidence of FGC.

In the introduction to this volume, Stanlie James and I emphasized the need to contextualize the practices I will call female genital cutting by analyzing their physical differences, their geographical distribution in Africa, and their varying cultural contexts. In this essay I will use that knowledge to critique some of the more popular U.S. literature on the topic of female genital cutting and analyze how these representations often reinforce widely held U.S. cultural convictions and attitudes about Africa, Africans, and African women in particular. After this analysis I will outline a third way to look at female genital cutting that moves beyond either a relativist or a militant confrontational feminist approach but encompasses elements of both.

My goal here is to promote better understanding among African, European, and American women by developing nuanced approaches that foster mutual respect in order to further cooperative efforts to diminish FGC. In pursuing this goal I am also respecting the feelings of many African women faced with the negative representations of all things African that have accompanied the controversy over FGC, as noted by Françoise Kaudjhis-Offoumou (my translation), "Controversies over the question of female genital mutilation have aroused impulsive and emotional reactions among Western women; African and other victims of excision have the impression that some of these women are trying to give us lessons, to accomplish a civilizing mission and are therefore shocked, even revolted." Such conflicts, she says, halt frank discussion of the problems and do not further the cause of getting rid of FGC.[2]

An Ethnography of Western Approaches to Female Genital Surgeries

The first Westerners to pay sustained attention to female genital surgeries in Africa (beyond occasional comments on curious practices by European travelers, including ancient historians) were anthropologists, who by about the 1940s were often imbued with a cultural relativist approach. Relativists were also generally functionalists, who viewed most "customs" as fundamental to the culture in which they existed and ethically neutral. Relativism was to some extent an attempt to move beyond nineteenth-century social Darwinist notions that classified societies according to their level of "civilization," which also meant skin color, and placed those with the darkest skin at the bottom of the heap. Harriet Lyons noted that nineteenth- and early-twentieth-century social Darwinians used "[a] people's propensity for violence, social degree of sexual interest, and perceived treatment of women, all of which have been seen to be involved in genital mutilations, . . . as convenient indices of depravity or virtue, and later on, of savagery or civilization."[3]

In an effort to correct such prejudicial notions, relativism and functionalism tried to avoid the negative valuation of culture and unfamiliar customs. Practitioners were to try to transcend their own cultures by being nonjudgmental toward the cultures of others with the goal of improving objectivity. One outgrowth of this view was the prescription that aspiring anthropologists doing fieldwork were not to interfere with the culture they were observing. They were definitely not to preach to the objects of their studies to get them to change their culture in any way. In an extreme relativist view, culture was sacred but many anthropologists and other social scientists, faced with distasteful aspects of a society, compromised by ignoring or skimming over them. Therefore, the representation of FGC performed in many societies was usually characterized by the use of the term *female circumcision,* de-sexualization, and a lack of attention to physical detail but an extensive discussion of the function of the custom within the social order. Male anthropologists often had difficulty in securing access to the site of the performance of FGC and often did not pay much attention to women anyway and so sometimes ignored the topic entirely.[4] A contemporary relativist view is expressed by Esther Hicks, who points out that in countries like Sudan, Somalia, and Ethiopia those who practice infibulation are in the vast majority and do not see the practice as a problem. Therefore, in her view, infibulation is only a problem in Western perceptions.[5] A relativist view of FGC is virtually absent from contemporary mass media and was never popular outside of academic circles.

The problems of perception in Western discourses surrounding FGC have a long history dating back to early modern Europe and may be rooted in the long-held conviction that deviant genital anatomy was conducive to deviant female sexual behavior. Perceptions are also a factor in the genital operations performed now in the U.S. to make ambiguous genitals, or sex, conform to gender (see Cheryl Chase, "'Cultural Practice' or 'Reconstructive Surgery'?" chapter 5 in this volume).[6] Western feminist discourses are not immune from these problems. In the 1970s and 1980s, with the rise of international feminism, American feminist scholars questioned the absence of women from academic discourse both as scholars and as subjects of research. From its inception, women's studies stressed a political agenda that was inclusive of women and critiqued disciplines and works that excluded women. The critique of male dominance pervaded all disciplines and pertained both to substance and personnel, theory and practice. Relativism and functionalism were discredited, both because of the false neutrality imposed (no one can transcend culture, and bias must be acknowledged and compensated for) and because practitioners failed to identify and critique patriarchal socioeconomic and ideological structures. This feminist critique thus opened the door once again to an assessment of cultures that ranked them according to, in this case, women's status within them.

In the popular press, a militant brand of feminism combined with old notions regarding Africans and Africa to make the issue of "female genital mutilation," a category that subsumed all the practices, a key catalyst in an ongoing media and legal campaign that often misrepresented what happened in Africa. Much feminist critique, more accustomed to dissecting complacent U.S. stereotypes, has been less than felicitous when dealing with an area of the world that has largely suffered from negative images in the Western media. The media campaign has taken on a life of its own with sensationalistic overtones and voyeuristic elements.

The legal campaign first pushed to make FGC illegal in the United States, a cause that attracted unlikely allies, because some conservative politicians, who would not vote for an equal rights amendment or international conventions against gender discrimination, could with impunity support a women's issue that affected no Americans, given the exclusion from the legislation of breast implants, tattoos, genital piercing, male circumcision, genital reconstruction to change sex or to remedy sexually ambiguous genitalia, and other procedures commonly practiced in the United States. Ultimately, clitoridectomy and infibulation practiced by foreigners were outlawed by the U.S. federal government in 1996 in a campaign led by Congresswoman Patricia Schroeder. The present legal focus is on asylum cases in which a few African women and their children have claimed asylum in the United States on account of genital cutting practiced in their countries.

Since this campaign has become trendy in certain circles and trickled down to *Vogue* and other, less chic, women's magazines, it is worth looking at the representations of Africa and African women it conveys. This brief survey is not intended to be comprehensive but rather representative of attitudes common in the media. This critique is also not intended as a blanket condemnation of those who publicize the issue of female genital surgeries; the media focus has proved invaluable for raising consciousness about FGC both in Africa and in the West with the pervasiveness of CNN for instance. In Egypt, a 1994 CNN special report had a galvanizing effect on efforts to get rid of FGC, despite its "painful and distressing" nature for those involved, resurrecting and strengthening an eradication movement that began in the 1950s.[7] I would maintain, however, that insofar as campaign participants have revived old racist stereotypes about Africans, sensationalized the issue to play into prurient interests, and conveyed misleading information about Africa, they have helped neither to further international understanding nor to eradicate FGC. These unproductive aspects of the campaign are due in most cases, I believe, to uncritical absorption of negative stereotypes and lack of exposure to well-informed research about Africa and Africans rather than malice. Lack of time due to deadline pressures and lack of space due to a short public attention span also afflict journalists, perhaps more than laziness.[8] This critique is therefore intended to move us beyond these aspects of the campaign onto more fruitful ground where international cooperation can work seriously on eradicating practices that are harmful to women without whole-sale condemnation of their practitioners and their cultural contexts.

The basic elements in U.S. racist stereotypes about Africa have a long and undistinguished pedigree in Western cultures, best encapsulated in Tarzan movies. Africa is presented as one place, usually a jungle inhabited by wild animals and primitive people belonging to an unchanging time warp worthy of Gene Roddenberry. These peoples are organized into "tribes" who lead isolated lives in rural settings and have implacable enmities toward each other. They exist on the remote periphery of the world. Africans' characteristics are presented as ranging from maliciousness to ignorance and naïveté. Even when they have some Western education they are not able to cope on their own (the infantilized stereotype). Women, in particular, are seen as victims. Africans therefore need the help of more advanced civilizations, a.k.a. European-Americans, to raise them out of their ignorance and poverty, which ancient rituals perpetuate by promoting "tradition." European colonialism was therefore good for Africa because it began bringing them the benefits of higher civilization, modernization, which is equated in this view with Westernization. In an analysis of Western films of the 1930s, including *Tarzan, the Ape Man,* Kevin Dunn concluded,

> [T]he growing film industries of the 1930s contributed further to their viewing audiences' misperception of Africa and Africans and helped to perpetuate . . . racist and colonialist modes of thinking. . . . The nightmare Africa is often populated by savage natives, which . . . illustrates the need for the colonization and civilization of the continent. . . . The . . . savage and the colonized servants were the 'before' and 'after' example of the effects of civilization. The colonized Africans, however, tended to be untrustworthy and shiftless, reflecting and reinforcing racial attitudes that existed both at home and abroad. If there was a 'good' African in the film, he was defined by the characteristics admired in servants: honesty, courage, submission and unflagging loyalty. . . . [T]he constant and consistent bombardment of these images, without any significant alternatives, undoubtedly had a shaping effect on how Western societies thought of Africa and Africans. The continuation of these representations in later popular films, even today, testifies to their accepted 'truthfulness' by audiences and film-makers.[9]

Films such as the "classic" *African Queen* and *Out of Africa* are typical representations that foregrounded white colonists' or adventurers' experiences in Africa and subordinated Africans to extras; they have had a powerful impact on many Americans.

Views of slavery are also heavily implicated in U.S. representations of Africa, a topic that deserves more extensive development elsewhere. Steven Spielberg's *Amistad,* while purportedly championing the cause of freedom-seeking, wrongfully imprisoned Africans in early-nineteenth-century New England, succeeded mainly in heaping more praise on the U.S. "founding fathers," ignoring the enshrinement of slavery in the Constitution. Only *Roots, Sankofa,* and *Beloved* foregrounded the experiences of slaves in representing slavery. The latter, although beautifully executed, was mostly ignored by Hollywood and by the U.S. public. It is worthwhile noting that although representations of slavery have been more often than not dominated by white male perspectives, white feminist perspectives on FGC until relatively recently have triumphed.[10] In the next section I will attempt to "enculture" some of those representations, as it were, while acknowledging that raising international awareness of FGC has been useful for campaigns to diminish the practices in some ways.

Representations of FGC: Feminism

I will begin by analyzing some sources commonly used in women's studies classes regarding FGC and then look at the print media. I will end by discussing legal discourses, which have increasingly dominated the representations. In all of these the three R's regarding representations of Africa and African women are evident: reducing all of Africa to one uncivilized place; reducing African women to the status of their genitals, presumed to be infibulated, and Africans to being sadistic torturers or victims; and reducing all FGC to its worst form, infibulation.

The contemporary U.S. feminist agenda regarding FGC was largely set by the seminal works of Mary Daly, Fran Hosken, and Hanny Lightfoot-Klein, despite the availability of works by African women such as Asma El Dareer, Raqiya Abdalla, Nahid Toubia, Olayinka Koso-Thomas, Aamina Warsame and Sadiya Ahmed, Efua Dorkenoo, and even Awa Thiam, whose militance most closely approximates that of Hosken and Lightfoot-Klein. Daly, Hosken, and Lightfoot-Klein at the time they wrote their works had very little experience in Africa, Daly none, and none were trained in African studies of any kind. Thus, we should not be surprised that these feminist representations of FGC share common assumptions with the dominant Western discourses regarding Africa. Feminists are no more immune from culture and ethnocentrism than anyone else.

The *Hosken Report* is the single most influential document responsible for raising Western consciousness of FGC. It is still cited by many sources as current information, although it dates from the 1970s and was flawed from its inception. Hosken began with uncompromising blame for those Africans involved in FGC and breathtaking generalizations: "The secrecy, the continuing evasiveness, and the unwillingness by all involved to face this reality confirms that they are aware of their complicity and guilt."[11] She continued to indicate how those who are enlightened can raise Africans up, Africans being presumed not to be able to cope with anything much. "We [presumably Westerners] are able to teach those who cling to distorted beliefs and damaging practices some better ways to cope with themselves, their lives, reproduction and sexuality." Africans do not know about each other either: There are "dozens who may be traditional enemies." African women are "the keepers of tradition in every society" and "blindly resist change." Nor can educated African women speak for African women in general. "It always amazes me how some African women, especially those trained at European and American universities, . . . take it upon themselves to speak for all the many millions of women living in Africa." Hosken thus arrogates to herself the right to speak for most African women, who are implied to be inarticulate or primitive, and specifically discounts the views of (Western) educated African women.

In the interest of proving that militant campaigns work, Hosken goes on to revise history, although not with facts in mind, "Neither missionaries [in Kenya] nor the British government attacked initiation or any other African customs." This is simply incorrect. Central Kenya of the 1920s is, in fact, the case continuously used by those stressing the retrogressive effects of forcible efforts imposed by foreigners to prohibit FGC. Missionaries attacked polygyny, FGC, and other practices they saw as being unacceptable; such attacks reinforced a nationalistic backlash that renewed FGC. Moreover, in Hosken's view anyone who says that the practice is gradually disappearing in Kenya is wrong and only trying to "soothe the conscience of the public." Thus, she refuses to accept any evidence that would indicate any amelioration of the situation lest people not pay attention to her campaign or to her construction of Africans as unregenerate practitioners of damaging rituals.

Hosken's belief in the widespread and unchanging nature of the problem may also have contributed to her methods of compilation of statistics to show the extent of FGC in Africa. What she seems to have done is to assume that all of the women in any group or even any country that ever practiced FGC have it done now. Esther Hicks in her study of infibulation estimated that Hosken had considerably exaggerated the areas in which it is practiced and noted that infibulation is not, in any case, geographically but culturally specific, meaning that those who practice it continue to do it wherever they are.[12] It is very difficult to compile accurate statistics, given the lack of reliable data, but there is no reason to assume, for instance, that because one group in Nigeria practiced clitoridectomy that everyone does so now. Many Igbo people in Nigeria abandoned the custom of clitoridectomy in the 1920s. Each successive generation of Kikuyu and Akamba, who together compose about half of Kenya's population, is diminishing the practice so that now perhaps a fifth or fewer of the girls participate in initiation rites that include clitoridectomy.[13]

The chief culprits in perpetuating FGC in Hosken's view are African men because they demand that women have the procedures. "The demands of a majority of African men are the real reason why the operations continue today." This statement is too broad and is more relevant to infibulation than to some other situations. The interpretation of FGC as having exclusively to do with male dominance places African and other women having experienced FGC in the position of victims, which is not always the case, as stated in a letter to the editor of the *The New York Times* by Bonnie Shullenberger, a teacher with three years of experience in Uganda, protesting A. M. Rosenthal's interpretation in his regular column on FGC. "A. M. Rosenthal's dream of eliminating female circumcision is one unlikely to be fulfilled as long as Euro-Americans insist on defining it in terms of male power and sexual repression."[14] Christine Walley's essay in this volume (chapter 1) describes her experiences in a Western Kenyan village where clitoridectomy with its associated puberty rites is practiced by a minority population and can be an empowering experience for many participants. Moreover, in some places young women have taken up genital cutting as a fad in the face of opposition from their elders, somewhat like bodypiercing in the United States.[15]

After the 1979 Khartoum Conference, where many African activists met to consider how best to eliminate such practices and Hosken presented a paper, she added a preface that moderated her tone a bit but did not alter the passages cited above; she called for support for the recommendations by country representatives at the conference but added that "the ignorant and misguided claims about a dubious 'cultural mystique' [supporting FGC] were clearly refuted in Khartoum."[16] The implication here is that in a militant campaign to eradicate FGC we do not need to pay attention to the cultural contexts of the practices, which did not interest Hosken much.[17]

Mary Daly's *Gyn/Ecology* came out in 1978 and drew heavily on Hosken's first edition. Mining *Gyn/Ecology* for references to FGC turned up an immediate terminological double standard. In the index under "clitoridectomy" are references to U.S. practices only, which are dealt with very briefly. Under "genital mutilation," however, are listed African practices, which are covered in a whole chapter entitled, "African Genital Mutilation: The Unspeakable

Atrocities." Typical of radical feminist thinking of the time, Daly provided her own version of "biology is destiny." Daly's impassioned approach un-equivocally reduces women's abilities and future to the status of their geni-tals. Thus, FGM (her term) involves, "profound silencing of the mind's imag-inative and critical powers" for its victims, who are taught "never to forget to murder their own divinity" and live their whole lives "preoccupied by pain." Echoing Hosken, she dismisses any consideration of the cultural con-text by calling that context rules for how to perform FGM. Although she recognizes that practices differ, she uses "it" throughout, as if only one prac-tice were involved. The function and consequences of the FGM rules, the "tribal" rituals, are to "distract the attention of the participants . . . from the victimized women's physical agony, mutilation, life-long deprivation, defor-mity, pain and premature death from complications." Those women who perform the operations are "mentally castrated"; they do it out of a form of false consciousness and are tools of men.[18] The image of African women presented, then, is as victims and puppets of men, who bear the ultimate responsibility.

Probably the most widely disseminated nonfiction work on FGC in col-lege libraries and elsewhere is that of Hanny Lightfoot-Klein. Both Hosken and Lightfoot-Klein became involved in the issue of FGC as short-term vis-itors to Africa. Lightfoot-Klein's title leaves no doubt as to how she views FGC and African women: *Prisoners of Ritual: An Odyssey into Female Genital Cir-cumcision in Africa.* African practitioners of FGC in her view do not bear guilt, but rather lack volition and initiative through being mired in old rituals. "I looked for villains in this conundrum and I found none. I found instead men and women entrapped in an antiquated ritual, dating heaven knows how far back into history, unable to free themselves from its centuries-old enmesh-ment, all of them its prisoners." Their inaction means that she, like Hosken, needs to speak for them. "I, as author, am only acting as their collective voice." Thus, Lightfoot-Klein purports to represent what all Sudanese think but just do not have the courage to say.

Lightfoot-Klein arrived in Africa by accident, having intended to go to Turkey, knowing nothing about "it" (we discover later that Sudan is meant). An American man she encountered at a hotel told her about infibulation, which information she reacted to with revulsion, incredulity, and curiosity. She then leads the reader through conversations with Sudanese, which she critiques in parentheses to show how ignorant the objects of her study are. African women are reduced to the status of their genitals. A photograph is captioned, after noting that it is a wedding party and the older women in it have "tribal scars," "Every female in this picture may be assumed to have been pharaonically circumcised."[19] As a central focus she provides the usual graph-ic description of the procedures performed and the medical complications from them without much differentiation or context, which adds to the ob-jectification of women's bodies.

The description, however, is somewhat complicated by Lightfoot-Klein's account of efforts to eradicate FGC in various countries. Unlike Hosken, she brings in female agency, "Although they are often made out to be dictatori-al, knife-wielding perpetrators of a practice for which neither they nor the men of this society will admit to having responsibility, in my opinion they are far better described as strong, proud, determined and sad survivors of the same rites that they defend so tenaciously."[20]

Perhaps the most popular account of FGC, however, is the more recent *Warrior Marks* by Alice Walker and Pratibha Parmar, which succeeded Walk-er's novel *Possessing the Secret of Joy.* Walker, like Hosken and Lightfoot-Klein, was clearly motivated by a humanitarian concern encouraged by empathy, although not free of stereotyping and careless ethnography.[21] Elsewhere in this volume Stanlie James and Christine Walley have analyzed Walker's in-terventions further; I will concentrate on those by Parmar. The book, *War-rior Marks* is the story of the making of the "documentary" film of the same name. The goal of the film is stated early on: "Without necessarily condemn-ing anyone, this film will present the facts about the horrors and hazards of a practice [*sic*] that is thousands of years old, with the intent to encourage people to re-evaluate their traditions in light of the fragile health of their societies and the planet." Thus, the putative audience is Africans for a film that was mostly shown to Americans, creating a situation where Americans once again critique African cultures, which are blamed for FGC. The prac-tice referred to is infibulation, so all procedures are reduced to the most ex-treme practice.

Warrior Marks is divided into separate sections expressing the views of Walker and of Parmar, who locates herself as a Kenyan-born expatriate In-dian. Some of her observations are unexceptionally representative of femi-nist perspectives that do not condemn but rather promote cooperation, but some are akin to those of Hosken and Lightfoot-Klein. She notes the offense taken by many African women at the colonial tone of Western feminists re-garding FGC at the End of the Decade for Women U.N. Conference in Nairo-bi in 1985. Since then, she says incorrectly, African women have undertaken grass-roots projects to stop FGM, as she calls the practices. She implies that nothing would have happened without the attention drawn to FGC by West-ern women. Yet in some places attempts to diminish or eradicate FGC go back to at least the 1920s and include Africans of both genders, as documented by Lillian Sanderson in *Against the Mutilation of Women*. Lorna Ng'ang'a describes those in Kenya, begun in the 1920s by missionaries. The failure of such attempts resulted in the furtherance of the Kikuyu Independent (non-Christian) School movement and the reinforcement of clitoridectomy as a marker of identity, which happened again during the 1950s' Land and Freedom movement, called Mau Mau by the British.[22]

Parmar calls the FGM issue "painful, complex and difficult . . . involving questions of cultural identities and sexuality, human rights, and the rights of women and girls to live safe and healthy lives." Accusations of cultural imperialism should not paralyze Western feminists into doing nothing about FGM, she says. She asks herself, "How can I create a sensitive and respectful representation of a people—and a continent—who have historically been misrepresented? . . . How can I work directly with African women in order to halt this violence against women and girls?" Parmar's awareness of cultural imperialism and desire to work with African women on an equal basis demonstrate progress in feminist thought in some fifteen years of widespread awareness of FGC. Yet her reduction of Africa to one people and of FGC to infibulation, and her claim to represent the whole continent in one short "documentary," once again give the impression that all Africans practice FGC.

More problems appear in the account of the filming, which was done in Senegal and the Gambia because, according to Walker, Sudan and Kenya are "just horrible."[23] Parmar describes walking down the street in Dakar and speculating that "so many of these women could well be genitally mutilated"— her interest focuses overwhelmingly on their genitals. Practices other than FGC come in for criticism—polygyny for example (Parmar uses the term *polygamy*, which means anyone having multiple spouses, although what she means is the custom of a man having many wives).[24] She is impatient with the slower pace of life in West Africa, the socializing that she views as wasting time, and she is surprised to discover that all peoples do not practice FGC. Although she stresses that "it is crucial to have voices of African feminists and activists like Awa Thiam who have been absent from previous documentaries on this subject," she objects to Thiam's request to include an interview of a political leader in the film. Parmar wrestles with the fact that senior women were complicit in an initiation ceremony she filmed. Any statement by her contacts that lack of resources impedes action to reduce FGC is viewed as an excuse for inaction, but she notes that poverty is a huge problem. To show sisterly solidarity, Parmar films Alice Walker walking down a road with a chance-met group of women. The "flamboyant" colors the women wear are seen as "a creative reflection of the women's pain." Once again, nothing is important about them other than the fact that they have undergone FGC.

For Parmar, Senegal and the Gambia form a poorly understood background only for what is important, FGM, which is defined as the torture of children. Different kinds of FGC are not well understood. Parmar asks an excisor about defibulation of girls at marriage, but infibulation is not the local practice, clitoridectomy is. When the excisor therefore responds that she does not know, Parmar blames her for being ignorant. This displacement of the practice of infibulation onto sub-Saharan Africa, which is common in U.S. literature and may hark back to Social Darwinian notions, was found to be offensive by Emmanuel Babatunde, whose own contemporary analysis of Yoruba female circumcision (removal of the prepuce) in Nigeria stresses its differences from practices in the Horn.[25]

The best element in *Warrior Marks* is the interview with Efua Dorkenoo, whose own book, *Cutting the Rose,* is one of the best recent works on FGC but has had relatively little circulation compared to *Warrior Marks.* Dorkenoo provides a badly needed normalization to counteract the prevalent construction of African women as dominated and overwhelmed by FGC and emphasizes the importance of the cultural context to efforts at change. Dorkenoo says that in the West people think that women are completely destroyed by FGC, but "you see women who have been stitched and cut and restitched, and yet you see them laughing, strong . . . that is the hope for the future, within this stream of survivors, that's where things are going to change and happen. . . . Through rituals [women] build sisterhood—sisterhood which lasts for a long time." Dorkenoo also emphasizes the power of African women's networks with a moving reference to cultural context and gender and identity formation, "But however we do it, we have to work through a cultural medium for women to find a new image of themselves. You see, genital mutilation is mixed up with how I see myself as a woman. Every society decides who is a woman."

Parmar herself is torn, "One of the worries I know I have is that it's very easy for Westerners to use genital mutilation as a way of describing Africa as being backward and savage and barbaric and feeding into all those sort of racist perceptions of Africa." She observes that people grow to think that things are beautiful that are about enslavement.[26] Parmar presents a more complex representation of FGC than the others already examined here, but it is problematic in terms of reductionist feminist matriarchal assumptions and ignorance of the cultural context.

Newspapers: The "Liberal" Media?

These problematic aspects come to the fore in considering contemporary representations of FGC in newspapers, even the most respected. The *New York Times* has given the issue of female genital mutilation, the term used in most of its articles, more prominence than have other major U.S. dailies.[27] A special column by A. M. Rosenthal in December 1992, for example, set the tone for the representations in the early 1990s. Rosenthal was unequivocally extreme in his use of language, calling all FGC "torture," a "crime," "sexual and social insanity." He stated, "I am all for violence on TV—the violence of reality, about war, drugs and real crime, including FGM." He recommended imposing economic sanctions as an incentive for getting governments to stop FGM.[28] He ignores the context completely in favor of condemnation.

Rosenthal's view of African women echoes an earlier article by Blaine Hardin of the *Washington Post*. In Nairobi to cover the 1985 Women's Conference, Hardin reported that going to Africa "to assess the progress of the world's women is akin to going to Beirut to assess the progress of world peace. For African women, to an extent greater than anywhere else in the world, are yoked to a traditional culture that keeps them pregnant and powerless and uses them and their children as draft animals to power the continent's faltering leading occupation—subsistence farming." Despite his reference to the importance of agriculture, he devoted much of his report to discussing what he calls "female circumcision." African women are constructed as overworked victims of their "cultures" (where are the men in this?), for whom "female circumcision" is the most pressing problem. No appreciation of African women's talents for organization or anything else is evident. He did conclude, however, by noting that African women activists who are working to abolish FGC "find criticisms of it [*sic*] by westerners to be patronizing and counterproductive."[29]

Much discussion of FGC was aroused by Celia Dugger's reporting about Fauziya Kassindja's efforts to be freed from a Pennsylvania prison, where she was being held as an illegal immigrant, and claim asylum in the U.S. on the basis of fleeing forced polygynous marriage and clitoridectomy in Togo. The headlines and prominent placement of the articles alone shape the reader's perspective on FGC: "Woman's Plea for Asylum Puts Tribal Ritual on Trial"; "U.S. Frees African Fleeing Ritual Mutilation"; "Rite of Anguish: A Special Report; Genital Ritual Is Unyielding in Africa"; "Tug of Taboos: African Genital Rite versus U.S. Law" and many more of the same gist.[30] Although the headlines omitted it, the substance of the stories included the facts that Kassindja had a secondary-school education and a father who refused to have his daughters excised. Her rebellion and flight were in the context of having been presented with other alternatives within Togolese society.

It was a stiff legal struggle to get Kassindja freed from prison, where the seventeen-year-old had been for over a year, which required widespread mobilization of public opinion and resources partly because of a judge's refusal to believe Kassindja. But the focus of the articles describing the case was mainly on the African practices, an excellent example of diversion of attention from U.S. civil rights abuses and maltreatment of immigrants. The African focus was strengthened when Celia Dugger went to Togo to investigate further rather than to the Pennsylvania and New Jersey prisons. At the latter, a riot caused by ill-treatment of the prisoners—illegal immigrants—forced the facility's closure and Kassindja's transfer to the Pennsylvania prison. The story of scandalous prison conditions, insofar as they affected Kassindja, did not emerge fully, however, until she published her own book, *Do They Hear You When You Cry?* Dugger missed an excellent opportunity for a good muckraking story.

Nowhere in the media is the reduction of FGC to one physical process so evident as in the CNN 1994 special report depicting a brutal infibulation of an Egyptian girl done by a barber and in the 1996 Pulitzer prize–winning photographs by Stephanie Welsh, a Syracuse University student, of a procedure performed on a Samburu secondary school student in northern Kenya. Welsh was given a hundred rolls of film by the photo editor of a Syracuse newspaper to do a pictorial essay on AIDS in Kenya. Instead, she decided that she wanted to focus on FGC but had trouble getting "the confidence of the tribe" so she could be an observer. Finally, she was allowed to do so and treated hospitably. She took many pictures, some of which were considered to be too explicit and bloody for the resulting feature published in *Newsday.* Sixteen of the pictures she took were used nationally and are in high demand internationally. Welsh speculated that Seita Lengila, the girl whose excision ceremony was shown in the photos, had inward doubts about the procedure, which in Welsh's view was "a brutal injustice." She sent all but the bloodiest photos to Lengila. What is not known is whether she secured her permission to distribute them or if, for instance, the profits from distributing the pictures are paying Seita Lengila's school fees.

Why did Welsh win a Pulitzer prize? The editor who gave her the film stated, "Honestly, there are people at newspapers today that [*sic*] could shoot circles around her from a technical standpoint . . . [but] You can't teach people how to open their eyes and their minds." In a country numb to violence of all kinds due to media overexposure perhaps this "exotic" variant could still attract attention; it certainly reinforced what many Americans think is important about Africa. In a scenario suspect to many alert Kenyans (in

Nairobi any foreign photographer is thought to be a journalist out to make money from exploitative photos of unsuspecting Kenyans), a novice photographer used Kenyan pain and celebration to build a career, abetted by U.S. preoccupations and profit motives. One of the Kassindja activists realized the irony of the situation and commented, "It is unbelievable that one woman is being honored for taking the pictures and a woman who ran away for fear of being actually mutilated is being treated like a criminal."[31]

Human Rights/Legal Discourses

It was with some relief that I turned to the human rights literature and found generally more balanced and less exploitative considerations of FGC. Some of the most thoughtful analyses of FGC have been written by human rights activists, prominent among these being Isabelle Gunning, another contributor to this volume (chapter 4). In considering some of the better examples of this literature I was also impressed with pieces by L. Amede Obiora, Adamantia Pollis and Peter Schwab, Rhoda Howard, Hope Lewis, and Kay Boulware-Miller.[32] Pollis and Schwab are concerned with the cultural specificity of supposedly universal human rights but do not deal specifically with FGC. Obiora and Lewis have good discussions of representations. Obiora has origins in a society where a form of FGC is or was practiced and therefore enters the debate from an emic perspective. Obiora, Howard, Lewis, and Boulware-Miller all differentiate the practices involved in FGC and problematize the construction of all FGC as torture and child abuse, while Lewis and Boulware-Miller also analyze African-American views on FGC. None of these authors favors the continuation of all forms of FGC, but several point out that all forms of FGC are not mutilating by Western standards, as does Walley (chapter 1). All stress the need for understanding enhanced by a thorough examination of particular cultural contexts and listening to and respecting the voices of the African participants and activists most closely involved with FGC.[33]

Two pieces cited more widely than those mentioned above are by Alison Slack and Robyn Cerny Smith. Slack, who lived in Mauritania as a Peace Corps volunteer, is wary about the unthinking imposition of foreign values and coercion of people. She differentiates among the practices and pays substantial attention to similar practices in Western cultures. She catalogs the various human rights proclamations (given their lack of provision for enforcement, calling them laws is too strong), such as the UN Declaration of Human Rights of 1948, the African Charter on Human and People's Rights of 1981, and the Arab Charter on Human and People's Rights, while analyzing their applicability to FGC, which she calls "female circumcision."

Yet Slack uses data from Hosken and Lightfoot-Klein uncritically, along with the term *tribe*, and unthinkingly creates oppositions between cosmetic surgeries in the United States and among Africans or Papuans that construct the latter as other. Forgetting fashions for whole-body tattooing and body-piercing in the United States, she mentions them only in connection with East Africans and New Guineans, while using facelifting in the United States as their opposite. She gets onto distinctly shaky ground when trying to make an argument that FGC can never be truly voluntary because practitioners do it without "full awareness of the possible outcomes," implying that African ignorance is universal. This argument can easily be applied to smoking and the use of breast implants in the United States, but she uses it only for Africans. Nonetheless, she backs off of stern proscriptions, opting instead for "reinforcement of already existing concerns [among Africans] by education and personal communication."[34]

Smith's essay is more problematic. At its heart is an oxymoronic argument best summarized by Smith's conclusion:

> The purpose [here] is to reshape the debate so that the international commu-
> nity can resolve the female circumcision issue in a way that reflects the true
> experiences, oppressions, and needs of women and girls subject to circumci-
> sion. The legal community must first start with the experiences of marginal-
> ized groups, here women and girls, in naming the terms of the debate. Only then
> will the constructed debate adequately address their oppressive experiences.
> Perhaps if these women and girls have the power to name their true oppres-
> sions and experiences in the international community, they may be able to work
> together to reevaluate the traditions that silence them. Then they may choose
> which traditions truly are necessary for tribal unity from their point of view
> and reject those traditions that continue to oppress them.

It is apparently up to the international community to solve the problem of FGC for those involved, who do not seem to be part of that community. In Smith's view, the chief obstacle to solving the problem is tradition. De-spite the wealth of sources available by 1992, she relies on Hosken and on Hosken's reading of Jacques Lantier, whose book *La cité magique et magie en Afrique noire* is a prime example of the three Rs regarding representations of FGC that we identified as being unproductive and prejudicial to dimin-ishing the practices.[35] Lantier reduces all FGC to one practice, the most ex-treme, infibulation; Africa is reduced to one uncivilized place mired in tra-dition; and Africans are either evil torturers or victims, constructed as others compared to modern civilized Westerners. Using sources critically is abso-lutely necessary for thoughtful discussion of FGC.

In a gesture to listening to the voices of actual Africans, she refers critically to Jomo Kenyatta's *Facing Mount Kenya* (first published in 1938) in taking on anthropological relativistic arguments. Although she recognizes that Kenyatta had a nationalist agenda, she condemns the Kikuyu for having patriarchy, of which girls' puberty rites, including clitoridectomy, are a part. She thus accepts Kenyatta's construction of Kikuyu patriarchy at face value.[36] Kenyatta's agenda, however, included the creation of the good Kikuyu-nationalist, excised woman (and docile wife), who was to be a virgin at marriage. It is not at all clear, however, that the latter was a widespread cultural expectation. Kenyatta also inveighed against women going to Nairobi to trade, lest that practice lead to prostitution. Nonetheless, trade had strong roots in the culture, and women kept going.[37] Smith fails to apply the deconstructive maxim to Kenyatta. Kikuyu patriarchy was, and is, a much more vexed entity than she has appreciated, especially since Kikuyu women have contested both its construction and its perpetuation fiercely.

In effect, Smith's piece has a pretense of objectivity when she dissects arguments about FGC, whether socialist-feminist or cultural-relativist, but in the end her views are also matriarchal-feminist and demonstrate that all FGC is oppressive and imposed by men on undifferentiated African othered victims, who belong to tribes. There is insufficient contextualization or differentiation of the practices—and no interrogation of the concept of human rights—to broaden the usual Western interpretation to include considerations of economic justice. Nonetheless, such thinking only puts Smith with most American feminists on the subject of women in non-Western cultures. We need to be more considerate and modest in our pretensions.

Legal Discourses: Criminalization?

If increasingly the human rights literature is moving away from the problems evident in the Smith article, what actually happens in the courts when issues concerning FGC arise and what images of Africa and Africans are presented? In the United States, the relatively recent criminalization of FGC performed by foreigners has not been followed by a show trial to test the law. The law remains a popular unenforced window dressing that allows even the most conservative U.S. lawmakers to assert their enlightenment, as illustrated by Gunning in chapter 4. In France, however, two cases in the early 1990s tested the public resolve to punish immigrant West Africans responsible for perpetuating customs widely perceived as unacceptably barbaric.

Both cases involved an *exciseuse* named Soko Aramata Keita and various parents of excised girls; one girl had died from the operation. The first trial featured eminent participation by several French women's groups. Prosecutor Commaret made it clear from the beginning that she intended to test "universal" principles. Maurice Peyrot in *Le Monde* described it as follows, "The trial was manifestly intended to be seen as a solemn condemnation of an indefensible practice, and the only real question at issue was how to put an end to an age-old initiation rite." He observed that the trial did not resemble the usual criminal proceeding: It was probable that the accused did not know that foreign forms of FGC were illegal in France; the court proceedings most often resembled a seminar with various Western "experts" promoting different views on the subject; and the interpreters were not instructed to, and did not, translate for the defendants anything except direct questions asked them. Indeed, Peyrot's interpretation is supported by Commaret's summation to the jury, "An unusual case, this. For beyond the persons and acts accused, there is a clash of ideas: law versus custom, the unacceptable versus the tolerable, the universality of certain values versus cultural relativism."

These oppositions require close examination. The first one constructs African custom as not equivalent to law, even though colonialists regularly erected patriarchal versions of African customs into laws enforced in lower colonial courts. In the interests of cheap and peaceful governance, and because of sexist and racist cultural relativism, colonial governments generally did not make strong efforts to change the customs they found barbaric. Africans were assumed to be so different from Europeans that change was impossible. Furthermore, women's affairs were not seen as affecting the colonial project of extracting profit from the colonies. Thus, the trial in Paris marked a certain decolonization of attitudes, but in the interests of requesting conformity of everyone on French soil.

"The unacceptable" of the second opposition claims civilized ground for French courts, while universality is proclaimed for French values as opposed to the (evil) cultural relativism of the third opposition, which is portrayed as allowing the unacceptable. The jury convicted both parents in the Malian Bambara Coulibaly family involved in the first trial and Keita as well, imposing a harsher penalty than requested. Raymond Verdier, in an article in *Droit et Cultures* critical of these proceedings, lodged the following objections to how clitoridectomy was presented by the prosecution: The procedure is not a mark of women's inferiority but of complementarity of the sexes and an act of social incorporation; excision is essential to social identity; there was no intent to harm the girls; there was widespread ignorance of the prohibition on foreign types of FGC at the time the procedures were performed, some eight or nine years before the trials; immigration officers had not informed the parents of its illegality; and the Coulibalys understood little French, the women of the family none. Verdier concluded by calling for adaptive solutions and tolerance, not condemnation.[38]

These proceedings once again invoked the three Rs in the form of testimony and summations that reduced the Coulibaly family and Soko Aramata Keita to the status of generic Africans mired in barbaric customs, people who could be kept ignorant of the proceedings to remove even their knowledge of the debate or of their probable fate from their hands.[39] The "civilization" of France was asserted over and against the otherness and "barbarity" of Africans, despite widespread French collaboration with Nazis during World War II and many colonial atrocities. The images of African women presented were either as villains (the *exciseuse* was also accused of running a cloth business to launder money from excisions) or as victims (the ignorant mothers blindly pursuing African customs, regardless of the harm to their daughters). The verdict demonstrated that the cultural contextualization provided by witnesses such as Claude Meillassoux, the respected anthropologist, was not regarded as important enough to mitigate the offenses.

Although a show trial on FGC has not occurred in the United States, there was a symbolic one in the form of an episode from the popular television show *Law and Order* entitled "Ritual." In it, a successful Egyptian immigrant patriarch pays for a prominent Egyptian male doctor to come to New York to excise his great-niece, the daughter of his niece and her American husband. The niece and her mother support having the procedure done, but the husband murders the patriarch in rage at the prospect. The district attorney, known for his implacable pursuit of murderers whatever their status or motives for committing murder, sides with the murderer and prosecutes him reluctantly. An "expert" witness, an African-American woman professor from Columbia, provides more displacement of infibulation to sub-Saharan Africa by testifying that infibulation is most common in Sierra Leone[!] As the episode ends, the prosecutors are congratulating themselves for doing their best to bring down a "three-thousand-year-old custom."

Thus, *Law and Order* takes an unprecedented position in justifying lethal violence if it can eradicate FGC performed by foreigners. The subject of genital cutting performed for reasons embedded in American culture was dealt with in another episode of *Law and Order* by the conviction of a doddery Jewish circumciser who accidentally castrates a baby. His punishment? Not execution or even a prison term but permanent removal of permission to practice. He is portrayed as a sympathetic character, whereas the murder victim in "Ritual" is not. The murder victim's women supporters are seen as requiring the enlightened intervention of the U.S. courts to educate them as to their misguided beliefs (the patriarchal imperialist assumption). The double standard is evident because the wisdom of routine ritualized circumcision of male babies is not questioned.

Legal Discourses: Asylum

This discussion brings up the last aspect I wish to analyze here, how African societies are being represented in the current campaign for U.S. asylum for those facing FGC. There are distinctly troubling aspects of the asylum cases that clearly reinforce stereotypes and promote the three Rs. In analyzing these aspects I do not mean to oppose asylum in any way. My chief point will be that each case is individual and must be based on sound knowledge of conditions pertaining to that individual rather than sweeping generalizations about Africa that are often inaccurate.

A persistent aspect of the cases involving Kassindja, the experiences of Waris Dirie, the model-turned-anti-FGC-activist, and Lydia Oluloro, a Nigerian woman fighting deportation for herself and her daughters, has been concentration on FGC to the exclusion of other subjects. Kassindja and Dirie both fled their countries as much because of the prospect of forced or arranged marriages as because of genital surgeries. Oluloro had exhausted her appeals of deportation when her lawyer came up with the FGC strategy. He discovered she had undergone clitoridectomy and then asked her about the probable fate of her daughters if they returned to Nigeria. Subsequently, the FGC issue became the chief focus of the case, which was ultimately won. Oluloro's initial case opposing deportation to Nigeria was based on her daughters' exposure to tropical diseases and a different family structure, their ignorance of the language spoken (Yoruba), different roles and expectations for women, a lower standard of living, and lesser educational opportunities. She also feared losing her economic independence.[40] The legal aspects of the cases made FGC the central issue, the *sine qua non* without which African women whose immigration status is questionable will be deported, in part because feminists are less likely to get involved in helping them fight deportation if FGC is not an issue. Immigration and Naturalization Service lawyers have said that the only grounds for asylum are that otherwise a woman would be subjected to a forced female genital surgery.[41]

Oluloro's claim that she would lose her economic independence is intriguing because Yoruba women are world-renowned for their economic independence, usually support themselves and often their children, and do not practice community of property in marriage. There are Muslim Yoruba, who

might seclude women, but it seemed likely that Oluloro's divorce would prevent co-residence with her former husband's family in any case (although
had his family pressed the matter, they could have gained custody of the girls).
At the same time it is notoriously difficult for those without green cards to
get decently paying jobs in the United States. Their victimization in low-paid
jobs is well known, and they are subjected to arrest and deportation as illegal immigrants or as aliens (a well-chosen word) without a work permit. It
was Oluloro's status as the divorced wife of a Nigerian student who had lost
her U.S. residency permit that created problems with the INS in the first
place.[42] Nevertheless, legal discourse constructed African women as helpless
victims of infamous practices, while the United States was being presented
as a liberated paradise for Africans.

A piece by Gregory Kelson, a lawyer, adduces evidence to support claims
of asylum based on a woman or girl being subjected to FGC and proves my
point. He uses as his hypothetical case a Nigerian woman applying for asylum and relies heavily on Oluloro's statements, as well as the U.S. Department
of State's *Report on Human Rights in Nigeria* (1993). Oluloro came to the
United States to marry a Nigerian man who became violent and abusive, and
she divorced him. Although Oluloro lived in the United States for the entire
duration of the marriage in which he repeatedly abused her, she stated that,
in Nigeria "husbands would have been able to control [women's] bodies like
my husband controlled mine." The Human Rights report on the case took
the opportunity to condemn polygyny, bridewealth (the ratification of a
marriage by giving gifts to the woman's parents), forced marriage (often
equated with arranged marriage), lesser women's inheritance rights, and
women's lower rate of involvement in wage labor than men's (most African
women work outside the home but many are self-employed and therefore not
included in labor force statistics).[43] Kelson's assertion that "many tribal customs dictate that a woman cannot own property in her own right or hold a
job" does not reflect the situation in southwestern Nigeria. Women are therefore second-class citizens in Nigeria, Kelson concludes, and "would have a
difficult time speaking out against the practice of female circumcision."

Kelson makes no distinction among Nigerians, who belong to more than
two hundred ethnicities. Citing a 1950 study of part of Igboland, he says,
"Tribal law and custom mandate that female circumcision is imposed on
women, and Nigerian law does little to protect women. Severe social penal-
ties reinforce this practice and essentially prevent women from resisting female circumcision." Further justification for Oluloro's asylum is to be found
in her membership in a persecuted group, namely "potential victims of [un-

defined] female circumcision," who could be but have not been protected by Nigeria's enforcement of its Constitution because in remote areas the government does not intercede in "tribal law" (those local customs codified into male-dominant laws by British efforts). Therefore, the Nigerian authorities condone violence against women; there is no adequate state protection. The state is incompetent or malicious (despite evidence of educational campaigns carried on in Nigeria against FGC). Kelson adds that female circumcision is cruel and inhumane and therefore a violation of a woman's basic human rights. He concludes with an apotheosis of the role of the United States in the world that allocates to Americans the power and responsibility for solving all of the world's problems. "As the last superpower in the world, we have a responsibility to lead the fight against the violation of women's human rights worldwide and to protect those within our borders should the need arise. This protection cannot occur unless we recognize that female circumcision is a form of persecution for which women should be granted political asylum."[44]

Sometimes when analyzing bias it is useful to employ the double-standard test. If the same standards were applied to the United States, how would we fare? Suppose that an American woman claimed asylum in Canada on analogous grounds to those Kelson adduces, only in this case X, as I will call her, will use as grounds violence from an abusive ex-husband to claim that she is part of a persecuted minority. She is from Idaho. What do we find? The state of Idaho does not protect women as a class, nor do the federal, state or local governments have adequate power to prevent her ex-husband from attacking her, as he has done repeatedly, even pistol-whipping her and otherwise threatening her with a gun. Furthermore, X complains, her ex-husband practices serial monogamy, having taken another wife, and refuses to relinquish the custody of his children with X, granted to him by the court because he earned more than she did. Courts in the United States often grant custody to a father if representations are made that the mother, who earns less, cannot adequately support them. Because women normally earn less than men and regularly sacrifice their earning power to family requirements, such decisions ratify and reinforce discrimination against women.

In addition, X's husband did not give back wedding gifts or her share of the marital property. Because he was able to afford a better lawyer than X's, the court awarded their property to him, although marital property now is customarily split more equally. Again, the state was not protecting her, this time because men and women often have unequal access to resources. In addition, if she returns to her former home in Idaho, neighbors, who have been tormenting her with petty acts of vandalism because he told them that she is a lesbian, will resume their persecution. Moreover, she finds customs such as serial monogamy and unequal division of property at divorce repugnant.

Therefore, X alleges through her lawyer, some women in the United States belong to a persecuted minority who object to violence from their husbands and ex-husbands, and the U.S. does not protect them adequately. U.S. law confers fewer rights on women than most African governments do (on paper). The Equal Rights Amendment did not secure enough state support to be added to the Constitution, and the United States did not ratify the international Convention on Elimination of All Forms of Discrimination against Women. As a result of the case X wins support from Canadian feminists, who demonstrate on behalf of oppressed U.S. women. The Canadian court sides with X, citing U.S. lack of constitutional and effective protections for women. Some U.S. women activists decide to revive the fight for the Equal Rights Amendment and to ratify international antidiscrimination conventions that would give women equal protection of the law.

If the judge in this case is to find for X she will have to grant asylum to any U.S. woman who wishes to emigrate to Canada because U.S. laws do not provide adequate protection to women as a class. In addition, the allegations of incompetence and discrimination on the part of the U.S. government would cause the ruling to foster a diplomatic rift between Canada and the United States. In some ways, then, U.S. courts are ill-equipped to assert that U.S. laws respecting women are superior to those of African nations. The displacement of violence against women in the Oluloro case from the U.S. to Nigeria is troubling and only made credible because of American assumptions of a superior U.S. civilization and African barbarity. It is also the pervasiveness of these assumptions that explains a set of U.S. laws that criminalizes genital operations done by Africans or for Africans but not those done by North Americans, even if the results are the same or similar. My initial question about why U.S. lawmakers have so unusually adopted militant feminist positions is thus answered.

The construction of asylum claims needs to be specific and not based on a widespread condemnation of all African laws and customs that assumes that everyone has always practiced FGC and will continue to do so. Reinforcement of negative cultural valuations of Africa and Africans serves no good purpose and ultimately does great disservice to the campaign to end FGC because it discourages working together to do so in an atmosphere of mutual respect. We also need better laws and protections for women in the United States.

Changing Discourses?

Is there evidence of lessening bias in contemporary discourses regarding FGC? Many Africans and Americans are struggling to make things better for women, and some African victories are being won, as emphasized in some media coverage in the United States. A scattering of articles from various newspapers across the country indicates the possibilities of presenting more positive aspects regarding FGC.[45] The *Chicago Tribune* carried a story in March 1998 about the beginning of the three-year U.N. campaign to eradicate FGC. Some of the stringers who formed the huge entourage that followed the Clintons on their April 1998 visit to Africa used their time well to do more thoughtful pieces than the usual.

The *New Orleans Times-Picayune* in April 1998 reported on the successful grass-roots efforts by a Senegalese village to stop FGC, an effort praised by Hillary Rodham Clinton. Vivienne Walt of the *Sacramento Bee* published a long and detailed article stressing these grass-roots elements, which included intensive literacy- and skills-training built around group discussions and classes in local languages. The issue of FGC was only broached once the other programs were established. The movement has forced Senegalese political leaders to take a stand against FGC. Molly Melching, one of the American activists working in UNICEF and U.S.-funded programs, said, "Making a political issue of female circumcision, or declaring it a barbaric act, does not convince many Africans." A similar report from Egypt filed by John Lancaster of the *Washington Post* concerned successful Egyptian Coptic efforts to get rid of infibulation. These also involved intensive long-term, educational, grass-root efforts: a two-person team that remains seven years in a town at the invitation of community leaders and trains local volunteers. Cesar Chelala in the *San Francisco Chronicle* discussed a Central Kenyan effort to reinvent female puberty celebrations that exclude clitoridectomy, described in chapter 3 of this volume by James.[46] Once in a while there is even an article about other images of African women, as when Elizabeth Fullerton of the *Washington Post* described Mauritanian women's successful efforts to achieve commercial independence for their businesses by opening their own market in Nouakchott, the capital.[47]

Unfortunately, none of these articles achieved the front-page placement accorded Dugger's articles by the *New York Times*. More pervasive now are small squibs in newspapers, the hair salon and dentist office magazines that appear routinely and praise the good works of American and other activist women trying to eradicate FGC. This common currency in missionary-view articles encourages Americans to feel superior as they lecture Africans about "barbaric" practices. A good example is from a Joyce Brothers column of May 4, 1999:

> Dear Dr. Brothers: I take up a matter with you because a friend told me to do so, and because I am very angry. I come from a country and people I love, and in my home we have certain customs. Like with my first daughter born there, she was set on the way to proper womanhood by cutting a private body part. This has always been. Now, I'm told that I can no longer do this to my daughters here, because it is against the law. How can this be? My wife, she also had this done when she a child [*sic*]. Without this cutting I would not have married her. What is wrong?—P.B.
>
> Dear P.B.: There are many different customs around the world. Many of these customs are ancient, passed on from one generation to another. Some are based in beliefs tied to local interpretations of religion. For instance, in Afghanistan Taliban men believe that a woman can be stoned to death for adultery. This is against our laws, as is genital mutilation. If you live in this country, it's necessary to obey those laws. Just because a custom is ancient, just because it's accepted in certain cultures, doesn't make it right. In the past, we have done terrible, cruel things in this country, but we've made changes and so must you. The "cutting" of girls is not allowed here.[48]

"P.B.'"s letter may not be genuine. The syntax does not resemble the excellent English employed by many Africans resident in the United States, and it is too conveniently glib about an issue many Africans hold to be private. It provides too ideal an opportunity for Brothers to join the smug consensus that considers the United States to be an enlightened place that has long abandoned "terrible, cruel" practices, unlike P.B.'s country (bringing in the stoning of Afghani women is a nice touch along these lines).

It would be wonderful if U.S. scholarly and media representations would be more accurate and contextually specific regarding FGC and not sensationalize and exaggerate the importance of such practices; if the efforts of African and other non-Western activists to end FGC were highlighted along with how Americans can help provide resources to help them; if African women's leadership on this issue was acknowledged and promoted; if more attention were devoted to non-FGC representations of African women; if the impacts of U.S. actions in the international economy that worsen the situation for all Africans and increase women's dependence on husbands were illustrated; and if more attention were given to the campaigns to focus attention on the harmful effects of U.S. genital and other unnecessary surgeries performed for cultural, cosmetic, or aesthetic reasons. Also needed is a renewed effort to better U.S. women's legal and economic status; a media campaign that emphasizes the defects of the present situation would be useful.

Conclusion: A Third Way

As teachers and private individuals, we can, then, profit from the mistakes of others and find a third way to deal with FGC in our classes or in our lives. When we want to learn or teach about FGC we can include it along with other topics about African women. We can contextualize FGC in terms of variations in practices, their distribution, meaning and trajectory, stressing the matrices of lack of economic opportunity and education, and the world economic role of the United States to make the connections. We can dedicate ourselves to finding the most effective ways to diminish those practices that have the most unhealthy psychological and physical complications. We can respect local knowledge and the leadership of local women. Most of us cannot or will not go to Africa to help in this effort; we can, however, give resources to those who are embarked on long-term, grassroots efforts that are finally, as in Senegal and Egypt, yielding results. Many resources are needed precisely because these are grass-roots efforts and not only require extensive education that includes health education but also economic development that benefits women and respects their input. Marking and pulling out FGC only as an abhorred phenomenon obscures the consideration of the whole socio-religio-economic context, which must be relied upon to foster change. If it is discounted, the efforts to get rid of FGC will fail.

The good news? African societies are much more resilient, creative, intelligent (which has nothing to do with level of formal education), and flexible than U.S. popular media representations make them. The magnitude of FGC has been exaggerated, and all forms are not severely mutilating. In some areas FGC has diminished substantially and continues to do so. There are many activist African men and women working to get rid of FGC in innovative ways, and changes are occurring daily, some of which include diminution in FGC. Many American women are well placed at home to help with resources to further the effectiveness of local efforts. A few of the very dedicated are devoting their lives to the effort, but not as missionaries.

The bad news? Some changes disempower women, especially changes connected to a rapacious world economy that persists in incorporating African economies as suppliers of cheap raw materials and labor.[49] Many Americans do not accept any responsibility for a world system that profits them daily and do not wish to rectify the maldistribution of wealth and resource over-use that make them comfortable. In some African countries, entrenched attitudes, tremendous poverty, local corruption, wars, and lip-service only by governments make any countrywide efforts to better the overall status of women impossible, including diminishing FGC. In some areas, infibulation in particular is spreading.

Therefore, the role of local and international non-governmental organizations is even more critical to eradicating practices, not confined to FGC and not confined to Africa, that are inimical to women's well-being. The cautionary news? Be careful to define those practices and consider the whole context before making representations. As Awa Thiam has said, "The question of excision and infibulation is so complex that it must be treated with the greatest possible sensitivity. Are we dealing with practices that women themselves want?"[50] Seble Dawit and Salem Mekuria have the last words: "A [biased sensationalized] media campaign in the West will not stop genital mutilation. Westerners and those of us living in the West who wish to work on this issue must forge partnerships with the hundreds of African women on the continent who are working to eradicate the practice[s]. Neither Alice Walker nor any of us here can speak for them: but if we have the power and the resources, we can create the room for them to speak with us as well."[51]

Appendix: Questions to Ask Yourself about Images of African Female Genital Cutting

1. Is Africa presented as one uncivilized place with no specific cultural context or explanation for the practice(s) being shown/discussed? Simplistic unexplained references to tradition/custom are not sufficient explanation.

2. Are the voices of African women heard and identified by name in this representation? If they are, are different viewpoints presented? Are dichotomous stances of pro- or anti-female genital cutting the only African views shown? Are African women who participate willingly in any procedure made into villains and those who have any kind of procedure performed on them made exclusively into victims?

3. Are the practices differentiated according to which procedure is being performed? Is there information about differences in procedures and their cultural and geographic locations? Are graphic depictions of procedures inserted or foregrounded unnecessarily, without explanation?

Notes

1. Efua Dorkenoo, *Cutting the Rose: Female Genital Mutilation, The Practice and Its Prevention* (London: Minority Rights Group, 1994), 1.

2. Françoise Kaudjhis-Offoumou, *Marriage en Côte d'Ivoire* (Abidjan: Éditions KOF, 1994), 159. Nahid Toubia has stated, "The attention of the world community on this issue

has, so far, produced mixed results. When Western feminists in the 1970s and 1980s expressed their empathy by making public statements, undertaking studies, or pressing for national laws or international resolutions, they were helpful in exposing the issue and removing the shroud of silence surrounding it. But others, particularly the less responsible elements of the popular press, mishandled the issue by sensationalizing it and treating African and Asian women in a condescending manner. Unfortunately, this crude approach to a complex issue has created a defensive reaction among many people involved with the practice, who might otherwise be allies in the fight for eradication" ("Female Genital Mutilation in the Perspective of Sexual and Reproductive Health," *Report from the Seminar on Female Genital Mutilation, Copenhagen, May 29, 1995* [Copenhagen: Danida, 1995], 7).

3. Harriet Lyons, "Anthropologists, Moralities, and Relativities: the Problem of Genital Mutilations," *Canadian Review of Sociology and Anthropology* 18, no. 4 (1981): 501. Analysis of penile subincision and vaginal introcision among Australian aborigines was particularly fascinating to Victorians. Thinkers from Freud and Durkheim to Bettelheim and Montagu offered analyses of various genital surgeries to support different theoretical points.

4. Lyons notes that deemphasis on sex was an attempt "to counter the racist sensationalism of earlier authors" ("Anthropologists," 507–9). Many of the older studies cited in Lillian Passmore Sanderson, *Female Genital Mutilation: Excision and Infibulation, A Bibliography* (London: Anti-Slavery Society for the Protection of Human Rights, 1986) were relativist. Denise Paulme, in *Femmes d'Afrique Noire* (Paris: Mouton, 1960), a pathbreaking book she edited on African women, included an annotated bibliography with seventy authors entered on the subject of female initiation, which in Africa does not always include FGC. Seventeen of the entries dealt with FGC in some manner, but only one of them was in any way critical of the practices, Y. E. Hills, "Female Circumcision in the Sudan," *Anti-Slavery Reporter* 5, no. 1 (1949): 13–15. A more recent relativist work is Jean-Pierre Ombolo, *Les mutilations sexuelles en Afrique Noire* (Yaoundé, Cameroon: printed by the author, 1981).

5. Esther Hicks, *Infibulation Female Mutilation in Islamic Northeastern Africa*, rev. ed. (New Brunswick: Transaction Publishers, 1996), 211.

6. Katherine Park, "The Rediscovery of the Clitoris in French Medicine and the *Tribades*, 1570–1620," in *The Body in Parts: Fantasies of Corporeality in Early Modern Europe*, ed. David Hellman and Carla Mazzio (New York: Routledge, 1997), 170–93. Prosecutor Commaret in successfully attacking FGC performed in France by an African *exciseuse* stated that the psychological damage would be great for girls when they "realize they will never again be like other women," thus constructing them as deviant from European standards. "The Summation of Prosecutor Commaret," Keita Case, Criminal Court of Paris, March 6–8, 1991, *Passages* (Northwestern University Program of African Studies), no. 3 (1992): 2. By Malian Bambara standards however, they would be regarded as deviant if they had not been excised

7. The ethics of CNN paying an operator to perform an infibulation for television are highly reprehensible, and the video was clearly exploitative of those involved. Marie B. Assaad, "Female Circumcision in Egypt a Harmful Practice Embedded in Culture and

Tradition," *Report from the Seminar on Female Genital Mutilation, Copenhagen, May 19, 1995* (Copenhagen: Danida, 1995), 24, 26ff.

8. Although journalists have these excuses, those who engage in more extensive studies and media production do not. African materials are becoming more accessible, but the will to access them has to be there.

9. Kevin Dunn, "Lights . . . Camera . . . Africa: Images of Africa and Africans in Western Popular Films of the 1930s," *African Studies Review* 39, no. 1 (1996): 169–70.

10. Isabelle R. Gunning has chronicled a grass-roots example of this phenomenon in California ("Female Genital Surgeries: Eradication Measures at the Western Local Level—A Cautionary Tale," chapter 4 in this volume).

11. For reasons of space, I have departed from conventional usage here and given only one extended note citing all of the relevant page numbers for works that are analyzed intensively. That note can be found at the end of the discussion of the source. Similarly, in a few cases I have used one note at the end of a paragraph to cite all of the sources referred to in it.

12. Hicks, *Infibulation*, 8. By Hosken's definition it seems that France should be included on her map of places where FGC is practiced, because some African immigrants practice FGC there and some French doctors practice "cosmetic" female genital surgeries.

13. Ifi Amadiume, *Male Daughters, Female Husbands: Gender and Sex in African Society* (Atlantic Highlands: Zed Press, 1987); Claire C. Robertson, "Grassroots in Kenya: Women, Genital Mutilation, and Collective Action, 1920–1990," *Signs: Journal of Women in Culture and Society* 21, no. 2 (1996): 615–42.

14. Bonnie Shullenberger, letter to the editor, *New York Times*, June 22, 1995, A26.

15. Lori Leonard, "'We Did It for Pleasure Only': Hearing Alternative Tales of Female Circumcision," *Qualitative Inquiry* (2000).

16. Fran P. Hosken, *The Hosken Report*, 2d ed. (Lexington, Mass.: Women's International Network News, 1979), 1–3, 12–13, 4, 15–16, preface.

17. The francophone analogue of Fran Hosken, only more extreme in her use of language, is probably Renée Saurel, who in *L'enterrée vive: Essai sur les mutilations sexuelles* (Geneva: Editions Slatkine, 1981), 1–3, 19, calls FGC "genocide of girls and women" and its victims "buried alive." She says that the reasons for the practices do not matter, and the consequences are "the spirit rent in pieces."

18. Mary Daly, *Gyn/Ecology* (Boston: Beacon Press, 1978), 155, 159, 164–67.

19. An African woman living in the United States told a researcher that mere acquaintances asked intrusive questions and that as a result she felt as if, to them, "all she was was a big genital that had been mutilated." Celia Dugger, "Tug of Taboos: African Genital Rite versus U.S. Law," *New York Times*, Dec. 28, 1996, 1:1.

20. Hanny Lightfoot-Klein, *Prisoners of Ritual: An Odyssey into Female Genital Circumcision in Africa* (New York: Haworth Press, 1989), ix, xii, 7, 199, 77.

21. Alice Walker and Pratibha Parmar, *Warrior Marks: Female Genital Mutilation and the Sexual Blinding of Women* (New York: Harcourt Brace, 1993), 340, refer to the "Tricoleur tribe" in Senegal. Senegalese do speak French, but they are independent and have abandoned the French tricolor flag. The reference may be to the Toucouleur or Tukolor people.

22. Lillian Passmore Sanderson, *Against the Mutilation of Women: The Struggle to End Unnecessary Suffering* (London: Ithaca Press, 1981), 63–111; Lorna Ng'ang'a, "Female Genital Mutilation Activities in Africa: Focus on Kenya—Using a Case History," in *Report from the Seminar on Female Genital Mutilation, Copehhagen, May 19, 1995* (Copenhagen: Danida, 1995), 35–37; see also Lynn M. Thomas, "'Ngaitana (I will circumcise myself)': The Gender and Generational Politics of the 1956 Ban on Clitoridectomy in Meru, Kenya," *Gender and Society* 8, no. 3 (1996): 338–63.

23. Walker and Parmar, *Warrior Marks*, 10.

24. I have also been critical of polygyny, but only insofar as those I work with in Ghana and in Kenya have criticized it.

25. Emmanuel D. Babatunde, *Women's Rights Versus Women's Rites: A Study of Circumcision among the Kentu Yoruba of South Western Nigeria* (Trenton: Africa World Press, 1997), 1–24.

26. Walker and Parmar, *Warrior Marks*, 7, 93–95, 139, 148, 154, 158–60, 179, 185, 210, 95, 318, 252–54, 275–77.

27. The use of Lexis/Nexis was most helpful here, but users beware—different sources are listed, depending on whether the term *female circumcision* or *female genital mutilation* is used.

28. A. M. Rosenthal, "On My Mind: Female Genital Torture," *New York Times*, Dec. 29, 1992, A15; Rosenthal, "The Torture Continues," July 27, 1993, 8:13.

29. Blaine Harden, "As UN Women's Decade Ends African Wives Still Exploited; Men Demand Pregnancies as Proof of Their Virility," *Washington Post*, July 6, 1985, A1.

30. Celia Dugger, "Woman's Plea for Asylum Puts Tribal Ritual on Trial," *Washington Post*, April 15, 1996, A1; Dugger, "U.S. Frees African Fleeing Ritual Mutilation," *Washington Post*, April 25, 1996, A1; Dugger, "Rite of Anguish: A Special Report; Genital Ritual Is Unyielding in Africa," *Washington Post*, Oct. 5, 1966, 1:1; Dugger, "Tug of Taboos: African Genital Rite versus U.S. Law," *Washington Post*, Dec. 28, 1996, 1:1

31. Rita Ciolli, "A Woman's Ritual of Anguish: A Look at the Pulitzer-Winning Photos of the Rite of Female Circumcision in Kenya," *Newsday*, April 23, 1996, B4.

32. L. Amede Obiora, "Bridges and Barricades: Rethinking Polemics and Intransigence in the Campaign Against Female Circumcision," *Case Western Reserve Law Review* 47, no. 2 (1997): 275–378; Adamantia Pollis and Peter Schwab, "Human Rights: A Western Construct with Limited Applicability," in *Human Rights Cultural and Ideological Perspectives*, ed. Pollis and Schwab (New York: Praeger, 1979): 1–18; Rhoda E. Howard, *Human Rights in Commonwealth Africa* (Totowa: Rowman and Littlefield, 1986); Hope Lewis, "Between *Irua* and 'Female Genital Mutilation': Feminist Human Rights Discourse and the Cultural Divide," *Harvard Human Rights Journal* 8 (1995): 1–55; Kay Boulware-Miller, "Female Circumcision: Challenge to the Practice as a Human Rights Violation," *Harvard Women's Law Journal* 8 (1988): 155–77.

33. Another well-informed piece with an overview and critique of human rights discourse is Noor J. Kassamali, "When Modernity Confronts Traditional Practices," in *Women in Muslim Societies Diversity within Unity*, ed. Herbert L. Bodman and Nayereh Tohidi (Boulder: Lynne Rienner, 1998), 39–61. Kassamali's title is, however, unfortunate, harking back to the old paradigm of Africans rooted in unchanging tradition.

34. Alison T. Slack, "Female Circumcision: A Critical Appraisal," *Human Rights Quarterly* 10 (1988): 437–86.

35. Jacques Lantier, *La cité magique et magie en Afrique noire* (Paris: Librairie Artheme Fayard, 1972).

36. Robyn Cerny Smith, "Female Circumcision: Bringing Women's Perspective into the International Debate," *Southern California Law Review* 65 (1992): 2449–504. In a list of scholars writing about Kikuyu history and customs, Smith (2477) misspells the last name of the only African scholar and gives his first name incorrectly. "George Muruiki" is, in reality, Godfrey Muriuki.

37. Claire C. Robertson, *Trouble Showed the Way: Women, Men and Trade in the Nairobi Area, 1890–1990* (Bloomington: Indiana University Press, 1997), ch. 1.

38. These proceedings plus extracts of articles from *Droit et Cultures* are available in *Passages* no. 3 (1992): 1–4 in English translation. See also Bronwyn Winter, "Women, the Law and Cultural Relativism in France: The Case of Excision," *Signs: Journal of Women in Culture and Society* 19, no. 4 (1994): 939–74.

39. In the second trial, the proceedings were translated for the defendants, and one of the lawyers spoke the language of some of the defendants.

40. Angela Neustatter, "It Cuts so Deep; Born a Somali Nomad, Waris Dirie Is Now a Top Model and a UN Ambassador Campaigning against Female Circumcision. Trouble Is, She's Locked Herself in Her Hotel Room and Won't Come Out," *London Independent,* March 22, 1998, 4–5 (features section). Neustatter infantilized Dirie and accused Africans of being bad parents. Stuart Wasserman and Maria Puente, "Female Genital Mutilation under Scrutiny at Hearing," *USA Today,* Feb. 11, 1994, 3A; Timothy Egan, "An Ancient Ritual and a Mother's Asylum Plea," *New York Times,* March 4, 1994, A25; Gregory Kelson, "Granting Political Asylum to Potential Victims of Female Circumcision," *Michigan Journal of Gender and Law* 3, no. 1 (1995): 266–69.

41. Dugger, "U.S. Frees African."

42. Sylvia Moreno, "For Her Daughter's Protection; Nigerian Fights Deportation, Fearing Mistreatment by Tribe," *Washington Post,* May 27, 1998, B1.

43. The statements of academics have sometimes been distorted to support the cause. Merrick Posnansky, professor emeritus of anthropology at UCLA (identified as "Polansky" by Celia Dugger), told Dugger that sometimes women were forced into polygynous marriages and into female genital surgeries. This is true, but the interpretation has usually left out the "sometimes" part. Dugger, "Women's Plea."

44. Kelson, "Asylum," 288ff. The impression that Kelson is overgeneralizing is heightened by a tendency to confuse practices in Nigeria with those in Kenya (286n124).

45. Celia Dugger's articles eventually included more nuanced approaches to FGC but never as featured initial items. "Tug of Taboos" contains a reference to the reduction of African women to their genital status, and "Rite of Anguish" a discussion of Ivoirian efforts to get rid of FGC. The latter even has a quote from anthropologist Ellen Gruenbaum that problematizes representation, "[Y]ou will not change people's minds by preaching to them or telling them they are primitive. They undertake the risks for reasons important to them." The article, however, was accompanied by one of Stephanie Welsh's Kenyan photographs, although Dugger does not mention Kenya in it. In "New Law Bans

Genital Cutting in U.S." (*New York Times*, Oct. 12, 1996, sec. 1:1) Dugger cites recent World Bank funding for eradication efforts and stresses the efforts of Rep. Pat Schroeder with their unlikely Republican support that finally succeeded in outlawing FGC for the estimated 150,000 African women and girls at risk in the United States, an estimate compiled by assuming that all African women immigrants are at risk.

46. *Chicago Tribune*, March 10, 1998, C7; Bruce Alpert, "Fight against Circumcision Praised," *Times-Picayune*, April 3, 1998, A18; Vivienne Walt, "Backlash in Africa against a Major Ritual," *Sacramento Bee*, July 12, 1998, F1; John Lancaster, "Village Gives Up a Painful Ritual; Drive to End Female Circumcision Gains Support among Egypt's Copts," *Washington Post*, June, 21 1998, A19; Cesar Chelala, "New Rite Is Alternative to Female Circumcision," *San Francisco Chronicle*, Sept. 16, 1998, A23.

47. Elizabeth Fullerton, "Women Gaining Stature in Business in Muslim Mauritania," *Washington Post*, Aug. 3, 1998, A17.

48. Joyce Brothers, "Despite Reality, You Gotta Have High Hopes," New Jersey *Star-Ledger*, May 4, 1999, 38.

49. One defeat for African and Caribbean economies came in the 1998–2000 banana war won by the U.S. government on behalf of companies like United Brands (Chiquita Banana) with strong interests in Central America and monopolistic dominance of the U.S. market. The United States successfully protested preferred treatment of other bananas in European markets, a loss that will undoubtedly reduce the standard of living in economies heavily dependent on banana exports.

50. Awa Thiam, *Speak Out, Black Sisters: Feminism and Oppression in Black Africa*, trans. Dorothy S. Blair (Dover, N.H.: Pluto Press, 1986), 84.

51. Seble Dawit and Salem Mekuria, "The West Just Doesn't Get It," *New York Times*, Dec. 7, 1993, A27.

3. Listening to Other(ed) Voices: Reflections around Female Genital Cutting

STANLIE M. JAMES

ALICE WALKER HAS brought her considerable talent and resources to bear on the critical problem of female genital cutting by retrieving the character Tashi from the margins of *The Color Purple* and centralizing her story in the novel *Possessing the Secret of Joy*.[1] Through Tashi's fictional story, along with the documentary film and accompanying text *Warrior Marks*, Walker has managed to focus attention on this issue in ways that have eluded human rights activists who have toiled unheralded for years to effect change.[2] In fact, Walker's successful efforts to generate national attention and discussion in the United States were cause for somber rejoicing and hope, although a variety of representatives from the mainstream media felt compelled to express horror and dismay that such "savage" practices continued to exist in those "exotic" places. Although I am delighted that my "shero" Alice Walker has become so publicly supportive of ongoing struggles to eradicate these practices harmful to women and girls, I am uneasy with the manner in which she has chosen to champion such a worthy cause.

Early in the film and companion text *Warrior Marks*, Walker recounts the unfortunate story of how her brother shot and blinded her in one eye; she rightly characterizes it as a "patriarchal wound." She suggests that her injury is analogous to the female circumcision/genital mutilation millions of women have experienced over thousands of years and that this "visual mutilation" has helped her to "see" more clearly the subject of genital mutilation. I find the analogy between her personal misfortune and pervasive practices of female genital cutting to be particularly problematic. Although little boys with BB guns are emblematic of violent patriarchal societies, the logic of the analogy suggests that boys shooting and blinding their sisters is a traditional ceremonial practice sanctioned by this society in much the same fashion as female circumcision is in other societies. Although Walker is certainly imbued with a sympathetic perspective, centering her own story within this international struggle for women's human rights seems to have the unintentional consequence of "othering" or marginalizing the very people she wishes her audience to support.

Walker compiled an impressive array of interviews for *Warrior Marks*, including women who have been circumcised/mutilated, the mother of a girl who will undergo the procedure, and activists who are struggling to eradicate these practices. Curiously, these interviews are interspersed with a dancer's almost erotic depiction of the horrors of circumcision. One stunning interview is with a weeping young woman, Aminata Diop, who had refused to undergo circumcision/mutilation and was seeking sanctuary in Europe. She had been disowned by her parents, and her father had divorced and thrown her mother into the street for failing to control her daughter's behavior, thereby bringing shame upon him. Meanwhile, Aminata's fiancé had broken their engagement. In another interview, Walker spoke with a woman who had traumatic memories of her own experience but felt compelled, albeit regretfully, to continue the tradition with her own daughter. Outraged and censorious, Walker interviewed circumcisers in a manner that fails to articulate or even recognize that such practices have provided some women with opportunities to attain respect and income in societies where there are often precious few avenues available to women to attain such critically limited resources.

Female circumcision, sometimes referred to as genital mutilation (FGM), depending on one's political perspective, are English terms used for practices that involve cutting away all or part of the external female genitalia.[3] Christine Walley has observed that the "act of naming these practices is controversial in and of itself."[4] Elsewhere in this volume, she argues that the use of the English term *circumcision* equates practices of removing the clitoris with removing the male foreskin and does not interrogate the differing physical and psychological ramifications. The phrase *female genital mutilation* was first used by feminists, women's health advocates, and human rights activists and later adopted by the Inter-African Committee in Addis Ababa, Ethiopia, in 1990. This term was used as a means of equating the custom with torture and carries an (at least) implicit assumption that parents and relatives deliberately intend to harm children and are therefore abusive—a charge, by the way, that particularly incenses many African women, even some working diligently to eradicate the practices. Thus Walley notes "circumcision signal(s) relativistic tolerance (while) mutilation impl(ies) moral outrage."[5]

Other English terms used for the range of female genital cutting practices include *clitoridectomy, excision, infibulation,* and *female genital surgeries* or *operations,* whereas African terminology is often euphemistic and, of course, varies from group to group. Thus, in Sudan, excision and infibulation practices are known as "going to the back of the house," while in parts of Nigeria genital cutting is called "having your bath." I choose to use the phrase *female genital cutting* (or *genital cutting*) because it seems a bit less fraught with the kind of implications that may hinder our capacities to engage in the careful listening that is so crucial to efforts to eradicate the practices.

Before Walker's widely publicized venture into this subject matter, female genital cutting had already elicited horrified responses from some colonial missionaries, outraged the sensibilities of a few informed Western feminists and activists, provided anticolonialists with fuel for nationalist struggles, and been almost surreptitiously defined as a health matter by the United Nations.[6] It is within that context that Walker shares these and other stories. She challenges deeply entrenched and difficult practices that are often detrimental to the health and well-being of women and girls, but she does so in a way that invites the characterization of African women as victims without agency. Indeed, Walker seems "possessed" of the pernicious notion that she can and must rescue those unfortunate women from themselves, from their ignorance, and from their patriarchal traditions.

Patricia Stamp has argued that third-world women have often been treated as "passive targets of oppressive practices and discriminatory structures," a conceptualization that "colludes with sexist ideologies that construct women as naturally inferior, passive and consigned to a private apolitical world."[7] Privileged Western women (and I must include myself at least at the margin of this particular category) must be mindful of the sin that Marilyn Frye has termed "arrogant perception" and that Isabelle R. Gunning describes as the view that one is the center of the universe, thus distancing herself from the other.[8]

In "The Discourse of the Veil at the Turn of Two Centuries," Leila Ahmed observed that nascent Western feminist stirrings were deflected from Western conditions to focus on the veil as the ultimate symbol of Islamic oppression of women.[9] This redirected emphasis communicates too readily that oppression occurs only "elsewhere" and that "native" women can be rescued by encouraging them to abandon their own religion, customs, and culture and adopt those of the West. Ultimately, this form of arrogant perception is supportive of colonialism and its institutions.

Arrogant perception is apparent in Western facile insensitivity to the unfamiliar. It is exhibited in the West's horrified, condemnatory responses to practices such as the Indian tradition of sati, Chinese footbinding, and Arab customs of veiling and purdah. Arrogant perception nourishes ethnocentrism even as it obscures visions of the multifaceted complexity of those characterized as oppressed others as well as their inter- and intra-relationships within and between societies.

This essay emerges from my concern about whether others outside the culture can appropriately engage in nonimperialist critiques of such unfamiliar traditions. Can outrage be legitimately expressed in a manner that does not other or alienate the very people within cultures who are engaged in efforts to promote change? I am convinced that the debates swirling around female genital cutting can and must move beyond troubling stances of arrogant perception. Such debates must be restructured in ways that are neither condemnatory nor demeaning but that foster the integrity of our perspicacity.

Illuminated by careful study of the nuanced complexities of cultures, perspicacious integrity requires a capacity to historicize and conceptualize culture as complex and dynamic. It emerges from the creative synthesis of multiple approaches and strategies, including cognizance of similarities in historical traditions and boundary-transgressive interconnections. It develops on multiple levels from attempts to listen carefully to rarely heard voices of marginalized women within cultures, to interrogate cultural specificities with sensitivity, and to make efforts to incorporate prohibitions against female genital cutting in international human rights legislation. To that end, this essay explores the literature for approaches that will inform and enhance the integrity of our perspicacity and can, in turn, be used to mount effective challenges that would ultimately result in the eradication of genital cutting.

For years, activist Fran Hosken struggled diligently and heroically to document, by means of her Women's International Network (WIN) news, female genital cutting practices. Her arrogantly perceptive work not only succeeded eventually in carving out a prominent space for this issue within the context of the UN Human Rights agenda but has also engendered a growing body of literature. Although it is not my intention to provide a comprehensive literature review of this subject, it should be noted that this literature incorporates a variety of approaches, some of which have been useful to, and others that could be characterized as detrimental to, efforts to eradicate such practices. The most useful works have also provided critical culturally specific information. For example, Nawal El Saadawi was one of the first to write (movingly) about her personal experience of circumcision and to situate that experience within the Egyptian context of feminist political struggles, and Olayinka Koso-Thomas, a Nigerian physician and author of *The Circumcision of Women: A Strategy for Eradication,* briefly examined the customary tradition of female excision or clitoridectomy as a womanhood and societal initiation rite within the context of Sierra Leone.[10] The value of Koso-Thomas's contribution lies in her development of a detailed practical proposal for a twenty-year plan to eliminate the practice. Although specific to the situation in Sierra Leone, the plan can also serve as a model that other countries could adopt to address the problem. Based on six years of travel through Sudan, Kenya, and Egypt, Hanny Lightfoot-Klein's stunning contribution to the literature, *Prisoners of Ritual: An Odyssey into Female Genital Circumcision in Africa,* focuses on the Sudanese custom of infibulation. Lightfoot-Klein incorporates remarkable interviews of women and men, educated and uneducated, professionals and laypersons, in a manner that starkly portrays the grim physical, psychological, emotional, and social consequences of the practice and reveals the social significance and cultural values of this tradition.[11] As Claire Robertson explains elsewhere in this volume, Lightfoot-Klein, much like Hosken, has an unfortunate tendency to reduce women to the status of their genital parts.

Perhaps the most famous discussion of the customary practice of clitoridectomy was provided in Jomo Kenyatta's ethnographic *Facing Mount Kenya* published originally in 1938. Kenyatta, Kenya's first postcolonial leader, describes Gikuyu circumcision ceremonies for girls and boys as a critical aspect of sacred rites of passage.[12] The ritual was embedded in a series of activities that symbolized the rebirth of a child not as a child of individuals but as a child of the entire "tribe" and culminated in the acceptance of the child as an adult member of the society.[13] Kenyatta argues that the tradition was critical to the identity of the Gikuyu and ultimately to the survival of the society. According to Kenyatta, no self-respecting Gikuyu woman or man would consider marrying an uncircumcised individual because that person was, by definition, an immature child. He also indicates that although male circumcision did not serve the same function, female circumcision provided a way of controlling the sexuality of girls and women.[14]

Kenyatta's study was conceived and written with at least two motives and audiences in mind. Presented to British academe in partial fulfillment of the requirements for an advanced degree in anthropology, Kenyatta's work endeavored to portray the Gikuyu as possessors of a rich and complex culture, comparable to albeit different from European culture. At the same time, writing as an anticolonial spokesperson and a self-appointed guardian of tradition, he offers his people an idealized version of precolonial life in which Gikuyus lived harmoniously in a democratic (and patriarchal) society. Exhorting his countrymen to return to the "correct" ways of their ancestors, he goes so far as to argue that those who would stray from his representations of their culture have been detribalized and should no longer consider themselves, or be considered, Gikuyu.

Kenyatta's ahistorical "official story" of precolonial Kikuyu society exposes his conceptualization of culture as a communally constructed consensus of homogeneous systems, beliefs, and values that are easily learned and transmitted from generation to generation. One must beware of official stories because, as Florencia Mallon reminds us, "they bury counterhegemonic elements in smoothed out discourses that purport to speak for the whole community."[15] Such conceptualizations, according to Gerald Sider, also are limited in use, especially when interrogating the role of culture in social change or when questioning how people participate "in the routine but . . . powerful and pervasive transformations of their social world." Sider goes on to argue that a culture adapts to conditions of imposed pressure and fragmentation while it is simultaneously a form of collective self-assertion that can be a part of struggle against domination and appropriation. Culture is situated within the social relations of daily life and production, thus enabling contradictions to emerge within culture, between culture and daily life, and among culture, the state, and production.[16]

Kenyatta failed to recognize that culture is neither monolithic nor static. Rather, culture is composed of a cacophony of voices and thus should be understood as the language of argument about identity.[17] Kenyatta's limited and limiting vision of history very likely conceals the discordant voices created by the "volatile paradoxes, disjunctions and contradictions" characteristic of all societies.[18] This orthodoxy inhibits creative efforts to interrogate Kikuyu traditions closely through, for example, retrieving women's history from the periphery. Such interrogations might extricate and explicate discourses of historical opposition to female circumcision and even patriarchy within the Kikuyu culture.[19] Although Kenyatta clearly loved his people and their traditions, his cultural vision was diminished not only by the silenced voices of women but also by his failure to acknowledge and ascertain the multiplicity of arguments about identity.

In contrast, Walker centralizes her own personal tragedy of being blinded by her brother and then presents her audience with a variety of women's voices that are divorced from the specificity of cultural and historical context. Throughout the film, Walker adopts a stance of arrogant perception, even as she exudes outrage that seems to obscure her vision of the multifaceted and nuanced nature of the range of practices involving female genital cutting that, in turn, serves to marginalize or "other" the very women she wishes to support.

Micere Githae Mugo, an African literary and cultural scholar, provides an important and informative critique of Alice Walker's novel *Possessing the Secret of Joy,* the documentary film and text of *Warrior Marks,* and their relationship. Mugo argues that Walker and Parmar made no attempt to engage in dialogue with the women they met in villages and filmed for the documentary. "Instead they imposed framed questions, interrogating their objectified subjects in order to elicit the answers they wanted from them."[20] Decrying Walker's depiction of the "victims" as denigrating rather than empowering, Mugo observes that "the African women subjects are presented to the reader as a collection of helpless bundles of mutilated creatures and as stereotypes who are far from the semblance of living dignified human beings. They are pitied and patronized, instead of being cherished, nurtured and invested with faith as human subjects, potentially capable of understanding and changing the conditions that dehumanize them." Mugo insists that "liberating feminist writing has the responsibility to expose not only the practices but also the institutions, structures and systems that embody and perpetuate the oppression of women."[21]

The superficiality of Alice Walker's insights into African social, political, and economic institutions obscures the rich heritage of its many cultures and societies, and that, in turn, suggests an (unintentional perhaps?) insensitivity to the complexities of the lives of African women. This crucial deficiency leads to the regrettable conclusion that both the text and the video *Warrior Marks* are contaminated by a not-very-subtle form of cultural imperialism. That conclusion is especially disappointing, because Walker's womanist writings are typically characterized by sophisticated analyses of the concept of multiple oppressions. For example, her haunting and complex short story "Advancing Luna—and Ida B. Wells" exhibits subtly nuanced insights into the impact of race, class, and gender on rape as it is played out within the context of African American communities and the broader American society.[22]

Evading the dubious position of arrogant perceiver requires the capacity to conceptualize culture as complex, competitive, dynamic, and historicized. Rigorous interrogation of the particulars of culture enables the development of sophisticated, contextualized analyses while allowing for critique with careful specificity. The writing of Isabelle Gunning, Robyn Cerny Smith, Jean-Claude Muller, and Jonathan P. Berkey provides intriguing examples of efforts to avoid the limitations of arrogant perception while enhancing understanding of this critical issue.

In "Arrogant Perception, World Traveling and Multicultural Feminism: The Case of Female Genital Surgeries," Gunning probes the issue of female genital cutting. In an exercise of sensitivity and conciliation, she chooses to refer to such practices as "genital surgeries" and elegantly characterizes them as "culturally challenging," a term she defines as any practice that someone outside a particular culture would view as negative, largely because she or he is culturally unfamiliar with the custom.[23] Gunning proposes to confront these culturally challenging practices by retrieving the obscure history of genital surgeries in Western societies and exploring similarities and interconnections across boundaries of nationality.

Citing Ben Barker-Benfield's article "Sexual Surgeries in Late Nineteenth Century America," Gunning alerts readers to the existence of clitoridectomies and other related surgeries in Western societies.[24] Following the Civil War, white American men were increasingly concerned about the rise of "hysteria" or "madness" among women and felt that this could be traced to their sexuality. These "disorderly women" were identified as women's rightsists, bloomer-wearers, midwives, and anyone who had a suspected aversion to men or who sought to rival men in manly sports and occupations. Within that context, gynecology, a new medical specialty, was developed to "cure" women's problems. Because women's "mental disorders" were equated with their sexual organs, one "cure" adopted in the late 1860s was clitoridectomy.

Although it would be easy to assume that this was "simply" an issue of gender oppression in the United States, Gunning's careful interrogation of the practice reveals the complexities of multiple oppressions. Evidence suggests that during the 1840s clitoridectomies and other related forms of surgery were tested by a Dr. Sims on enslaved women borrowed from their masters or purchased for purposes of experimentation. Later, during the 1850s, destitute white immigrant women in New York's Woman's Hospital were also subjected to experimentation. Once he had "perfected" his methods, Sims employed these surgeries in his private practice to cure white middle- and upper-class women whose male guardians (i.e., fathers and husbands) could afford his fees.[25]

Gunning's strategy of moving beyond stances of arrogant perception emerges from her efforts to uncover interconnecting similarities across boundaries of nationality and culture. She argues that becoming familiar with these hitherto obscured aspects of Western history facilitates Westerners' ability to understand that although most of these specific practices have been discontinued, the attitudes and assumptions about gender roles that were used to justify the surgery remain largely in place within contemporary Western society.[26] In this volume, Gunning interrogates the odd responses of U.S. legislative bodies to foreign practices of female genital cutting and juxtaposes those responses to domestic practices of male circumcision.

In "Female Circumcision: Bringing Women's Perspectives into the International Debate," Robyn Cerny Smith examines prevalent anthropological arguments that defend such traditional practices as crucial to the continued survival of "tribal" groups as distinct cultural entities. Noting that female circumcision has often been characterized by authorities as ritual, Smith explores the work of anthropologists such as Victor Turner and Clifford Geertz on rites of passage and ritual in order to explicate analytical frameworks that have often been employed to determine whether a practice was indeed central to a group's identity.[27] Smith notes that on the basis of such analyses, ethnographies of the Kikuyu often support the notion that the practice of female circumcision that accompanies "the *irua* ceremony is crucial to the maintenance of the Kikuyu as a separate, distinct entity. . . . [and that] the . . . tribe's distinct values and structure would probably disappear without the circumcision ceremony or age-sets."[28] The nomadic Darod of Somalia, in contrast, base their practice of infibulation on their understanding of Islam and its emphasis on controlling female sexuality. Unlike the Kikuyu, female circumcision among the Darod is neither a rite of passage nor embedded in ritual. Therefore, Smith argues, "tribal" unity cannot be dependent on female circumcision, but the practice "may contribute to the maintenance of a gender hierarchy, in which women are subordinate to men. It is not clear, however, that tribal identity would disintegrate in the absence of hierarchy in the long term."[29]

Although Smith's review of this body of ethnographic literature is important, the significance of her work emerges from her willingness to explore feminism, postmodernism, and international human rights as alternative approaches to restructuring the debates surrounding genital cutting. She observes that feminist perspectives have managed to facilitate the understanding that "female circumcision," in addition to maintaining "tribal identity," is employed to sustain male dominance and control female sexuality. At the same time, Smith reminds readers that some feminist theories "were [also] developed by Western white women and are therefore "insufficiently attentive to . . . cultural diversity, and they falsely universalize features of the theorist's own era, society, culture, class, sexual orientation, and ethnic, or racial group."[30] Smith restates Nancy Hartsock's important admonition to postmodernists who would criticize feminist theories while failing to replace them with theories "that will help oppressed and marginalized groups name their experiences and guide their actions in their fight against oppression."[31]

An alternative approach to restructuring debates around female genital cutting is provided by international human rights law. Its purpose is to establish international standards of human rights and to oblige states to protect them. The United Nations charter mentions human rights, but these rights are continuing to attain specificity through the promulgation of a variety of multilateral conventions (treaties) and resolutions. The human rights of women have recently achieved heightened visibility within the international system. One example, the 1993 Vienna Declaration and Programme of Action, emphasizes women's equality and the necessity of integrating their human rights into the mainstream of UN activities. The declaration recognizes the importance of eradicating a litany of violations of women's human rights, including sexual harassment and violence against women. It also makes oblique references to genital cutting by stressing the need to eliminate "any conflicts which may arise between the rights of women and the harmful effects of certain traditional or customary practices, cultural prejudices and religious extremism."[32] In 1996 the World Health Organization (WHO) issued a definitive technical report critiquing the euphemistic use of the term *female circumcision* and deliberately naming these practices "genital mutilation."[33]

Although the right to be free from genital cutting has yet to be enshrined within a specific declaration or convention, reference to such practices within the Vienna Declaration and the WHO technical report are indicative of international efforts to move toward the inclusion of what they termed "female genital mutilation" (FGM) as a violation of women's human rights. These efforts were significantly advanced in 1995 at the Fourth World Conference on Women in Beijing. FGM was referenced several times in the Beijing Declaration and the Platform for Action, which included sections on health, the girl child, and violence. Recognizing female genital cutting as a grave health risk that is also discriminatory toward the girl child, and conceptualizing such practices as an aspect of violence against women, the Beijing document has advanced the international community toward the establishment of FGC as a violation of women's human rights.[34] Thus, as Smith has observed, women may receive some protection from genital cutting through their rights to health, to be free of cruel and degrading practices, to sexual and corporal integrity, and to reproduction.[35] Additional protection for women's human rights is, of course, found in the UN Convention on the Elimination of All Forms of Discrimination against Women (1981), which appears to provide the strongest support for women's rights to sexual and corporal integrity. A convention, however, is considered legally binding only on those states that ratify it. Therefore Kenya, which has ratified this convention, should be subject to international pressure to eradicate FGC, whereas Somalia, which has not ratified it, is not legally obligated to eradicate the practice.[36]

Smith engages the struggle to move beyond arrogant perception by encouraging reliance on the voices of marginalized women and to seek redress within the international human rights system. Only when the experiences of these women become central to that discussion, she argues, will the debate be restructured in a manner that adequately expresses their oppression. "Perhaps if these women and girls have the power to name their true oppressions and experiences in the international community, they may be able to work together to reevaluate the traditions that silence them. Then they may choose which traditions truly are necessary for tribal unity from their point of view and reject those traditions that continue to oppress them."[37]

The efforts of Gunning and Smith to restructure debates surrounding practices of female genital cutting resonate with cultural specificity and historicized voices of women within an international context. At first glance, Jean-Claude Muller's fascinating ethnography on the Dii of North Cameroon seems irrelevant to these discussions because the emphasis appears to be on male circumcision.[38] The variation in focus, however, serves to enhance the reader's understanding of the multifaceted implications of these practices and the accompanying debates.

Muller's examination of the male circumcision practices of the Cameroonian Dii reveals that the objectives of the practice include the separation of men from women and the transformation of young boys into men. The latter is accomplished through the infliction of intense suffering, especially circumcision. Boys between the ages of nine and fifteen are collectively taken to the bush for a period of several months; during this time they are subjected to humiliations of pain, privation, and hazing. They also periodically undergo painful washing of their penises with abrasive substances, and eventually the foreskins are removed in a circumcision ceremony. The newly circumcised are separated from women through sharing "secrets" reserved for men, especially the most important secret of the removal of the foreskin.[39] Muller's informants felt that such treatment—the humiliations and the painful washings—were designed to teach respect for elders and make men capable of controlling their wives. The Dii believe that an uncircumcised man would be unable to make his wife obey and would therefore be dominated by her.

Muller found that unlike many who practice male circumcision, the Dii do not subscribe to the belief that the foreskin is anatomically feminine and needs to be removed in order to transform boys into men. Rather, the Dii believe that a true masculine character develops out of pain and suffering. In fact, the foreskins of boys who exhibit bravery during the operation are desiccated and later placed in the ritual drink used in subsequent ceremonies. Because circumcision is above all concerned with marking the masculine, the boy who has been designated to be the village leader is required to undergo a second circumcision in which the penis is partially peeled lengthwise. Muller mentions that this procedure is similar to an operation practiced by several neighboring groups of the Dii, including the Dowayos, who are noted for removing all the skin of the penis bit by bit over the course of a day. Dii awareness of the Dowayo practice supports the notion that traditional practices not only cross ethnic and geographic boundaries but are also modified during that process, thus providing additional support for conceptualizations of societies as dynamic, complex, and historicized. The Dii believe that the pain accompanying the second circumcision will render the prospective leader patient, virtuous, and capable of resolving all difficult leadership problems by virtue of the stoicism instilled in him through his additional suffering.

In some societies, clitoridectomy accompanies male circumcision, whereas in others one can be practiced without the other. Among the Dii, however, female genital cutting is not practiced. They do, however, subscribe to a form of genital manipulation in conjunction with male circumcision. Four days prior to the return of the young boys from their bush camp, women are notified to prepare themselves for their own ceremony. Young girls who have yet to be initiated are chosen to become "jesting relatives" of the newly circumcised. The evening before the boys return, the women perform their own version of the dances of circumcision, which also include bullying and hazing. The following morning the girls undergo a "circumcision" ceremony. After they are undressed, a female circumcisionist uses a pair of clips to poke the sides of the vagina and pull out the clitoris. This "operation" is repeated four times (a sacred number for women), and the girl is then asked if she feels any pain. Giving an affirmative response, the girl is told that she will suffer more pain later if she lets men practice sex without first doing *hen male* (resist, delay). She is instructed that to make love hurriedly and without preliminaries will cause as much pain as is inflicted on her in this moment.

After this short sexual initiation, the girls are bathed and return to the village, where a small ceremony is held to designate a "jesting relationship" for each girl with a boy returning from the bush. This relationship is reserved only for boys and girls who have participated in the parallel ceremonies on the same occasion and at the same location. These boys and girls are considered equal, so much so that a man would never, or very rarely, marry his jesting partner, because the norms of female obedience and marital respect would be contradictory to the equality implied within this relationship.[40]

Dii practices of male circumcision and what Muller calls female pseudo-excision are designed to sustain patriarchy by producing (socially) gendered men and women.[41] For men, this goal is achieved through the removal of the foreskin. There is no corresponding practice of clitoridectomy, because, unlike some other ethnic groups that believe the clitoris is a male appendage that must be removed, the Dii believe that the very essence of femininity resides in the clitoris. According to Muller, the clitoris is perceived as an essential organ because it regulates sexual relations between men and women. Through the ceremony of pseudoexcision, a young girl is taught that she will feel no pain if she behaves appropriately but will suffer if she misbehaves. Muller's sources also stressed their belief that the clitoris reveals whether a woman behaves with dignity and in a feminine manner.

Muller notes that for divergent reasons a man must have his foreskin removed while a woman retains her clitoris as representations of the quintessence of masculinity and femininity. Both men and women must endure the unifying principles of pain and suffering, which, according to Muller, serve to increase masculinity in men while curbing the savage sexuality of women.[42]

Some Western feminists have often understood female genital mutilation as a consequence of patriarchal dominance perpetrated by men on women.[43] Muller's study indicates that mutilation is not confined to the female body, nor does it serve only to enforce patriarchal dominance. Thus, deceptively simple assumptions must be revisited and revised within the specificities of cultural context.

Cleanliness, aesthetics, hygiene, birth control, and fear that the "untrimmed" clitoris would grow down past a woman's knees are among the many reasons expressed for a range of female genital cutting practices. Transgressing geographical and cultural boundaries, the most frequently mentioned rationale for such practices is the need to control women, especially their sexuality. Clearly, female genital cutting must be recognized as a patriarchal practice embedded within the complexity of gender hierarchy.

Muller's (perhaps unintentional) contribution to perceptions of the deeply entrenched and pervasive nature of patriarchy and gender hierarchy arises from his careful depiction of male circumcision among the Dii and the accompanying rite of passage (and the additional circumcision of the prospective leader). While other ethnographies (including Kenyatta's) have described male circumcision, Muller's work exposes a critical connection between male circumcision and female subordination through his exploration of the Dii conviction that an uncircumcised male would be unable to make his wife obey. Even the emphasis on equality between the sexes found in the jesting relationship could be viewed as a metaphorical safety valve designed to neutralize or institutionalize incipient challenges to male dominance. With the institution of these two distinctive characteristics, the Dii can afford to respect women's human right to bodily integrity, because the maintenance of patriarchy in their society is not dependent on the mutilation of women. Rather, male privilege within this particular version of gender hierarchy is upheld by a tradition of penis mutilation.

Jonathan P. Berkey has examined the history of genital cutting practices where it was common in the Muslim world.[44] He observes that scholars and others who often remark that female excision is not an explicitly Islamic custom are usually referring to the fact that the practice is not mentioned in the Qur'an, nor did medieval commentators who approved of the practices make reference to any specific passages in the Qur'an to support their claims. In fact, Berkey asserts, the practice of female excision was unknown in many Muslim societies, and in some societies where it was practiced its origins were clearly pre-Islamic; thus, the custom was often shared by both Muslims and non-Muslims. In Egypt, for example, both Coptic Christians and Muslims engaged in the practice, although, Berkey notes, it was not an ancient universal custom among Egyptians. Some females were mummified with their external genitalia intact.

Berkey argues that the important question is not the debate over whether excision is or is not Islamic but the way in which female excision "interacts with different cultural strata within the broader Islamic framework, how it attaches itself to certain values within the framework as a method of legitimization and finally how it contributes . . . to the process of redefining Islam."[45] According to Berkey, Islam incorporated and accommodated the ancient and popular practice of excision into its religious and legal worldview.

Berkey observes that in some parts of the world male circumcision in Islam is synonymous with being a Muslim. The consensus of four accepted "schools" of Sunni law (Shafi'is, Hanfis, Malikis, and Hanbalis) was that circumcision was a component of the *Sunna,* an Arabic word that refers to the normative speech and behavior of the Prophet Muhammad.[46] Most jurists characterized circumcision as obligatory, although at least some Hanafis considered it commendable if not absolutely required.[47] Jurists' positions regarding female excision were more equivocal. The consensus of the Islamic legal community never objected to the practice, and where it had deep cultural roots (as in Egypt) attempts were made to invest the operation with all the authority of a religious obligation. Thus "many Hadiths list circumcision, along with the shaving of pubic hair, trimming of the moustache and fingernails . . . as among . . . practices associated with *fitra,* the idealized practice of the prophet which, according to Muslim doctrine, the religion of Islam preserves."[48]

"In the absence of an explicit Qur'anic statement discussions of female excision by Islamic jurists begins with those hadiths which deal specifically with the issue." They generally fell into one of three categories:

1. Those enjoining ablutions after sex.
2. Although there is some uncertainty about its authenticity, the second category includes a hadith in which it was reported that the Prophet enjoined a female circumcisor in Medina, "Do not destroy it completely [i.e., don't cut away too much in the course of the operation] for it is more favorable for the woman and preferable for the husband." This hadith, however, is said to rely on a "weak" chain of transmitters from the Prophet, which, in turn, has led at least one commentator to conclude that the uncertainty over its authenticity obviates the requirement for the operation.[49] Despite this caveat, the hadith (and several variants) have been cited by medieval jurists and provided the basis for much later discussions on the practice.
3. Important tradition in the Musnad of Ibn Hanbal, which described circumcision as sunna for men and a "noble deed" (*makruma*) for women, which appeared frequently in later juristic literature.[50]

Berkey argues that based on these hadiths, medieval Islamic jurists constructed a variety of nuanced opinions that were overwhelmingly favorable to the practice of female excision. The tradition from the Musnad of Ibn Hanbal, for example, formed the basis for the consensus of the Hanbali school of law on the matter, reflected in Ibn Qayyim's description of the cutting of the clitoris as a sign of the veneration of God and in the opinion of Hanbali scholar Ibn Qudama that "circumcision is required of men and recommended as correct for women but not required of them."[51]

The scholars of the other three Sunni schools of law developed independent positions on this issue. The Safi'i school, for example, which predominated in Egypt, adopted what Berkey describes as the most strident position of all. The prominent thirteenth-century Shafii jurist al Nawawi wrote that "circumcision is required [*wajib*] for both men and women."[52] Thus the discourse within this juristic tradition generally approved of female excision and in some cases held it to be mandated by Islamic law.[53] Berkey observes, "There is compelling evidence, therefore that medieval Muslims, or at least those Muslims among whom female excision was practiced perceived the custom as one that had religious sanctions."[54] He goes on to suggest that even in the present day the wide range of distinctions in female genital cutting practices implies a different set of underlying reasons for the operation, ranging from a simple "cleansing," to a rite to ensure fertility, to a severe enforcement of chastity.

Berkey found that in both the medieval and modern periods, female genital cutting was and is practiced, at least in part, "to control women's sexuality by limiting their sex drive or more precisely by limiting the physical pleasure which they can receive from sexual intercourse."[55] Medieval Islamic writers linked excision, pleasure, and chastity and believed that the operation was necessary to preserve a woman's virtue and protect a man's honor. Al-Jahiz wrote, "The uncircumcised woman finds pleasure which the circumcised woman does not. . . . Chastity," according to Al-Jahiz, was "limited to circumcised women."[56]

Berkey asserts that such pre-Islamic practices as excision "might survive the transition to a new religion" (in this case Islam) "by attaching itself to, and constructing a justification on, some ethical concern of the new faith." Incorporation of these practices actually accommodated the "misogynistic conviction" common to patriarchal societies in the Near East and the Mediterranean that women are possessed of extraordinary sexual appetites, a condition that is in turn linked to the presumed deficiency in their capacity to reason and consequently to behave in ethical fashion.[57] Restraining women's sexuality was therefore directly related to male honor, which could only be protected by preserving the modesty of those women for whom a man bore responsibility. Thus, Berkey argues that the practice of female excision in the medieval world is best understood within the context of the tension that permeates Islamic sexual ethics. On the one hand, reports Berkey, sexual desires of men and women are recognized and even approved; on the other hand, those desires must be appropriately channeled. Islamic jurists feared above all a woman's passion, even as they recognized a wife's right to be sexually satisfied by her husband. Although that desire and need had to be recognized, she only attained her rights through the jurists' principal goal of confining sexual relations to certain specified, circumscribed situations. Berkey observes that there was an ambiguity perceived in the sexual passion of women. It needed to be restricted through excision in order to enforce ethical standards, but it was also crucial to preserve it by limiting the operations.[58]

While Islamic writers were making the critical linkages among excision, a woman's pleasure, and chastity, they also emphasized moderation. Al-Jahiz cited the hadith of the Prophet urging that the operation be a limited one; the problem was in striking a delicate balance that would preserve a woman's chastity and therefore a man's honor. An excision could not be so radical as to decrease a woman's pleasure to a point where she could lose her sexual desire for her husband. In fact, Berkey claims, all the various hadiths implied that the restrictions must be physically and emotionally beneficial to both partners.[59]

This perspective continues to be apparent in contemporary society, as evidenced by the remarks of an Egyptian woman: "We are told that circumcision is necessary because drinking the water of the Nile as a child makes a girl passionate when she grows up. So this helps her to get hold of herself so that she doesn't tire her husband or need these things if she's a widow or divorced."[60] Both men and women are believed to be endowed with exceedingly strong, potentially disruptive, sexual energy. Both, therefore, need to be restrained, but it is the woman who in effect is expected to assume the burden of restraint for both—for the man by remaining an object of his sexual passions and for herself—through the practice of female excision.[61]

Our understanding of the nuanced complexities of patriarchal customs is richly informed by Berkey's historicized analysis of Islam and female excision, by the specificity of Gunning's and Smith's treatments of genital cutting, and by Muller's examination of male circumcision practices. Alice Walker contributes a palpable sense of outrage to these discussions. While she enjoys a wide latitude for the expression of that outrage in the fictitious *Possessing the Secret of Joy,* outrage almost obscures her laudable intentions of eradicating such practices in the text and the film *Warrior Marks.* That is, her outrage nudges her dangerously close to demonizing women circumcisers while characterizing African women as both bad mothers and child abusers. Such cultural insensitivity invites the animosity of many African women who have struggled so valiantly to bring about change and is viewed by some as cultural imperialism. Outrage may be necessary, but it is certainly not a sufficient condition for fostering perspicacious integrity. In fact, one must take care to see that outrage does not support the arrogant perception deemed detrimental to the struggle for change.

The diversity of texts suggests that the task of achieving the necessary perspicacious integrity so crucial not only to the elimination of genital cutting but also to struggles to eradicate patriarchy will emerge from a creative synthesis of multiple approaches and strategies and from efforts to foster boundary-transgressive interconnections, including the movement to incorporate specific prohibitions against female genital cutting into international human rights legislation. It may also be facilitated through the adoption of perspectives and strategies developing among black feminists.

Black feminisms have emerged from the margins of society and academe to express disaffection with common unilateral analytical frameworks of race-, gender-, and class-based discrimination. The failure of these analytical frameworks to capture the subtle complexities of experiences of oppression has served effectively to "other" black women. As a response, American black feminists have sought to place African American women at the center of analyses through the critical examination of their everyday lives.[62]

Careful readings of African American women's histories reveal them to be political actors who have striven to forge what Chandra Mohanty refers to as "communities of resistance" in order to engage in profound struggles to eradicate oppressions and transform society.[63] As active subjects who have transgressed arbitrary boundaries of objectification and victimology, pragmatic African American women, when they have deemed it appropriate, have developed strategic alliances with other groups, including African American men, white women (sporadically), and other women of color who have had similar experiences of oppression. These alliances have been sensitive to political maneuverings designed to privilege certain groups or issues. Despite the fragility of such alliances, they represent critical efforts to transgress the boundaries of race, class, and gender and are instructive to the processes of developing sophisticated analyses of issues of multiple oppression. Lessons gleaned from this labor will not only enhance efforts to transcend the boundaries of nationality, ethnicity, and religion but also facilitate attempts to articulate the complexities of patriarchy.

Just as many African American theorists and activists continue to engage in analyzing the relations of gender, race, and class in order to resist and eradicate multiple oppressions, African women are likewise engaged in developing their own communities of resistance that have profound implications at both the material and ideological levels for the institutions of patriarchy. For example, Africa News Service reported after years of research and discussion with villagers that a growing number of rural Kenyan families are participating in an alternative rite, Ntanira na Mugumbo (Circumcision through Words). Thirty families participated in the first Circumcision through Words program, which occurred in August of 1996 in the village of Gatunga near Mount Kenya. In December of that same year, some fifty more families participated, and the following August, seventy families ushered their daughters through this new rite of passage.[64]

Circumcision through Words is a product of collaborations among rural families and Maendeleo ya Wanawake (MYWO), the Kenyan national government's women's group, which is committed to the eradication of female genital cutting, and receives technical support from the Program for Appropriate Technology in Health (PATH), headquartered in Seattle. Circumcision through Words developed out of recognition that the practice of clitoridectomy was deeply entrenched in beliefs, values, assumptions, and taboos of the culture that have been integral to a woman's social status and personal identity. "Indeed, it seems the central defining achievement of [this new rite] is not that it saves young women from the dangers of [genital cutting] but that it captures the cultural significance of female circumcision while doing away with the dangerous practices itself."[65] Leah Muuya of MYWO observes, "People think of the traditions as themselves. They see themselves in their traditions. They see they are being themselves because they have been able to fulfill some of the initiations."[66]

PATH distributes a MYWO-produced videotape entitled *Secret and Sacred,* which explores the personal dangers and harmful social results of clitoridectomy. The tape points out that the puberty rite has traditionally signaled a young woman's readiness for the responsibilities of adulthood. Circumcision through Words, rather than subjecting young women to the traditional rites of passage that include genital cutting, brings candidates together to spend a week in seclusion, where they are taught about assuming their roles as women, parents, and adults in the community. They are also taught about personal health, hygiene, reproductive issues, communication skills, self-esteem, and how to deal with peer pressure. The week concludes with a community celebration of song, dance, and feasting to affirm the girls and their new place in the community.[67]

Kenya is not the only location where changes are occurring. In July 1998, National Public Radio's *All Things Considered* reported on thirty-one rural villages in Senegal that had renounced the practice of excision through a program called Tolstan, which means "breaking through" in Wolof. Composed of eight modules, each of which is two months in length, Tolstan is a nongovernmental organization (NGO) run by Senegalese for Senegalese and part of an ongoing campaign to raise awareness around this custom. It has been organized jointly by the government, religious groups, and UN organizations, including UNICEF and the United Nations Development Fund for Women (UNIFEM). Through storytelling, proverbs, role-playing, and discussions, a respectful, nurturing atmosphere is created so that education about a variety of topics critical to the welfare of the entire village can occur. About a year into the course, the seventh module focuses on women's health and incorporates the topic of excision. Rather than criticizing the practice or insisting that it should be stopped, the health effects of the procedure are laid out. As the creator of the program, Mollie Melching, a white woman from Texas who had lived in Senegal for twenty-three years, explained, "I think what succeeded in our program is that we never told people to stop. We gave them the facts. We gave them the information. We said you are adults. You love your children. You care about your family. You care about the future of the family and the village. You, when given the facts, will make the right decision. And they did. They made the right decision."[68]

In one village that has stopped the practice a woman explained, "We do not want any more blood, any more suffering for our girls on their wedding night, no more girls dying from infection, hemorrhage or AIDs caused by excision." Kerthio Diara, another woman from the same village, observed that the course made women aware of their rights. "We studied the rights of the individual and we focused on the right to health that involves a woman's freedom to make decisions about her body and to keep her body intact." Diara went on to add, "This was an astonishing revelation for us because this right questioned the ancient custom of excising all girls in the community. Any woman who was not excised became everyone's laughing stock." Another woman said, "Those who do it now will be ridiculed by others. Those who feel they cannot give it up will be forced to hide to do it as in the case of any another [sic] shameful practice."[69]

In order to convince the members of their community to do away with the practice of excision, members of the group spoke with the elders and religious leaders as was suggested in the modules of their training program. They also spoke to their husbands, who understood their concerns. Encouraged by that support, they produced a play on individual rights that incorporated messages about the negative effects of excision, and over many months they performed the play throughout all parts of the village; those performances provided, in turn, the basis for extensive discussions. Eventually, the village came to a consensus around giving up the practice forever.

Despite this progress, efforts to eradicate excision continue to be contentious. The National Public Radio report concluded by describing what happened when one group of villagers who had successfully completed the program visited a second village to present a play about their decision to change the tradition. The play was not well received in the second village. One elderly woman yelled that no one there had ever gotten sick or died, because "we know how to do the cutting correctly." A man stormed out of the play, shouting, "This village has more pressing problems, like poverty and disease." Many villagers denounced their visitors for abandoning a sacred tradition for money, while one of their elders accused Tolstan of attempting to turn women into prostitutes for foreigners. Although the practice continues in many villages that Tolstan has not yet targeted, the course is now underway in 250 villages across Senegal. Five other West African nations have requested Mollie Melching's assistance in establishing similar programs.[70]

Although deep entrenchment of practices of female genital cutting is apparent in these stories from two sides of the African continent, both cases are illustrative of the potential to eradicate such practices through forging partnerships between women within their villages and countries, from north and south, and across such boundaries as race, ethnicity, religion, nationality, and class. Soraya Mire, a Somali American who endured the Somali tradition of excision and infibulation at the age of thirteen, has produced, written, and directed a film that challenges Somali traditions. The documentary *Fire Eyes: Female Circumcision,* which ironically has been reputed to have been partially funded by Alice Walker, has been described as "a highly contextualized piece which portrays the specificity of a particular African culture."[71] The film begins with Mire recounting her experience and later, in an extremely difficult and courageous act, allowing her altered genitalia to be shown so the audience has some sense of the extensive damage that results from practices of excision and infibulation. Unlike Walker's story of being blinded, Mire's experience directly relates to the issue of female genital cutting. *Fire Eyes* includes segments in which women describe their own experiences and their intentions for their daughters and men discuss their positions on the practice. She also includes interviews with an imam about the religious implications and with two African American doctors, who describe the harmful physical ramifications of excision and infibulation and successful corrective surgery procedures. Like Walker, Mire is emphatically opposed to the practices and characterizes them as a form of child abuse that must be eradicated. Unlike Walker, she recognizes the mitigating cultural constraints upon women and makes the critical argument that one must take "a leap of faith to recognize the incredible amount of love involved in this experience—when you do this to young girls."

Other films that contribute to efforts to contextualize and historicize female genital cutting include *Rites* and *In the Name of God: Helping Circumcised Women.*[72] Directed by Penny Dedman, the major premise of *Rites* is that female genital mutilation has been commonplace throughout history and throughout the world. The term *mutilation* is used because it is understood to be a medical term that refers to any removal of a healthy organ. This documentary identifies and describes eighteenth- and nineteenth-century practices of female genital cutting in Western societies, discusses the elaborate gadgets devised to stop masturbation, shows pictures of chastity belts from the Middle Ages, and provides footage of an Oprah Winfrey interview of a victim of Dr. James C. Burt's "surgery of love" in Ohio. In addition to providing such crucial information about Western practices, *Rites* also includes information about genital cutting in various parts of Africa. For example, several prominent activists, including Efua Dorkenoo, Berhane Ras-Work, Olayinka Koso-Thomas, and Nawal El Sadaawi are interviewed. Saadawi provides important information about genital cutting in Egypt and the religious and patriarchal rationale for the tradition. The documentary also includes rare footage of a secret excision ceremony of Maasai girls in Kenya undergoing a rite of passage. Legislative responses to genital cutting are also analyzed and critiqued. This film, with the appropriate reading assignments and discussion, should be especially helpful to instructors who find it necessary to discuss this topic in their undergraduate courses.

The second documentary, *In The Name of God: Helping Circumcised Women*, may be most useful to more advanced students, particularly for those in medical and nursing schools. This film focuses on infibulation in Ethiopia. It is estimated that more than 90 percent of all Ethiopia women undergo that procedure. The film provides graphic descriptions of scars, deinfibulation at marriage and reinfibulation after the birth of a child, and problems with childbirth as a result of infibulation. It then focuses on the unique Fistula Hospital in Addis Ababa. Fistulas are holes that develop between the bladder and the vagina, through which urine leaks as a result of infibulation. Women who suffer from fistulas have a strong odor and often become smelly outcasts, trying to survive on the outskirts of their society. The hospital, staffed by former patients and two white doctors, attempts to repair the fistulas. Often the damage is so extensive that the operations are unsuccessful; at other times, although the repairs are successful the woman is rendered sterile. The film also includes information about the Ethiopia National Committee against Circumcision (NCTPE), which has begun an education campaign against circumcision.

Unfortunately, many of the struggles to eradicate genital cutting have been rendered invisible by unsympathetic, unconcerned, or ill-informed outsiders. As these stories are retrieved from the margins sometimes referred to as the "third world," previously concealed domestic challenges to female genital cutting and gender hierarchy at the level of individual households and within specific countries may be revealed. Knowledge of African women's agency, their varied and multiple challenges, will in turn inform conceptualizations of those broader, ongoing internal arguments over critical issues of cultural identity.

The Tolstan Project in Senegal, the Circumcision with Words Program in Kenya, Soraya Mire's *Fire Eyes: Female Circumcision, Rites,* and *In the Name of God: Helping Circumcised Women* illustrate Gunning's concept of "world travelling" and the potential of collaborative feminist efforts to address a particularly contentious and complex issue. They are indicative of women's assertion of oppositional agency that is occurring all over the world, sometimes surreptitiously and at other times with great fanfare, individually and/ or in groups, and more and more often transgressing a multitude of boundaries. Attentive listening to other(ed) voices informs our efforts to recognize the many ways women choose to resist the disabling characterizations of victim, acknowledge the integrity of the interrogations and analyses of their/ our cultural traditions, and respect their endeavors to mobilize, strategize, and challenge the practices of female genital cutting that have been so detrimental to health, well-being, and autonomy.

In the momentous struggle to move beyond arrogant perception and toward perspicacious integrity, theorists and activists are challenged to understand the nuances of their own cultures, even as they are becoming cognizant of the complexities and subtleties of other cultures. They must engage in multiple and multicultural dialogues in order to embrace ever-more-expansive roles as sensitive, knowledgable, non-imperialist people who recognize that African and "othered" women around the world are making priorities among hard choices as they design their own struggles. Only after toiling to create necessary, profound insights into the interconnections of similarities and differences can the ultimate task commence of constructing the transformational, transnational consensus so critical to dismantling all aspects of multiple oppressions, including but not limited to female genital cutting.

Notes

This essay is a revised and expanded version of "Shades of Othering: Reflections on Female Circumcision/Genital Mutilation," which was published in *Signs: Journal of Women in Culture and Society* 23, no. 4 (1998): 1030–48. © 1998 by the University of Chicago. All rights reserved.

1. Alice Walker, *The Color Purple* (New York: Washington Square Press, 1982); Alice Walker, *Possessing the Secret of Joy* (New York: Harcourt Brace, 1992).

2. Alice Walker and Pratibha Parmar, eds., *Warrior Marks: Female Genital Mutilation and the Sexual Blinding of Women* (New York: Harcourt Brace, 1993); *Warrior Marks: Female Genital Mutilation and the Sexual Blinding of Women* (1993), video produced by Pratibha Parma and Alice Walker (color, fifty-four minutes).

3. There are four basic forms of this practice. (1) Mild *sunna* is a rarely practiced ritualistic circumcision in which the prepuce of the clitoris is nicked, slit, or removed, thus leaving the gland and body of the clitoris intact. This form is often equated with male circumcision because the clitoris is not generally damaged. (2) Modified *Sunna* (or Muslim) circumcision is a partial or total excision of the body of the clitoris. (3) Excision or clitoridectomy, the most common form, usually involves the removal of the entire clitoris and sometimes parts of the labia minora, often resulting in extensive scar tissue that can obstruct the vaginal opening. In Sudan this form of circumcision is referred to as

Sunna. (4) Infibulation or pharonic circumcision, the most severe form, involves the removal of virtually all external female genitalia, including the entire clitoris and the labia minora, while much of the labia majora is also cut or scraped away. The remaining raw edges of the labia majora are held together and then sewn so the remaining skin will form a bridge of scar tissue over the vaginal opening. The entire area is closed, leaving only a tiny opening about the size of a matchstick. Sometimes a straw is inserted into the opening so that urine and menstrual blood can be passed. See Hanny Lightfoot-Klein, *Prisoners of Ritual: An Odyssey into Female Genital Circumcision in Africa* (New York: Haworth Press, 1989), 33, for an excellent description of these procedures; see also Alison T. Slack, "Female Circumcision: A Critical Appraisal," *Human Rights Quarterly* 10 (1988): 438–87.

4. Christine J. Walley, "Searching for 'Voices': Feminism, Anthropology and the Global Debate over Female Genital Operations," *Cultural Anthropology* 12, no. 3 (1997): 470.

5. Walley, "Searching for 'Voices,'" 408.

6. Cora Ann Presley, *Kikuyu Women, the Mau Mau Rebellion and Social Change in Kenya* (Boulder: Westview Press, 1992); Slack, "Female Circumcision"; Robyn Cerny Smith, "Female Circumcision: Bringing Women's Perspectives into the International Debate," *Southern California Law Review* 65, no. 5 (1992): 438–87. Female circumcision was first brought to international attention in 1979 at a World Health Seminar in Khartoum, Sudan. The seminar "Traditional Practices Affecting the Health of Women and Children" sought the eradication of female genital mutilation through stressing education and formulating recommendations for governmental interventions (Slack, "Female Circumcision," 480).

7. Patricia Stamp, "Burying Otieno: The Politics of Gender and Ethnicity in Kenya," *Signs: Journal of Women in Culture and Society* 16, no. 4 (1991): 845.

8. Marilyn Frye, "In and Out of Harm's Way: Arrogance of Love," in *The Politics of Reality: Essays in Feminist Theory* (Trumansberg, N.Y.: Crossing Press, 1983), 52–83; Isabelle R. Gunning, "Arrogant Perception, World Traveling and Multicultural Feminism: The Case of Female Genital Surgeries," *Columbia Human Rights Law Review* 23, no. 2 (1992): 189–248.

9. Leila Ahmed, "The Discourse of the Veil at the Turn of Two Centuries," presented at the University of Wisconsin, Madison, Nov. 21, 1993.

10. Nawal El Saadawi, *The Hidden Face of Eve: Women in the Arab World,* trans. and ed. by Sherif Hetata (London: Zed Press, 1980); Olayinka Koso-Thomas, *The Circumcision of Women: A Strategy for Eradication* (London: Zed Press, 1985).

11. Lightfoot-Klein, *Prisoners of Ritual.*

12. Consistently throughout *Facing Mount Kenya,* Kenyatta spells his ethnic group with the letter G. In deference to him, I have used that spelling when discussing his book. At other times in the text, I revert to the common spelling: Kikuyu I see this as another opportunity, albeit minor, to enhance perspicacious integrity. Kenyatta, *Facing Mount Kenya: The Tribal Life of the Gikuyu* (1938, repr. New York: Vintage, 1965).

13. I have used the term *tribe* here despite its current disfavor because it is the term that was used by Kenyatta.

14. Kenyatta, *Facing Mount Kenya,* 132–33, 162.

15. Florencia Mallon, *Peasant and National: the Making of Postcolonial Mexico and Peru* (Berkeley: University of California Press, 1995), 90.

16. Gerald Sider, *Culture and Class in Anthropology and History: A Newfoundland Illustration* (New York: Cambridge University Press, 1986), 4, 193.

17. Author communication with Florencia Mallon, Madison, Wisc., Feb. 1994. I am grateful to Florencia Mallon for a conversation clarifying this point.

18. Sider, *Culture and Class*, 7.

19. Claire Robertson, "Grassroots in Kenya: Women, Genital Mutilation and Collective Action," *Signs: Journal of Women in Culture and Society* 21, no. 2 (1996): 615–42.

20. Micere Githae Mugo, "Élitist Anti-Circumcision Discourse as Mutilating and Anti-Feminist," *Case Western Reserve Law Review* 47, no. 2 (1997): 461–79.

21. Mugo, "Elitist Anti-Circumcision Discourse," 478, 467.

22. Alice Walker, "Advancing Luna—and Ida B. Wells," in *You Can't Keep a Good Woman Down* (New York: Harcourt Brace, 1981), 85–104.

23. Gunning, "Arrogant Perception," 191.

24. Ben Barker-Benfield, "Sexual Surgery in Late Nineteenth Century America," *International Journal of Health Services* 5, no. 2 (1975): 279–98.

25. Barker-Benfield, "Sexual Surgery," 288–89: Gunning, "Arrogant Perception," 205–9; see also Slack, "Female Circumcision."

26. In her 1994 keynote address to the Women's Caucus of the African Studies Association, Seble Dawit observed that in 1979 the medical license of James C. Burt was revoked for performing clitoridectomies and a form of infibulation on five hundred unconsenting, and frequently unconscious, U.S. women. In his book *Surgery of Love* (New York: Carlton Press, 1975), Burt argued, ironically, that the procedure was designed to stimulate sexual response in women and their partners, an idea diametrically opposed to African rationales for such procedures.

27. Victor Turner, *The Forest of Symbols: Aspects of Ndembu Ritual* (Ithaca: Cornell University Press, 1967); Clifford Geertz, "Religion as a Cultural System," in *Reader in Comparative Religion: An Anthropological Approach*, ed. William A. Lessa and Evon Z. Vogt, 4th ed. (New York: Harper and Row, 1972), as quoted in Smith, "Female Circumcision," 2453–56.

28. Smith, "Female Circumcision," 2470.

29. Ibid., 2472.

30. Ibid., 2488.

31. Ibid., 2489.

32. "UN Vienna Declaration and Programme of Action" (A/CONF.157/24 13 Oct. 1993), in *The Vienna Declaration and Programme of Action* (New York: United Nations, 1933), sec. 11, para. 38.

33. World Health Organization, *Female Genital Mutilation: Report of a WHO Technical Working Group, Geneva, 17–19 July 1995* (Geneva: World Health Organization, 1996).

34. "Beijing Declaration and the Platform for Action of the Fourth World Conference on Women" (A/CONF.177/20, Oct. 17, 1995), in *The United Nations and the Advancement of Women, 1945–1996*, rev. ed. (New York: Department of Public Information, United Nations, 1996).

35. Smith, "Female Circumcision," 2490–96.

36. Elsewhere I have discussed the range of responses by African nations to the U.N.

Convention on Women. See Stanlie M. James, "Challenging Patriarchal Privilege through the Development of International Human Rights," *Women's Studies International Forum* 17, no. 6 (1994): 563–78.

37. Smith, "Female Circumcision," 2503. For a more critical reading of Smith, see Claire C. Robertson, "Getting beyond the Ew! Factor: Rethinking U.S. Approaches to African Female Genital Cutting" (chapter 2 of this volume).

38. Jean-Claude Muller, "Les deux fois circoncis et lest presque excisées: Le cas des Dii de l'Adamaoua Nord Cameroun," *Cahiers d'Études Africaines* 33, no. 4 (1993): 531–44. I am grateful to Nadia Turk, University of Colorado, Boulder, for translating this important article.

39. Muller observes that even though women are aware of this "secret," they would never mention it. Men know that women know, and women know that men know that they know.

40. If they should marry, it is only with the stipulation that the jesting relationship will be forgotten.

41. Muller differentiates genital manipulation from practices of excision and genital elongation, which has as its goal the elongation of the labia majora and minora as well as the clitoris for the playful, hedonistic purpose of increasing sexual pleasure.

42. Muller, "Les deux fois circoncis."

43. Robertson, "Getting beyond the Ew! Factor."

44. Jonathan P. Berkey, "Circumcision Circumscribed: Female Excision and Cultural Accommodation in the Medieval Near East," *International Journal of Middle East Studies* 28, no. 1 (1996): 20. I am grateful to Michael Chamberlain for advising me of this very important article.

45. Berkey, "Circumcision Circumscribed," 28.

46. Ibid., 37.

47. Ibid., 21.

48. Ibid., 24.

49. Ibid.

50. Ibid., 25.

51. Ibid.

52. Ibid.

53. Ibid., 26

54. Ibid., 27.

55. Ibid., 30.

56. Quoted in ibid., 30.

57. Ibid., 30.

58. Ibid., 34.

59. Ibid., 31–32.

60. Ibid., 30.

61. Ibid., 34.

62. See, for example, bell hooks, *Feminist Theory: From Margin to Center* (Boston: South End Press, 1984); Deborah K. King, "Multiple Jeopardy, Multiple Consciousness: The Context of a Black Feminist Ideology," *Signs: Journal of Women in Culture and Society* 14, no. 11 (1988): 42–72; Patricia Hill Collins, *Black Feminist Thought: Knowledge, Conscious-*

ness and the Politics of Empowerment (Boston: Unwin Hyman, 1990); Paula Giddings, *When and Where I Enter . . . : The Impact of Black Women on Race and Sex in America* (New York: William Morrow, 1984).

63. Chandra Talpade Mohanty, "Introduction: Cartographies of Struggle, Third World Women and the Politics of Feminism," in *Third World Women and the Politics of Feminism,* ed. Chandra Talpade Mohanty, Ann Russo, and Lourdes Torres (Bloomington: Indiana University press, 1991), 1–47.

64. Africa News Service, "Alternative Rite to Female Circumcision Spreading in Kenya," Nov. 19, 1997.

65. Africa News Service, "Alternative Rite."

66. Ibid.

67. Ibid.

68. Mollie Melching on NPR Radio's *All Things Considered,* July 22, 1998.

69. Melching on *All Things Considered.*

70. Ibid.

71. *Fire Eyes: Female Circumcision* (Soraya Mire), New York: Filmakers Library, 1994; Isabelle Gunning, "Uneasy Alliances and Solid Sisterhood: A Response to Professor Obiora's Bridges and Barricades," *Case Western Reserve Law Review* 47, no. 2 (1997): 445–59.

72. *Rites* (Penny Dedman), New York: Filmakers Library, 1991; *In the Name of God: Changing Attitudes towards Mutilation* (Leyla Assas-Tengroth), New York: Filmakers Library, 1997.

4. Female Genital Surgeries: Eradication Measures at the Western Local Level—A Cautionary Tale

ISABELLE R. GUNNING

THIS ESSAY EXPLORES the development and impact of criminal laws, de-signed arguably to eradicate the practice of female genital surgeries, on the actual citizens and resident African women they are designed to help.[1] I, like the other authors in this book, oppose the various practices of female geni-tal surgeries (FGS) or female genital mutilation (FGM).[2] A careful, critical look at the political process by which American laws—for this essay, federal and California state bills—that now criminalize the surgeries, however, re-veals disdain and disrespect for African women and their cultures. The pro-cess, along with the language in these bills, raises questions about their ef-fectiveness in eradicating the surgeries.

Many themes can be gleaned from the essays in this volume, and two are closely related. The first is that African men and women (particularly wom-en) are the rightful leaders and primary theoreticians/strategists in the move-ment to eradicate the surgeries. Although no one in this book argues that non-Africans cannot be involved, a common theme is that African activists—especially those who are part of the cultures in which the surgeries are per-formed—are more likely to be familiar with the detailed, complicated, and complex cultural meanings and tensions that embed and surround the sur-geries. Those who are not part of such cultures must educate themselves about the historical and cultural contexts surrounding the surgeries. Close-ly related to the theme of encouraging Westerners to seek advice, informa-tion, and leadership on eradicating such practices from African women ac-tivists is the idea of the invisibility of these activists' historical and current eradication efforts and the need to reveal and acknowledge them. African

women from countries where the surgeries are performed are natural leaders because so many have been effective in battling against that tradition.[3]
Many continue to do so.[4] Rather than be "othered," ignored, or demonized
for their unheralded efforts, these activists need to be recognized, admired,
and emulated as role models.

Understanding these important themes in the abstract may still leave feminists who are not Africans to be concerned about what to do and still remain
part of the eradication movement. The issue is of particular concern when
the geographical focus is not on the performance of surgeries by people in
African countries but on the performance of the surgeries "at home" (i.e.,
in a Western country).

What Are These Laws, and Who Did
the Legislators Consult?

Both the federal and the California bills passed in 1996 are called female genital mutilation acts and criminalize the cutting of the female genitalia except
in certain circumstances, when authorized by a medical professional, for girls
below the age of eighteen.[5] The federal bill is more cleanly written than California's and criminalizes the actual and "knowing" performance of a "circumcision, excision, or infibulation." The California bill covers any person
who "causes" *and* "permits" a child to suffer the physical harm of female
genital mutilation. The federal bill is directed at circumcisers, whereas the
California bill would also reach parents. Both laws make the acts they cover
felonies (i.e., the prison-time exposure is greater than one year). Non-citizen
parents or circumcisers who are convicted likely would be subject to deportation. These convictions could be considered "aggravated felonies" under U.S.
immigration laws, which would trigger removal procedures for both permanent residents and refugees.[6] Both bills direct the appropriate federal or state
agency to carry out research on the numbers of circumcised girls and wom-
en in the United States and develop educational and outreach policies to target immigrant communities.

One would have thought that research might have been done and educational and outreach plans developed before the bills' passage. Typically, one
studies whether there is a problem, its extent, and the array of possible solutions before choosing to implement any particular solution. That was not the
case here, however.

I became involved with the anti-FGM bill in California soon after it and
the federal bill became law. Before this I conducted extensive research on FGS

and wrote an article critical of typical and popular Western approaches to FGS, the "arrogant perception" used to discuss and criticize the surgeries.[7] When a local African refugee community group asked me to become involved, I was working on FGS for a conference that was to focus on African women refugees. Upon learning of the new bills and reading my earlier work, the group's executive director asked for my help in efforts to change the law. As I researched the legislative history on the bills, I noticed a glaring absence of input from African women.

In California, hearings were, allegedly, held. I say "allegedly," because several legislative aides told me and my research assistant that the hearings had occurred, but we were unable to locate written or videotaped evidence of them. Who testified at these hearings is unclear. What was clear was that no African American organizations, neither women oriented nor general, were among the sponsoring organizations, and there was only one African organization, which although affiliated with a large international group was actually extremely small and new to the state. Although there are other African immigrant groups throughout the state, typically in cities such as Los Angeles and San Diego and in the Bay Area, none were informed or questioned. The executive director of the Los Angeles group with which I work, for example, was ignored. She is well known in parts of Sacramento and Washington, D.C., those circles dealing with refugee and African matters, yet none of her contacts and colleagues thought to inform or consult her as the California bill made its way through the legislative process. Several feminist and community organizations, largely white, were consulted or contacted for input and support.

At the federal level, there is no list of supporting organizations. The federal government had gathered experts and concerned activists in a conference rather than in a congressional hearing to provide information and various perspectives on the problem the bill was designed to address. The array of invitees to the Department of Health and Human Services "Workshop on Female Circumcision/Female Genital Mutilation," held in Rockville, Maryland, on October 3, 1996, were far more diverse than the California's list of supporters and included several African feminists, among them the executive director from Los Angeles. Unfortunately, the day the symposium was held was also the very day that the president signed the bill into law. Participants had little, if any, impact on the bill's creation and substance. Even well-meaning American feminists—black and white—did not apparently think it important to consult with African feminists in any serious fashion or even to inform the rightful and knowledgeable leaders of the struggle against FGM.

What Difference Would Consultation Have Made?

True consultation with African experts would certainly have led to more informed legislating, but perhaps the result would have been the same. We should do something. At the international level, FGS has become a symbol of harmful traditional practices against women. Typically, once a practice or situation becomes recognized as an international human rights violation or a problem of some kind, individual nations should take some action to enforce that global norm or determination. This global norm was developed at the instigation and with the participation of African activists and feminists at the international level.

Although it is undeniably important to do "something"—not merely because an international human rights norm is evolving, but, more important, the lives and health of women and girls demand action—the response to the international concern for FGS is criminal legislation rather than a public health-care and educational plan and program, as is the case in many African countries. That is an interesting reaction given the problems and moral valuations involved in coercing people to change and the complexities of what kind of a symbol such a law would provide. In the mid-1970s, when the American Academy of Pediatrics (AAP) determined that male circumcision had no health benefits whatsoever, one could have asked, Then why not pass a law outlawing the practice of male circumcision under threat of fines and imprisonment?[8] Perhaps that option was raised, but in light of deep-seated religious, aesthetic, and cultural norms that existed the approach was educational. Indeed, the educational approach had some effect. Male circumcision, of course, is still performed in the United States despite an unheralded opposition movement that claims male circumcision poses health risks, but the number of such procedures has dropped since the AAP encouraged members to discourage their members from performing the unnecessary surgery.[9] For FGS performed by foreigners in Western countries, however, the solution has been criminalization.

The difference in treatment between a practice that affects "us" (and men) and a practice affecting "others" (blacks and women) is perhaps not accidental or coincidental.[10] Process is important. Some cultures and groups are respected enough that their knowledge and views are solicited, heard, and considered; other cultures and groups are treated as more childlike and in less respectful ways.

What's in a Name?

I became involved with the anti-FGM bills after the bills had become law. The Los Angeles group with which I work had to decide how to respond to the new bills, especially the California law. A series of meetings were held with the organization's board of directors, which included a number of local African people, and the organization's women's focus group, which included current and former clients as well as other local African women activists who took great interest in the issue. A number of general meetings (small and large) involving local refugee and immigrant African communities in Los Angeles and San Diego were also held. Most but not all who attended the various meetings were women. Out of these meetings, consensus developed.

Not all the women opposed the surgeries; some invoked in all sincerity the usual rationales involving matters of health, sex, cleanliness, aesthetics, and religion.[11] Others were quite opposed to the surgeries, although the tenor of their opposition would be considered muted by Western standards. Sometimes the quietness of their opposition reflected general discomfort in speaking about such matters. Sometimes the quietness was a reflection of fear, of being criticized or ostracized by the remnants of the familiar African community that they have managed to piece together in their new, often hostile, home, America. At still other times, quietness indicated gentle concern about getting too far ahead of the people they lead, love, and connect with. They were willing to slow down and speak in understandable terms so friends, family, and constituents would hear them. However they approached the issue, the consensus was to support the law. Some did so because they opposed the surgeries, and although a legal approach would not have been their first choice they supported the symbol of opposition. Others who might otherwise have supported the surgeries were clear about being "good citizens." I use that term not in the legalistic sense of whether they were in fact naturalized but in its true, social sense. They wanted to be a part of their new home and doing so meant respecting its laws.

The women did have concerns, however. Foremost among these was the use of the term *female genital mutilation*. It was not an easy decision. There was loud, sometimes angry, debate among the board members—all of whom present were immigrant or refugee Africans—over the choice of language. Some women felt that FGM was the correct characterization of the procedures and the proper political symbol. Others felt that the term *mutilation* would offend many in the immigrant and refugee African communities and repel them from seeking education and health information. Ultimately, the group agreed. The term *female circumcision* would be more appropriate.

As a result of these meetings and consensus decision making, I drafted a new version of the California anti-FGM bill. Among other things, in our version the legislation's name was changed to the California Immigrant Women's Health Act and the word *circumcision* was substituted for most references to FGM. Other changes involved removing some of the more inflammatory language in the text of the bill suggesting that African people are egregious child abusers and moving the bill itself from the criminal legislation section dealing with child abuse to the general crimes section.[12] Once we had an agreed-upon substitute for the current bill, we started the process of lobbying for the change.

Legislators and insiders we knew might support us were swamped at the time by the issue of welfare "reform." Indeed, the Los Angeles organization was distracted from sustained lobbying efforts by constituents' and clients' immediate needs following passage of welfare reform and related immigration reforms.[13] In the final analysis, political comity dictated that the original author of the bill needed to make the first move to alter or amend it. Although the process was surprisingly long and arduous, we eventually received an audience with the Latina legislator who had written and sponsored the bill. She was personable and sympathetic but responded to our concerns by noting that she had relied upon international usage.

Her response was simple and straightforward enough and represented, at some level, a victory for international feminists who have struggled against the surgeries. Still, it masked the complex issues involved in the symbolic nature and value in law and language. An international human rights norm exists, but what's in a name? What should this "illegal" thing (or things) be called? Who is being addressed? At the international level, the term *female genital mutilation* has its virtues. At U.N.–related conferences and committees (e.g., the Fourth World Conference on Women in Beijing in 1995), the use of severe language, such as "torture," that invoked uncontested international human rights violations was an effective approach to moving the topic of surgeries from a private, cultural norm to a public political practice. To be recognized as a human rights violation is, symbolically, to take women's lives seriously and, as a practical matter, to attract resources from international organizations to local, grass-roots groups conducting health and educational efforts. It is not at all clear, however, whether using such an inflammatory term as *mutilation* would be effective in convincing those most in need of changing their ways. Insulting people's parents and elders and demeaning their entire cultures is more likely to breed resentment than responsiveness.

Naming must go on at multiple levels for different audiences. Harsh and blunt language at the international level reveals respect for the lives of women and girls by placing their pain and suffering on the same level, internationally, with acknowledged public harm. At the grass-roots, educational level, however, more muted tones carry respect for the cultural contexts and tensions in which particular women and girls struggle to survive.[14] Whatever the name and whatever the level, the ultimate goal, eradicating surgeries, remains the same.

We were unable to convey the full contours of our concern. The legislator, her aides, and the several department of women's health employees in attendance all agreed that more culturally sensitive language could be used in educational material. But that material was seen as separate from the law. They seemed surprised that regular people, especially those who "don't speak English anyway," would ask about the law or want to see it.

I teach the law and am accustomed to going from the actual text to helping students decipher what it means. I used the same pedagogical approach in discussing the anti-FGM law with the Los Angeles group's board and its members. It seemed to me that people were entitled to know the legislation's actual language. Then they could know something about the terms of the debate surrounding the issue. What images were evoked, for example, and which symbols enshrined? Moreover, even if one is not a law student, it is useful and empowering to know how to decipher and make sense of "the law."

The legislator noted, however, that many other bills have a formal name yet are called something else. Everyone except us agreed that people do not have to know the actual content or specific language of a law, nor do they have to be told everything as part of their educations. They should be told what they need to hear. These are the voices of supporters and allies who would probably consider themselves feminists and see themselves as supporting the rights of girls and women. Some have acted on those principles in positive ways. Yet the disrespect involved in that maternalistic (née paternalistic) attitude is not apparent to them.

The disrespect runs deep. Lack of concern for the attitudes and issues of the targeted group suggests that even supporters were not focused on whether the legislation would be an effective weapon for eradicating the surgeries. The beauty of focusing on domestic laws as opposed to international laws regarding FGS lies precisely in the fact that law, as a tool for change at the national or domestic level, is a reality. By and large, it is not about symbolism, as is the case at the international level. In examining the federal and California state anti-FGM bills, however, legislators and supporters seemed to focus on symbolism—what their support for the bill ostensibly means they stand for.

Elsewhere in this volume, Claire Robertson has analyzed a similar situation—the largely symbolic criminal show trial of an excisor in France (chapter 2).

Ironically enough, conservative legislators also used this symbolic support for a vague kind of racial and gender equality. The bills passed with ease. There was little debate, discussion, research, mark-up, or controversy. Sacramento, California, or Washington, D.C.—cities where the needs of elite white women can occasionally be met—are not places where women of color, immigrants, and poor people have been welcomed in recent years. The ease with which the bills passed meant that conservatives—otherwise busy trashing welfare, health care, and other issues of vital importance to women, immigrants, minorities, and working and poor people—had suddenly found concern for colored women.

The bills are of cynical and symbolic value. A vote for such a bill was a way for conservatives who had little interest in women or people of color, as shown by voting records, to claim concern for racial and gender issues. Moreover, the vote often provided an opportunity to make a comfortable speech, safely denouncing African culture and people. At the California and federal level that meant an opportunity to label Africans as the most egregious of child abusers. In addition, such a vote was and remains cost-free. It would not divert resources from their "real" constituents. Although both bills call for the creation of health and educational materials, no money has been allocated for such programs, either in California or at the federal level, by the end of the 1990s.

Do the Laws Work?

The true measure of concern for women of color involves using fewer symbols, speeches, and profiling and achieving more substance and results. Perhaps, in spite of my complaints and concerns about symbolism and cynicism, the laws are working to stop the surgeries in the United States. It is unclear. It has never been clear how prevalent the surgeries actually are in the United States. I have seen cited only one study of their incidence in California—and that study's methodology is questionable.[15]

Still, the laws' presence may well discourage people from having the surgeries performed in California. It is unclear whether the process of enactment and the language used in the statutes have the moral authority and suasive power to educate people against performing the surgeries at all. Perhaps that will come when the promised but unfunded educational programs develop. In the meantime, the California bill has created much anxiety and anger in the African immigrant and refugee communities. Micro aggressions appear to be on the rise. There are more and more stories of strangers stopping African women to ask whether they are mutilated and accounts of doctors who decide to perform genital examinations on girl children of African immigrants—even if the health problem they present is a sore throat. Pregnant circumcised women have been gawked at and humiliated in hospitals. Accounts of such incidents spread and contribute to a dangerous health situation: African women of all classes and levels of education are increasingly reluctant to seek medical attention, least of all gynecological.

For feminist and human rights activists who supported the bills out of a sincere desire to see a symbolic, effective measure against FGS taken in the United States, initial results are surely not what they intended. Had greater attention been paid to seeking leadership from African women activists, especially those from nations or groups where FGS is performed, some, although perhaps not all, of these difficulties could have been avoided. A knowledge of, and respect for, the history of FGS would have revealed a history of struggle against it. Attempts to impose colonial laws against the practice of FGS proved less effective than laws or programs developed by women intimately involved with the surgeries. Understanding that fact might have encouraged American feminists concerned with the issue to conduct research and consult African activists before deciding on a solution.

The American feminists might have been encouraged to view African women in more realistic and respectful ways had they understood and respected the complex cultural contexts within which the surgeries are embedded. Rather than focusing on criminal laws and rushing to punish someone, there might have been a focus on the context within which too many African immigrant and refugee women live—isolated and alienated in a new and strange country; in varying degrees of financial difficulty; and all too often, like so many American citizens and residents, in great need of adequate overall health care for themselves and their families. When American feminists learn to respect other women and the current and historical cultural complexities of those women, there can be a truly multicultural, feminist, unity. That will create laws or processes both respectful and effective in eradicating FGS and all practices harmful to women everywhere.

Notes

1. In this essay, I will employ an approach understood in legal academic circles as "critical race theory" or "critical race feminism." For a general idea of these two interrelated schools of legal thought, see *Critical Race Theory: The Key Writings That Formed the*

Movement, ed. Kimberlé Crenshaw et al. (New York: New Press, 1995), and *Critical Race Feminism: A Reader,* ed. Adrian Wing (New York: New York University Press, 1997).

2. These practices are also commonly called female genital mutilation, as the laws I will discuss name them. I have explained elsewhere, in part, my preference for the term *FGS* over either *FGM* or *female circumcision.* Isabelle R. Gunning, "Arrogant Perception, World-Traveling and Multicultural Feminism: The Case of Female Genital Surgeries," *Columbia Human Rights Law Review* 23, no. 2 (1992): 189, 193n15. Although I respect African activists who oppose the surgeries and use either the term *circumcision* (to underscore respect for the larger culture out of which the practice comes) or the term *mutilation* (to underscore the unnecessary and high degree of damage that is often done to the female body through the surgeries), I wanted a term that is "neutral." The term *surgeries* also is designed to convey two other points. First, not every ritualized cutting is the most extreme and most harmful form, as is often suggested in Western accounts of FGM. Types of cuttings vary, although all are unnecessary because they are performed on healthy human tissue. Second, the "cuttings" are analogous to any number of unnecessary cosmetic surgeries performed in Western cultures with little organized feminist opposition.

3. Claire C. Robertson, "Getting beyond the Ew! Factor: Rethinking U.S. Approaches to African Female Genital Cutting" (chapter 2 in this volume); see also Robertson, "Grassroots in Kenya: Women, Genital Mutilation and Collective Action, 1920–1990," *Signs: Journal of Women in Culture and Society* 21, no. 2 (1996): 615–42.

4. Stanlie M. James discusses Ntanira na Mugumbo (Circumcision through Words) in "Listening to Other(ed) Voices: Reflections around Female Genital Cutting" (chapter 3 of this volume).

5. Crimes and Criminal Procedure, 18 U.S.C. section 116 (Supp. 1999) of the Crimes and Criminal Procedure section of the U.S. code outlawing FGM, was amended by the Illegal Immigration Reform and Immigrant Responsibility Act of 1996 (IIRIRA), Public Law 104–208 (110 Stat. 3009). It notes that the effective date of the enactment was September 30, 1996.

The California Penal Code section 273.4a was added through the California Health and Safety Code, title 8, chapter 3, section 124170, which was passed through the bill numbered AB 2125. The governor of California approved the bill on September 22, 1996, and it was filed with the California secretary of state the next day.

The exception concerning medical authorization was designed to allow Western-trained doctors to continue to surgically manipulate the genitalia of intersexed individuals (i.e., people with ambiguous genitalia), whether or not the surgery is necessary for the child's physical health. The Intersex Society of North America, a group of intersexed people who oppose such surgeries on minors, lobbied unsuccessfully to have such procedures, their mutilation as they understand it, included in the bill. Cheryl Chase, "Hermaphrodites with Attitude: Mapping the Emergence of Intersex Political Activism," *GLQ: A Journal of Gay and Lesbian Studies* 4 (1998): 189.

6. Immigration and Nationality Act (INA), 8 U.S.C.A. section 1227. Under section 237(a)(2)(A)(iii), this act states, "Any alien who is convicted of an aggravated felony at any time after admission is deportable." Section 101(a)(43)(F) of the INA defines an aggravated felony as "a crime of violence . . . for which the term of imprisonment is at least

one year." It is not clear how the Immigration and Naturalization Service (INS) will interpret the law, but as a technical matter (and given the violent imagery generally used to describe the surgeries) the acts criminalized by these laws could easily be considered crimes of violence and thereby subject circumcisers and even parents to deportation, regardless of the length of time they had been in the United States or the citizenship status of their children.

Some African immigrants come as refugees or asylees. That means they are allowed to stay in the United States because they face persecution in their home countries. Immigration laws would allow circumcisers or parents, if convicted of the acts covered, to be returned to their dangerous homelands. Section 208 of the Immigration and Nationality Act (8 U.S.C.A. sec. 1158) gives the attorney general discretion to grant asylee status to aliens who have a well-founded fear of persecution; section 241(b)(3) of the Immigration and Nationality Act (8 U.S.C.A. sec. 1231) mandates that the attorney general not deport aliens to countries where their lives or freedom would be threatened, but an alien convicted of a serious crime may be denied the life-saving benefits of asylee or refugee status. In both sections, a "serious crime" is specifically to include what is termed an "aggravated felony" under the INA.

7. Gunning, "Arrogant Perception."

8. "Reconsidering Circumcision: North Dakota Woman Challenges Male Circumcision," Minneapolis *Star Tribune*, May 19, 1997, 7A. This article discusses health arguments against male circumcision that were raised in a constitutional challenge to a North Dakota statute banning female circumcision. It notes that the American Academy of Pediatrics supported its position by determining that there was no medical reason for these surgeries. In 1989, however, the academy adopted a position of neutrality, having acknowledged a study suggesting that male circumcision may prevent a few rare diseases.

9. See, for example, Tim Hammond, "Long-Term Consequences of Neonatal Circumcision," in *Sexual Mutilations: A Human Tragedy*, ed. George C. Denniston and Marilyn Fayre Milos (New York: Plenum Press, 1997), 125, and "Reconsidering Circumcision."

10. Although it is commonly believed that such surgeries were brought to the United States by immigrant "others," they are very much a part of U.S. history. In "African Women in the Diaspora and the Problem of Female Genital Mutilation," presented to the Women's Caucus of the African Studies Association in November 1994, Seble Dawit observed that surgeries or mutilations were performed in the United States on nonimmigrant Americans in the nineteenth century and into the twentieth. Moreover, physicians routinely continue to perform them on intersexed individuals.

11. For a collection of some of the work that documents the array of rationales used to support the surgeries, see Gunning, "Arrogant Perception," 195–96 (including the notes).

12. The shift in sections was designed to erase the symbol of African immigrant and refugee parents being labeled as child abusers. It also increased the amount of jail time that a convicted person would serve. The current bill exposes violators to up to one year in a county jail and up to six years in a state prison (Ca. Penal Code sec. 273.4). The proposed California Immigrant Women's Health Act (a draft of which is in my files) would have added the crime of female circumcision to the section of the California penal code outlawing "mayhem" (dismemberment or physical mutilation of various parts of the

body, for example, tongue, eyes, nose, ears, or lips) and would have imposed a maximum state-prison term of up to eight years.

13. By welfare and immigration "reform," I refer to three acts passed in 1996 that imposed significant changes on immigrants and poor citizens: the Antiterrorism and Effective Death Penalty Act of 1996 (AEDPA, Pub. L. 104–132, 110 Stat. 1214); the Illegal Immigration Reform and Immigrant Responsibility Act of 1996 (IIRIRA, Pub. L. 104–208, 110 Stat. 3009); and the Personal Responsibility and Work Opportunity Reconciliation Act (PRWOR, Pub. L. 104–193, 110 Stat. 2105). The AEDPA and IIRIRA "worked the most dramatic changes in immigration law and procedure in thirty years," streamlining and accelerating the removal of aliens and drastically limiting judicial review for even refugee claimants. Thomas Aleinikoff, David Martin, and Hiroshi Motomura, *Immigration and Citizenship: Process and Policy*, 4th ed. (St. Paul: West Group, 1998), 173–74. The IIRIRA also made a significant change in the concepts of exclusion and deportation and made it more difficult for aliens who surreptitiously enter the United States to invoke certain procedural mechanisms and forms of relief because of the length of their stay. The PRWOR, commonly understood to be "Welfare Reform," had an impact on poor citizens. It also "severely restricted the access of [lawful] permanent resident aliens to most means-tested benefits programs and affirmed the exclusion of undocumented migrants from such programs" (174).

14. The issue of whether a particular naming conveys respect or disdain is a contextual one. At the grass-roots level, more muted, respectful tones are more persuasive in explaining the illegality of the procedures among foreign newcomers to the United States who may want to have the surgeries performed on their daughters. The routine performance of such surgeries on indigenous intersexed Americans, however, may present a different context. For some, recognition that the surgeries performed on them were wrong is so far behind that of the "African" FGM that they feel they must introduce the term *intersexed genital mutilation* (IGM) to a skeptical world—especially the medical community—in order to be heard at any level. Chase, "Hermaphrodites with Attitude."

15. Even the California State Department of Health may be developing doubts about this study's accuracy. One women's rights activist reported that the department had refused to provide her with a copy.

5. "Cultural Practice" or "Reconstructive Surgery"? U.S. Genital Cutting, the Intersex Movement, and Medical Double Standards

CHERYL CHASE

ONE OF THE FORMS of power that maintains gender boundaries in the United States is the surgical "correction" of infants whose genitals are deemed by medical professionals to be socially unacceptable. Media and scholarly discourses on "female genital mutilation," however, have not engaged these surgeries, instead serving up only representations of African women. These discourses continue a long tradition of making Africans into the "other," suggesting that ethnocentrism is a key factor in the sometimes purposeful maintenance of ignorance about contemporary U.S. genital surgeries. This essay will describe how Americans participate in the production of normatively sexed bodies from those born intersexed, the consequences of such genital surgeries for those subjected to them, the efforts of intersex people to organize to eliminate pediatric genital surgeries and how those efforts have been treated by many feminists, and the double standard regarding representations of genital cutting, depending upon who is cutting and where in the world the cutting is done.

"New Law Bans Genital Cutting in United States" read the headline on the front page of the *New York Times*.[1] The law seems clear enough: "Whoever knowingly circumcises, excises, or infibulates the whole or any part of the labia majora or labia minora or clitoris of another person who has not attained the age of eighteen years shall be fined under this title or imprisoned not more than five years, or both."[2] Yet this law was not intended and has not been interpreted to protect the approximately five children per day in the United States who are subjected to excision of part or all of their clitoris and inner labia simply because doctors believe their clitoris is too big.[3]

Sexual anatomies, genitals in particular, come in many sizes and shapes.

U.S. doctors label children whose sexual anatomies differ significantly from the cultural ideal "intersexuals" or "hermaphrodites" (a misleading term because these children are born with intermediate genitals, not two sets). Medical practice today holds that possession of a large clitoris, or a small penis, or a penis that has the urethra placed other than at its tip is a "psychosocial emergency."[4] The child would not be accepted by the mother, would be teased by peers, and would not be able to develop into an emotionally healthy adult. The medical solution to this psychosocial problem is surgery—before the child reaches three months of age or even before the newborn is discharged from hospital. Although parental emotional distress and rejection of the child and peer harassment are cited as the primary justifications for cosmetic genital surgery, there has never been an investigation of non-surgical means—such as professional counseling or peer support—to address these issues.

The federal Law to Ban Female Genital Mutilation notwithstanding, girls born with large clitorises are today routinely "normalized" by excising parts of the clitoris and burying the remainder deep within the genital region.[5] And boys with small penises? Current medical practice holds that intersex children "can be raised successfully as members of either sex if the process begins before 2½ years."[6] Because surgeons cannot create a large penis from a small one, the policy is to remove testes and raise these children as girls. This is accomplished by "carv[ing] a large phallus down into a clitoris, creat[ing] a vagina using a piece of [the child's] colon," marveled a science writer who spoke only to physicians and parents, not to any of the intersex people subjected to this miracle technology.[7] Efforts to create or extend a penile urethra in boys whose urethra exits other than at the tip of the penis—a condition called hypospadias—frequently lead to multiple surgeries, each compounding the harm.[8] Heart-rending stories of physical and emotional carnage are related by victims of these surgeries in "Growing up in the Surgical Maelstrom" and, with black humor, in "Take Charge: A Guide to Home Catheterization."[9]

"Reconstructive" surgeries for intersex infant genitals first came into widespread practice in the 1950s. Because intersexuality was treated as shameful and physicians actively discouraged open discussion by their patients—indeed, recommended lying to parents and to adult intersex patients—until recently most victims of these interventions suffered alone in shame and silence.[10]

By 1993 the accomplishments of a progression of social justice movements—civil rights, feminism, gay and lesbian, bisexual and transgender—helped make it possible for intersex people to speak out. Initially, physicians scoffed at their assertions that intersexuality was not shameful and that medically unnecessary genital surgeries were mutilating and should be halted. One surgeon from Johns Hopkins, the institution primarily responsible for developing the current medical model, dismissed intersex patient-advocates as "zealots."[11] Others cited the technological imperative. Doctors "don't really have a choice" about whether or not to perform surgery insists George Szasz.[12]

By 1997 the intersex movement had gathered enough strength to visit Congress and ask that the Law to Ban Female Genital Mutilation be enforced to protect children not only against practices imported from other cultures but also against this uniquely American medicalized form of mutilation. Their work won coverage in the *New York Times* and on *Dateline NBC,* and by the following year the *Urology Times* was reporting a small but growing "new tidal wave of opinion" from physicians and sex researchers supporting the activists.[13] Sad to report, the struggle of intersex activists against American medicalized genital mutilation has yet to attract significant support or even notice from feminists and journalists who express outrage over African genital cutting.

Hermaphrodites: Medical Authority and Cultural Invisibility

Many people familiar with the ideas that gender is a phenomenon not adequately described by male/female dimorphism and that the interpretation of physical sex differences is culturally constructed remain surprised to learn how variable sexual anatomy is.[14] Although the male/female binary is constructed as natural and therefore presumably immutable, the phenomenon of intersexuality offers clear evidence that physical sex is not binary. Intersexuality therefore furnishes an opportunity to deploy "the natural" strategically as a means for disrupting heteronormative systems of sex/gender/sexuality. The concept of bodily sex, in popular usage, refers to multiple characteristics, including karyotype (organization of sex chromosomes); gonadal differentiation (e.g., ovarian or testicular); genital morphology; configuration of internal reproductive organs; and pubertal sex characteristics such as breasts and facial hair. These characteristics are assumed and expected to be concordant in each individual—either all-male or all-female.

Because medicine intervenes quickly in intersex births to change the infant's body, the phenomenon of intersexuality has been, until recently, largely unknown outside specialized medical practices. General public awareness of intersex bodies slowly vanished in modern Western European societies as medicine gradually appropriated to itself the authority to interpret—and eventually manage—the much older category of "hermaphroditism." Victorian medical taxonomy began to efface hermaphroditism as a legitimated status by settling on gonadal histology as the arbiter of "true sex."[15] The Victorian taxonomy (still in use by medical specialists) required both ovarian and testicular tissue types, microscopically confirmed, to be present in a "true hermaphrodite." Conveniently, given the limitations of Victorian surgery and anesthesia, such confirmation was impossible in a living patient. All other anomalies were reclassified as "pseudo-hermaphroditisms" masking a "true sex" determined by the gonads.[16]

With advances in anesthesia, surgery, embryology, and endocrinology, however, twentieth-century medicine moved from merely labeling intersexed bodies to the far more invasive practice of "fixing" them—altering their physical appearance to conform with a diagnosed true sex. The techniques and protocols for physically transforming intersexed bodies were developed primarily at Johns Hopkins University in Baltimore during the 1920s and 1930s under the guidance of urologist Hugh Hampton Young. "Only during the last few years," Young enthused in the preface to his pioneering textbook *Genital Abnormalities,* have we begun "to get somewhere near the explanation of the marvels of anatomic abnormality that may be portrayed by these amazing individuals. But the surgery of the hermaphrodite has remained a terra incognito." The "sad state of these unfortunates" prompted Young to devise "a great variety of surgical procedures" by which he attempted to normalize the their bodily appearances to the greatest extent possible.[17]

Quite a few of Young's patients resisted his efforts. Emma T., a "'snappy' young negro woman with a good figure" and a large clitoris, had married a man but found her passion only with women. Emma refused surgery to "be made into a man" because removal of her vagina would mean the loss of her "meal ticket" (i.e., her husband).[18] By the 1950s, the principle of rapid postnatal detection and intervention for intersex infants had been developed at Johns Hopkins, with the stated goal of completing surgery early enough so the child would have no memory of it.[19] One wonders whether the insistence on early intervention was not at least partly motivated by the resistance offered by adult intersex people to "normalization" through surgery. Frightened parents of ambiguously sexed infants were much more open to suggestions of normalizing surgery than were intersex adults, and the infants themselves could, of course, offer no resistance whatsoever.

Most of the theoretical foundations justifying these interventions are attributable to psychologist John Money, a sex researcher invited to Johns Hopkins by Lawson Wilkins, founder of pediatric endocrinology.[20] Wilkins's numerous students subsequently carried these protocols from Hopkins to hospitals throughout the United States and abroad.[21] In 1998 Suzanne Kessler noted that

Money's ideas enjoyed a "consensus of approval rarely encountered in science."[22] But the revelation in 2000 that Money had grossly misrepresented and mishandled the famous "John/Joan" case (in which an infant was castrated and raised as a girl after his penis was destroyed in a circumcision accident) sent Money's stock into a steep decline.[23]

In keeping with the Hopkins model, the birth of an intersex infant is today deemed a "psychosocial emergency" that propels a multi-disciplinary team of intersex specialists into action. Significantly, they are surgeons and endocrinologists rather than psychologists, bioethicists, intersex peer support organizations, or parents of intersex children. The team examines the infant and chooses either male or female as a "sex of assignment," then informs the parents that this is the child's *true* sex. Medical technology, including surgery and hormones, is then used to make the child's body conform as closely as possible to the assigned sex.

Current protocols for choosing a sex are based on phallus size: to qualify for male assignment the child must possess a penis at least one inch long; clitorises may not exceed three-eighths inch. Infants with genital appendages in the forbidden zone of three-eighths to one inch are assigned female and the phallus trimmed to an acceptable size. The only exception to this sorting rule is that even a hypothetical possibility of female fertility must be preserved by assigning the infant as female, disregarding masculine genitals and a phallus longer than one inch.[24]

The sort of deviation from sex norms exhibited by intersex people is so highly stigmatized that emotional harm due to likely parental rejection and community stigmatization of the intersex child provides physicians with their most compelling argument to justify medically unnecessary surgical interventions. Intersex status is considered to be so incompatible with emotional health that misrepresentation, concealment of facts, and outright lying (both to parents and later to the intersex person) are unabashedly advocated in professional medical literature.[25]

The Impact of "Reconstructive" Surgeries

The insistence on two clearly distinguished sexes has calamitous personal consequences for the many individuals who arrive in the world with sexual anatomy that fails to be easily distinguished as male or female, who are labeled "intersexuals" or "hermaphrodites" by modern medical discourse.[26] About one in one hundred births exhibits some anomaly in sex differentiation, and about one in two thousand is different enough to render problematic the question, Is it a boy or a girl?[27] Since the early 1960s, nearly every medium-sized or larger city in the United States has had at least one hospital with a standing team of medical experts who intervene in these cases to "assign"—through drastic surgical means—a male or female status to intersex infants. The fact that this system for enforcing the boundaries of the categories "male" and "female" existed for so long without drawing criticism or scrutiny from any quarter is an indication of the extreme discomfort that sexual ambiguity excites in our culture. Pediatric genital surgeries literalize what many might otherwise consider a purely theoretical operation—the attempted production of normatively sexed bodies and gendered subjects through constitutive acts of violence. Since the early 1990s, however, intersex people have begun to politicize intersex subjectivity, thus transforming intensely personal experiences of violation into collective opposition to the medical regulation of bodies that queers the foundations of heteronormative gender identifications and sexual orientations.

This system of hushing up the fact of intersex births and using technology to normalize intersex bodies has caused profound emotional and physical harm to intersex people and their families. The harm begins when the birth is treated as a medical crisis, and the consequences of that initial treatment ripple out ever afterward. The emotional impact of this treatment is so devastating that until the middle of the 1990s people whose lives have been touched by intersexuality maintained silence about their ordeal. As recently as 1993, no one publicly disputed surgeon Milton Edgerton when he wrote that in forty years of clitoral surgery on children *not one has complained of loss of sensation, even when the entire clitoris was removed*" (emphasis in the original).[28]

The tragic irony in all this is that while intersexual anatomy occasionally indicates an underlying medical problem such as adrenal disorder, ambiguous genitals are, in and of themselves, neither painful nor harmful to health. The often debilitating pediatric genital surgeries are entirely cosmetic in function. Surgery is essentially a destructive process. It can remove tissue and to a limited extent relocate it, but it cannot create new structures. This technical limitation, taken together with the framing of the feminine as a condition of lack, leads physicians to assign 90 percent of anatomically ambiguous infants as female by excising genital tissue. Surgeons justify female assignment because "you can make a hole, but you can't build a pole."[29] Heroic efforts shore up a tenuous masculine status for the one-tenth assigned male, who are subjected to multiple operations—twenty-two in one case—with the goal of straightening the penis and constructing a urethra to enable standing urinary posture.[30] For some, the surgeries end only when the child grows old enough to resist.[31]

Children assigned female are subjected to surgery that removes the troubling hypertrophic (i.e., large) clitoris. This is the same tissue that would have been a troubling micropenis (i.e., small penis) had the child been assigned male. Through the 1960s, feminizing pediatric genital surgery was openly labeled "clitoridectomy" and was compared favorably to the African practices that have now become the focus of such intense scrutiny. As three Harvard surgeons noted, "Evidence that the clitoris is not essential for normal coitus may be gained from certain sociological data. For instance, it is the custom of a number of African tribes to excise the clitoris and other parts of the external genitals. Yet normal sexual function is observed in these females."[32] Authors Robert E. Gross, Judson Randolph, and John F. Crigler apparently understand normal female sexual function only as passive penetration and fertility. A modified operation that removes most of the clitoris and relocates a bit of its tip is variously (and euphemistically) called clitoroplasty, clitoral reduction, or clitoral recession and described as a simple cosmetic procedure in order to differentiate it from the now-infamous clitoridectomy. The operation, however, is far from benign.

Johns Hopkins surgeons Joseph E. Oesterling, John P. Gearhart, and Robert D. Jeffs have described their technique.[33] They make an incision around the clitoris, at the corona, then dissect the skin away from its underside. Next they dissect the skin away from the upper side and remove as much of the clitoral shaft as necessary to create an "appropriate size clitoris." Then they place stitches from the pubic area along both sides of the entire length of what remains of the clitoris; when they tighten these stitches, the tissue folds, like pleats in a skirt, and recesses into a concealed position behind the pubic mound. If they think the result still "too large," they further reduce the tip of the clitoris by cutting away a pie-shaped wedge.

For many intersex people, this sort of arcane, dehumanized medical literature, illustrated with close-ups of genital surgery and naked children with blacked-out eyes, is the only available version of *Our Bodies, Ourselves*. Thus, even as fierce arguments over gender identity, gender role development, and social construction of gender rage in psychology, feminism, and queer theory, we have literally delegated to medicine the authority to police the boundaries of male and female, leaving intersex people to recover as best they can, alone and silent, from violent normalization.

My own case, as it turns out, was not unusual. I was born with ambiguous genitals. A doctor specializing in intersexuality deliberated for three days—and sedated my mother each time she asked what was wrong with her baby—before concluding that I was male, with micropenis, complete hypospadias, undescended testes, and a strange extra opening behind the urethra. A male birth certificate was completed for me, and my parents began raising me as a boy. When I was a year and a half old, my parents consulted a different set of intersex experts, who admitted me to a hospital for "sex determination." "Determine" is a remarkably apt word in this context, meaning both to *ascertain* by investigation and to *cause* to come to a resolution. It perfectly describes the two-level process whereby science produces through a series of masked operations what it claims merely to observe. Doctors told my parents that a thorough medical investigation, including exploratory surgery, would be necessary to determine (that is, ascertain) what my "true sex" was. They judged my genital appendage to be inadequate as a penis: too short to effectively mark masculine status or to penetrate females. As a female, however, I would be penetrable and potentially fertile. My anatomy having now been re-labeled as vagina, urethra, labia, and outsized clitoris, my sex was next determined (in the second sense) by amputating my genital appendage—clitoridectomy. Following doctors' orders, my parents then changed my name; combed their house to eliminate all traces of my existence as a boy (photographs, birthday cards, etc.); engaged a lawyer to change my birth certificate; moved to a different town; instructed extended family members to no longer refer to me as a boy; and never told anyone else—including me—just what had happened. My intersexuality and change of sex were the family's dirty little secrets.

At age eight, I was returned to the hospital for abdominal surgery that trimmed away the testicular portion of my gonads, each of which was partly ovarian and partly testicular in character. No explanation was given to me then for the long hospital stay or the abdominal surgery, nor for the regular hospital visits afterward in which doctors photographed my genitals and inserted fingers and instruments into my vagina and anus. These visits ceased as soon as I began to menstruate. At the time of the sex change, doctors had assured my parents that their once-son/now-daughter would grow into a woman who could have a normal sex life and babies. With the confirmation of menstruation, my parents apparently concluded that that prediction had borne out and their ordeal was behind them. For me, the worst part of the nightmare was just beginning.

As an adolescent, I became aware that I had no clitoris or inner labia and was unable to experience orgasm. By the end of my teens, I began to research in medical libraries, trying to discover what might have happened to me. When I finally determined to obtain my personal medical records, it took three years to overcome the obstruction of the doctors whom I asked for help.

When I did obtain a scant three pages from my medical files, I learned for the first time that I was a "true hermaphrodite" who had been my parents' son for a year and a half, with a name that was unfamiliar to me. The records also documented my clitoridectomy. This was the middle 1970s, when I was in my early twenties. I had come to identify myself as lesbian at a time when lesbianism and a biologically based gender essentialism were virtually synonymous. Men were rapists who caused war and environmental destruction; women were loving beings who would heal the earth; lesbians were a superior form of being uncontaminated by "men's energy." In such a world, how could I tell anyone that I had actually possessed the dreaded "phallus"? I was an impostor, not really a woman but rather a monstrous and mythical creature. And because my hermaphroditism and long-buried boyhood were the history that underlay the clitoridectomy, I could never speak openly about that either, or about my consequent inability to orgasm. I was so traumatized by discovering the circumstances that produced my embodiment that I could not speak of these matters with anyone.

Nearly fifteen years later, in my middle thirties, I suffered an emotional meltdown. In the eyes of the world I was a highly successful businesswoman, a principal in an international high-tech company. To myself, I was a freak, incapable of loving or being loved, filled with shame about my status as a hermaphrodite, about the imagined appearance of my genitals before surgery (I thought "true hermaphrodite" meant that I had been born with a penis), and about my sexual dysfunction. Unable to make peace with these facts about myself, I finally sought help from a professional therapist, only to find my experience denied. She reacted to each revelation about my history and predicament with some version of "no it's not" or "so what?" I'd say, "I'm not really a woman." She would say, "Of course you are. You look female." I'd say, "My complete withdrawal from sexuality has destroyed every relationship I've ever entered." She would say, "Everybody has their ups and downs." I tried another therapist and met with a similar response. Increasingly desperate, I confided my story to several friends who shrank away in embarrassed silence. I was in emotional agony and found myself utterly alone, with no possible way out. I decided to kill myself.

Confronting suicide as a real possibility proved to be my personal epiphany. In contemplating my own death, I fantasized killing myself quite messily and dramatically in the office of the surgeon who had sliced out my clitoris, forcibly confronting him with the horror he had imposed on my life. But in acknowledging that desire to put my pain to some use, not to waste my life completely, I turned a crucial corner, finding a way to direct my rage productively out into the world rather than aim it destructively at myself. My breakdown became my breakthough, and I vowed that, whatever it took, I would heal myself. Still, I had no conceptual framework for developing a more positive self-consciousness. I knew only that I felt mutilated, not fully woman, less than fully human even, but I was determined to heal. I struggled for weeks in emotional chaos, unable to eat or sleep or work. I could not accept my image of a hermaphroditic body any more than I could accept the butchered one left me by the surgeons. Thoughts of myself as a Frankenstein patchwork alternated with longings for escape by death, only to be followed by outrage, anger, and determination to survive. I could not accept that it was just or right or good to treat any person as I had been treated—my sex changed, my genitals cut up, my experience silenced and rendered invisible. I bore a private hell within me, wretchedly alone in my condition without even my tormentors for company. Finally, I began to envision myself standing in a driving rain storm but with clear skies and a rainbow visible in the distance. I was still in agony, still alone, but I was beginning to see the painful process in which I was caught up in terms of revitalization and rebirth, a means of investing my life with a new sense of authenticity possessing vast potentials for further transformation. Since then I have seen this experience described by other intersex and transsexual activists.[34]

I slowly developed a newly politicized and critically aware form of self-understanding. I had been the kind of lesbian who at times had a girlfriend but who had never really participated in the life of a lesbian community. I felt almost completely isolated from gay politics, feminism, and queer and gender theory. I did possess the rudimentary knowledge that the gay civil rights movement had gathered momentum only when it could effectively deny that homosexuality was sick or inferior and assert to the contrary that "gay is good." As impossible as it then seemed, I pledged similarly to affirm that "intersex is good" and that the body I was born with was not sick or shameful, only different. I vowed to embrace the sense of being "not a woman" that I had initially been so terrified to discover.

I began a search for community that brought me to San Francisco in the fall of 1992 on the theory that people living in the "queer Mecca" would have the most conceptually sophisticated, socially tolerant, and politically astute analysis of sexed and gendered embodiment. I found what I was looking for, in part because my arrival in the Bay Area corresponded with the rather sudden emergence of an energetic transgender political movement. At the same time, a vigorous new wave of gender scholarship had emerged in the academy. In this context, Morgan Holmes could analyze her own clitoridectomy for her master's thesis and have her study taken seriously as academic work.[35] Openly transsexual scholars, including Susan

Stryker and Sandy Stone, were visible in responsible academic positions at major universities.[36]

Into this heady atmosphere, I brought my own experience. I started telling my story to everyone I met. Before long I learned of six other intersex people—including two who had been fortunate enough to escape medical attention. Realizing that intersexuality, rather than being extremely rare, must be relatively common, I decided to create a support network. Soon I was receiving several letters per week from intersex people throughout the United States and Canada and a few from further afield. Although details varied, the letters gave a remarkably coherent picture of the emotional consequences of medical intervention:

> All the things my body might have grown to do, all the possibilities, went down the hall with my amputated clitoris to the pathology department. The rest of me went to the recovery room—I'm still recovering.
> —Morgan Holmes

> I am horrified by what has been done to me and by the conspiracy of silence and lies. I am filled with grief and rage, but also relief finally to believe that maybe I am not the only one.
> —Angela Moreno

> As soon as I saw the title *Hermaphrodites with Attitude* I cried aloud for sheer joy. . . . Finally I can say, 'I'm hermaphrodite, I'm intersex, I'm transgender, I'm queer and damn proud,' as tears of joy and belonging stream down my face.
> —Lee

> Doctors never consulted me. . . . [T]he idea of asking for my opinion about having my penis surgically altered apparently never occurred to them. . . . Far too many people allow social stigma to cloud their judgment. It's OK to be different.
> —Randy

> I pray that I will have the means to repay, in some measure, the American Urological Association for all that it has done for my benefit. I am having some trouble, though, in connecting the timing mechanism to the fuse.
> —Thomas

Toward Social Justice

The peer support network that I formed grew into the Intersex Society of North America (ISNA). ISNA's long-term and fundamental goal is to change the way intersex infants are treated. We advocate that surgery not be performed on children born with ambiguous genitals unless there is a medical reason (to prevent physical pain or illness) and that parents be given the conceptual tools and emotional support to accept their children's physical differences. We also advocate that children be raised either as boys or girls, according to which designation seems likely to offer the child the greatest future sense of comfort. Advocating gender assignment without resorting to normalizing surgery is a radical position given that it requires the willful disruption of the assumed concordance between body shape and gender category. However, this is the only position that prevents irreversible physical damage to the intersex person's body, that preserves the intersex person's agency regarding their own flesh, and that recognizes genital sensation and erotic functioning to be at least as important as reproductive capacity. If an intersex child or adult decides to change gender or to undergo surgical or hormonal alteration of his/her body, that decision should also be fully respected and facilitated. The key point is that intersex subjects should not be violated for the comfort and convenience of others.

One part of reaching ISNA's long-term goal has been to document the emotional and physical carnage resulting from medical interventions. As a rapidly growing literature (see the bibliography on our Web-site, <http://www.isna.org>) makes abundantly clear, the medical management of intersexuality has changed shockingly little in the more than forty years since my first surgery—doctors still cut up children's genitals and still perpetuate invisibility and silence around intersex lives. Kessler expresses surprise that "in spite of the thousands of genital operations performed every year, there are no meta-analyses from within the medical community on levels of success."[37] Surgeons admit to not knowing whether their former patients are "silent and happy or silent and unhappy."[38] There is no research effort to improve erotic functioning for adult intersex people whose genitals have been cut, nor are there psychotherapists who specialize in working with adult intersex clients trying to heal from the trauma of medical intervention. To provide a counterpoint to the mountains of professional medical literature that neglect intersex experience and to begin compiling an ethnographic account of that experience, ISNA has worked to make public the lives of intersex people through our own publications (including our video, *Hermaphrodites Speak!*) and by working with scholars and the popular media.[39]

ISNA's presence has begun to be effective. It has helped politicize the growing number of intersex organizations as well as intersex identities themselves. When I first began organizing ISNA, I met leaders of the Turner's Syndrome Society, the oldest known support group focusing on atypical sexual differentiation founded in 1987. (Turner's Syndrome is defined by an XO genetic karyotype that results in a female body morphology with nonfunctioning ovaries, extremely short stature, and, variably, a variety of other visible physical differences still described in the medical literature with such stigmatizing labels as "web-necked" and "fish-mouthed.") Each of these women told me what a profound, life-changing experience it had been simply to meet another person like herself. I was inspired by their accomplishments (they are a national organization serving thousands of members) but wanted ISNA to have a different focus—less willing to think of intersexuality as a pathology or disability, more interested in challenging the medicalization of sexual difference entirely, and more interested in politicizing a pan-intersexual revolt across the divisions of particular etiologies in order to destabilize the heteronormative assumptions that underlie the violence directed at our bodies.

Public Discourse on Pediatric Genital Surgeries

Because the politicized intersex community is still quite young, and most intersex people remain too burdened by the crippling emotional consequences of what has been done to them to come out publicly, ISNA has deliberately cultivated a network of non-intersexed advocates who command a measure of social legitimacy and can speak in contexts where uninterpreted intersex voices will not be heard. Because there is a strong impulse to discount what intersex people have to say about themselves (as if we are too close to the issues to offer objective opinions), this sort of sympathetic representation has been welcome—especially in helping intersex people reframe intersexuality in nonmedical terms.[40] Some gender theory scholars, feminist critics of science, medical historians, and anthropologists have been quick to understand and support intersex activism. Feminist biologist and science studies scholar Anne Fausto-Sterling—who wrote, years before ISNA came into existence, about intersexuality in relation to intellectually suspect scientific practices that perpetuate masculinist constructs of gender—became an early ISNA ally.[41] Likewise, social psychologist Suzanne Kessler wrote a brilliant ethnography of surgeons who specialize in treating intersex. After speaking with a number of the normalized "products" of these medical programs, she, too, became a strong supporter of intersex activism.[42] Historian of science Alice Dreger, whose work focuses not only on hermaphroditism but also on other forms of atypical embodiment that become subject to destructively normalizing medical interventions (as in her discussion of conjoined twins in "Limits of Individuality"), has been especially supportive.[43] Fausto-Sterling, Kessler, and Dreger have each written books that analyze the medical treatment of intersexuality as being culturally motivated and criticize it as often harmful to its ostensible patients.[44]

Allies who help contest the medicalization of intersexuality have been especially important, because ISNA initially found direct, nonconfrontational interactions with medical specialists who determine policy on the treatment of intersex infants and actually carry out the surgeries to be both difficult and ineffective. Joycelyn Elders, the Clinton administration's first surgeon general, is a pediatric endocrinologist with many years of experience in managing intersex infants. In spite of a generally feminist approach to health care and frequent overtures from ISNA, she rejected the concerns of intersex people themselves.[45]

Surgeon Richard Schlussel, at a pediatric plastic surgery symposium (which had rejected ISNA's offer to provide a patients' panel) at Mount Sinai Medical Center in New York City in 1996 proclaimed, "The parents of children with ambiguous genitals are more grateful to the surgeon than any—more grateful even than parents whose children's lives have been saved through open heart surgery."[46]

Another pediatrician remarked in an Internet discussion on intersexuality, "I think this whole issue is preposterous. . . . To suggest that [medical decisions about the treatment of intersex] are somehow cruel or arbitrary is insulting, ignorant and misguided. . . . To spread the claims that [ISNA] is making is just plain wrong, and I hope that this [on-line group of doctors] will not blindly accept them." Yet another physician participating in that same chat, in a marvelous example of the degree to which practitioners of science can be blind to their complicity in constructing the objects they study, asked what was for him obviously a rhetorical question: "Who is the enemy? I really don't think it's the medical establishment. Since when did we establish the male/female hegemony?" Johns Hopkins surgeon Gearhart, quoted in a *New York Times* article on ISNA, summarily dismissed us as "zealots," but professional meetings in the fields of pediatrics, urology, genital plastic surgery, and endocrinology are abuzz with anxious and defensive discussions of intersex activism.[47] In response to a 1996 protest by Hermaphrodites with Attitude at the American Academy of Pediatrics annual meeting, that organization felt compelled to hold a press conference and issue a statement: "The Academy is deeply concerned about the emotional, cognitive, and body image development of intersexuals, and believes that successful early genital surgery minimizes these issues." The academy refused, however, to speak with intersex people picketing its meeting.

The roots of resistance in the medical establishment to the truth-claims of intersex people run deep. Not only does ISNA's existence imply a critique of the normativistic biases couched within most scientific practice but it also advocates a treatment protocol for intersex infants that disrupts conventional understandings of the relationship between bodies and genders. On a level more personally threatening to medical practitioners, ISNA's position implies that they have—unwittingly at best and through willful denial at worst—spent their careers inflicting a profound harm from which their patients will never fully recover. ISNA's position threatens to destroy the foundational assumptions motivating an entire medical subspecialty, thus jeopardizing their continued ability to perform what surgeons find to be technically fascinating work. Science writer Melissa Hendricks notes that Gearhart is known to colleagues as an "artist" who can "carve a large phallus down into a clitoris" with consummate skill.[48] Given these deep and mutually reinforcing reasons for opposing ISNA's position, it is hardly surprising that medical intersex specialists have, for the most part, turned at deaf ear toward us.[49]

Thus, the most important aspect of our current activities is the struggle to change public perceptions. By using the mass media, the Internet, and our growing network of allies and sympathizers to make the general public aware of the frequency of intersexuality and of the intense suffering that medical treatment has caused, we seek to create an environment in which many parents will have already heard about the intersex movement when their intersex child is born. Such informed parents have proved better able to resist medical pressure for unnecessary genital surgery and secrecy and to find their way to a peer-support group and counseling rather than to a surgical theater.

The Double Standard: First-World Feminism, African Clitoridectomy and Intersex Genital Mutilation, and the Media

African practices that remove the clitoris and other parts of female genitals have lately been a target of intense media coverage and feminist activism in the United States and other industrialized Western societies, and the euphemism *female circumcision* has been largely supplanted by the politicized term *female genital mutilation* (FGM). Analogous medical (rather than folk) operations performed on intersex people in the United States have not been the focus of similar attention—indeed, attempts to link the two forms of genital cutting have met with multiform resistance. Examining the way that first-world feminists and mainstream media treat African practices and comparing that treatment with their response to intersex genital mutilation (IGM) in North America exposes some of the complex interactions between ideologies of race, gender, colonialism, and science that effectively silence and render invisible intersex experience in first-world contexts. Cutting intersex genitals becomes yet another hidden mechanism for imposing normalcy upon unruly flesh, a means of containing the potential anarchy of desires and identifications within oppressive heteronormative structures.

In 1994 the *New England Journal of Medicine* paired an article on the physical harm resulting from African genital cutting with an editorial denouncing clitoridectomy as a violation of human rights but declined to run a reply drafted by University of California at Berkeley medical anthropologist Lawrence Cohen and two ISNA members detailing the harm caused by medicalized American clitoridectomies.[50] In response to growing media attention, Congress passed the Federal Prohibition of Female Genital Mutilation Act in October 1996.[51] That act specifically exempted from prohibition medicalized clitoridectomies of the sort performed to "correct" intersex bodies. The bill's principal author, feminist Congresswoman Pat Schroeder, ignored multiple letters from ISNA members and Brown University professor of medical science Anne Fausto-Sterling asking her to recast the bill's language. "New Law Bans Genital Cutting," the *New York Times* proclaimed and refused to address documentation from ISNA and Michigan State University professor Alice Dreger pointing out that genital cutting continues to be standard medical practice in the United States.[52]

The *Boston Globe*'s syndicated columnist Ellen Goodman has been one of the few journalists covering African genital cutting to make any response to ISNA overtures. "I must admit I was not aware of this situation," she wrote to me in 1994. "I admire your courage." She continued, however, to discuss African genital cutting in her column without mentioning similar American practices. Ironically, Goodman is based in Boston, a Mecca of sorts after Johns Hopkins for the surgical management of intersex children, with prominent specialists operating at Harvard, Massachusetts General Hospital, and Boston Children's Hospital. An October 1995 Goodman column on genital cutting was promisingly entitled "We Don't Want to Believe It Happens Here" but discussed only practices imported to the United States by immigrants from third-world countries.

While anti-excision African immigrant women within the United States have been receptive to the claims made by intersex opponents to medicalized clitoridectomies, first-world feminists and organizations working on African genital cutting have totally ignored us. Only two of the many anti-genital-cutting activist groups contacted have bothered to respond to repeated overtures from intersex activists. Fran Hosken, who since 1982 has regularly published a catalog of statistics on female genital cutting worldwide, wrote me a terse note saying that "we are not concerned with biological exceptions."[53]

Forward International, a London-based, anti–female-genital-cutting organization, replied to German intersex activist Heike Spreitzer that her letter of inquiry was "most interesting" but they could not help because their work focuses only on genital cutting "that is performed as a harmful cultural or traditional practice on young girls."

As Forward International's reply to Spreitzer demonstrates, many first-world, anti-FGM activists seemingly consider Africans to have "harmful cultural or traditional practices," whereas we in the modern industrialized West presumably have something better. We have science, and science is linked to the meta-narratives of enlightenment, progress, and truth. Genital cutting is condoned to the extent that it supports these cultural self-conceptions.

Robin Morgan and Gloria Steinem set the tone for much of the first-world feminist analysis of African genital cutting with their pathbreaking article in the March 1980 issue of *Ms.* magazine, "The International Crime of Genital Mutilation." A disclaimer atop the first page warns, "These words are painful to read. They describe facts of life as far away as our most fearful imagination—and as close as any denial of women's sexual freedom."[54] For *Ms.* readers, whom the editors apparently imagine are more likely to experience the pain of genital mutilation between the covers of their magazine than between their own thighs, clitoridectomy is presented as a fact of foreign life whose principal relevance to their readership is that it exemplifies a loss of "freedom," that most cherished possession of liberal Western subjects. One-half of the article's first page is filled with a photograph of an African girl seated on the ground, her legs held open by the arm of an unseen woman to her right. To her left is the disembodied hand of the midwife, holding the razor blade with which she has just performed a ritual clitoridectomy. The girl's face is a mask of pain, her mouth open, her eyes bulging.

In some twenty years of coverage, Western images of African practices have changed little although they have found their way into more mainstream publications. "Americans made a horrifying discovery this year," the January 1997 issue of *Life* soberly informed readers.[55] The two-page photo spread shows a Kenyan girl held from behind, a hand clamped over her mouth, her face contorted in pain as unseen hands cut her genitals. Interestingly, the girl in this photo is adolescent, her breasts are shown, covered with rivulets of sweat, and there is a definite air of sensuality in the presentation. The 1996 Pulitzer prize for feature photography went to yet another portrayal of a Kenyan clitoridectomy.[56] And, in the wake of Fauziya Kassindja's successful bid for asylum in the United States after fleeing clitoridectomy in Togo, the number of related images from her country skyrocketed. One wonders if Western photojournalists in search of sensational clitoridectomy photos do not represent a veritable tourism boom for a country the size of West Virginia.

These representations manifest a profound act of "othering" African clitoridectomy that contributes to the silence surrounding similar medicalized practices in the "modern," industrialized West. "Their" genital cutting is barbaric ritual; "ours" is scientific. Theirs disfigures; ours normalizes the deviant. The colonialist implications of these representations of genital cutting are even more glaringly obvious when contemporaneous images of intersex surgeries are juxtaposed with images of African practices. Medical books describing how to perform clitoral surgery on intersex children are almost always illustrated with extreme genital close-ups, disconnecting the genitals not only from the individual intersexed person but also from the body itself. Full body shots always have the subject's eyes blacked out. Why is it considered necessary—or at least polite—to black out the eyes of American girls but not the eyes of the African girls used to illustrate Steinem's "International Crime" or *Life*'s more recent "Ritual Agony"? I suspect one reason is that a Western reader is likely to identify with an American but not an African girl. Blacking out the American girl's eyes allows the reader to remain safely on this side of the camera.

First-world feminist discourse locates clitoridectomy not only elsewhere in Africa but also "elsewhen." An *Atlantic Monthly* article on African clitoridectomy, for example, asserted that the "American medical profession stopped performing clitoridectomies decades ago," and the magazine declined to publish a letter from ISNA contradicting that claim.[57] Academic publications are as prone to this attitude as the popular press. Feminist Martha Nussbaum, in a discussion of judging other cultures, acknowledges, "If two abuses are morally the same and we have better local information about one and are better placed politically to do something about it, that one seems to be a sensible choice to focus on in our actions here and now." But then she counter-factually locates U.S. genital surgeries solely in the past: "As recently as the 1940s, [genital surgeries] were performed by U.S. and British doctors to treat female 'problems' such as masturbation and lesbianism."[58] By collaborating in the silence about intersex genital surgeries, Nussbaum excuses first-world feminists from any obligation to challenge their own cultural practices as rigorously as they do that of others.[59]

In the influential *Deviant Bodies* anthology, visual artist Susan Jahoda's "Theatres of Madness" juxtaposes nineteenth- and twentieth-century material depicting "the conceptual interdependence of sexuality, reproduction, family life, and 'female disorders.'" To represent twentieth-century medical clitoridectomy practices, Jahoda quotes a 1980 letter to the editor of *Ms.* magazine prompted by the Steinem and Morgan article. The writer, a nurse's aid in a geriatric home, says she had been puzzled by the strange scars she saw on the genitals of five of the forty women in her care: "Then I read your article. . . . My God! Why? Who decided to deny them orgasm? Who made them go through such a procedure? I want to know. Was it fashionable? Or was it to correct 'a condition?' I'd like to know what this so-called civilized country used as its criteria for such a procedure. And how widespread is it here in the United States?"[60]

While Jahoda's selection of this letter does raise the issue of medicalized American clitoridectomies, it again safely locates the cutting in the past, as something experienced a long time ago by women now in their later stages of life. Significantly, Jahoda literally passes over an excellent opportunity to comment on the continuing practice of clitoridectomy in the contemporary United States. Two months earlier, in the April 1980 issue of *Ms.*, noted feminist biologists Patricia Farnes (a medical doctor) and Ruth Hubbard also replied to Morgan and Steinem:

> We want to draw the attention of your readers to the practice of clitoridectomy not only in the Third World . . . but right here in the United States, where it is used as part of a procedure to "repair" by "plastic surgery" so-called genital ambiguities. Few people realize that this procedure has routinely involved removal of the entire clitoris and its nerve supply—in other words, total clitoridectomy. . . . In a lengthy article, [Johns Hopkins intersex expert John] Money and two colleagues write, "There has been no evidence of a deleterious effect of clitoridectomy. None of the women experienced in genital practices reported a loss of orgasm after clitoridectomy." The article also advises that "a three-year old girl about to be clitoridectomized . . . should be well informed that the doctors *will make her look like all other girls and women*" (our emphasis), which is not unlike what North African girls are often told about their clitoridectomies. . . . But to date, neither Money nor his critics have investigated the effect of clitoridectomies on the girls' development. Yet one would surely expect this to affect their psychosexual development and their feelings of identity as young women.[61]

Although Farnes and Hubbard's prescient feminist exposé of medicalized clitoridectomies in the contemporary United States sank without a trace, there has been a veritable explosion of work like Nussbaum's and Jahoda's that keeps "domestic" clitoridectomy at a safe distance. Such conceptualizations of clitoridectomy's cultural remoteness—both geographically and temporally—allow feminist outrage to be diverted into potentially colonialist meddling in the social affairs of others while hampering work for social justice at home.[62]

Conclusion

Feminism represents itself as being interested in unmasking the silence that surrounds violence against women and in providing tools to understand the personal as political. Most medical intersex management is a form of violence based on a sexist devaluing of female pain and female sexuality: Doctors consider the prospect of growing up male with a small penis to be a worse alternative than living as a female without a clitoris, ovaries, or sexual gratification. Medical intervention literally transforms transgressive bodies into ones that can safely be labeled female and subjected to the many forms of social control with which women must contend. Why then have most feminists failed to engage the issue of medical abuse of intersex people?

I suggest that intersex people have had such difficulty generating mainstream feminist support not only because of the racist and colonialist frameworks that situate clitoridectomy as a practice foreign to proper subjects within the first world but also because intersexuality undermines the stability of the category "woman" that undergirds much first-world feminist discourse. We call into question the assumed relation between genders and bodies and demonstrate how some bodies do not fit easily into male/female dichotomies. We embody viscerally the truth of Judith Butler's dictum that "sex," the concept that accomplishes the materialization and naturalization of culturally constructed gender differences, has really been "gender all along."[63] By refusing to remain silenced, we queer the foundations upon which depend not only the medical management of bodies but also widely shared feminist assumptions of properly embodied female subjectivity.

In 1990 Suzanne Kessler noted, "[T]he possibilities for real societal transformations would be unlimited [if physicians and scientists specializing in the management of gender could recognize that] finally, and always, people construct gender as well as the social systems that are grounded in gender-based concepts. . . . Accepting genital ambiguity as a natural option would require that physicians also acknowledge that genital ambiguity is 'corrected' not because it is threatening to the infant's life but because it is threatening to the infant's culture."[64]

To the extent that we are not normatively female or normatively women, we are not the proper subjects of feminist concern. Western feminism has represented African genital cutting as primitive, irrational, harmful, and

deserving of condemnation. The Western medical community has represented its genital cutting as modern, scientific, healing, and above reproach. When
will Western feminists realize that their failure to examine either of these
claims "others" African women and allows the violent medical oppression
of intersex people to continue unimpeded?

Notes

My appreciation goes to Susan Stryker for her extensive contribution to the development
of this essay. An earlier version appeared as "Hermaphrodites with Attitude: Mapping the
Emergence of Intersex Political Activism," *GLQ: A Journal of Gay and Lesbian Studies* 4, no.
2 (1998): 189–211. © 1998. All rights reserved. Used by permission of Duke University Press.

1. Celia Dugger, "New Law Bans Genital Cutting in the United States," *New York Times*,
Oct. 12, 1996, 1.

2. Department of Defense Appropriations Act, Public Law 104–208, Sept. 30, 1996.

3. Alice Domurat Dreger, "'Ambiguous Sex'—or Ambivalent Medicine? Ethical Issues
in the Medical Treatment of Intersexuality," *Hastings Center Report* 28, no. 3 (1998): 24–
35, available from <http://www.isna.org/articles/dregerart.html>.

4. American Academy of Pediatrics Section on Endocrinology and Section on Urology Committee on Genetics, "Evaluation of the Newborn with Developmental Anomalies
of the External Genitalia," *Pediatrics* 106, no. 1 (2000): 138–42, available from <http://
www.aap.org/policy/re9958.html>; Cynthia H. Meyers-Seifer and Nancy J. Charest, "Diagnosis and Management of Patients with Ambiguous Genitalia," *Seminars in Perinatology* 6, no. 5 (1992): 332–39; American Academy of Pediatrics Section on Urology, "Timing
of Elective Surgery on the Genitalia of Male Children with Particular Reference to the Risks,
Benefits, and Psychological Effects of Surgery and Anesthesia," *Pediatrics* 97, no. 4 (1996):
590, available from <http://www.aap.org/policy/01306.html>; Leslie A. Parker, "Ambiguous Genitalia: Etiology, Treatment, and Nursing Implications," *Journal of Obstetric,
Gynecologic,and Neonatal Nursing* 27, no. 1 (1998): 15–22.

5. Joseph E. Oesterling, John P. Gearhart, and Robert D. Jeffs, "A Unified Approach to
Early Reconstructive Surgery of the Child with Ambiguous Genitalia," *Journal of Urology* 138, no. 4, pt. 2 (1987): 1079–84. The following video trains surgeons in the procedure:
Richard Hurwitz, H. Applebaum, and S. Muenchow, *Surgical Reconstruction of Ambiguous Genitalia in Female Children*, Ciné-Med Inc., 1990 (the video can be ordered from
Ciné-Med at MACROBUTTON HtmlResAnchor <http://www.cine-med.com> as video number ACS-1613).

6. American Academy of Pediatrics Section on Urology, "Timing of Elective Surgery," 590.

7. Melissa Hendricks, "Is it a Boy or a Girl?" *Johns Hopkins Magazine* 45, no. 5 (1993): 10.

8. John F. Stecker, Charles E. Horton, Charles J. Devine, and John B. McCraw, "Hypospadias Cripples," *Urologic Clinics of North America: Symposium on Hypospadias* 8, no. 3
(1981): 539–44.

9. Howard Devore, "Growing up in the Surgical Maelstrom," and Sven Nicholson,
"Take Charge: A Guide to Home Catheterization," both in *Intersex in the Age of Ethics*,
ed. Alice Domurat Dreger (Hagerstown: University Publishing Group, 1999), 78–81.

10. Anita Natarajan, "Medical Ethics and Truth Telling in the Case of Androgen Insensitivity Syndrome," *Canadian Medical Association Journal* 154, no. 4 (1996): 568–70, available from <http://www.cma.ca/cmaj/vol-154/0568e.htm>; Dreger, ed., *Intersex in the Age of Ethics.*

11. Natalie Angier, "Intersexual Healing: An Anomaly Finds a Group," *New York Times,* Feb. 4, 1996, E14.

12. Ian Mulgrew, "Controversy over Intersex Treatment," *Vancouver Sun,* April 7, 1997, 1; Edna Durbach and George Szasz, "Spare the Knife, Spoil the Child," *Globe and Mail,* Feb. 27, 1996, 76.

13. Natalie Angier, "New Debate over Surgery on Genitals," *New York Times,* May 13, 1997, B7; "Gender Limbo," *Dateline NBC,* June 17, 1997; Anne Scheck, "Intersexuality Takes a Conservative Turn," *Urology Times* 26, no. 1 (1998): 1, 32–33.

14. Judith Butler, *Gender Trouble: Feminism and the Subversion of Identity* (New York: Routledge, 1990); Thomas Laqueur, *Making Sex: Body and Gender from the Greeks to Freud* (Cambridge: Harvard University Press, 1990).

15. "Histology" refers to the structure of the tissue of the sex glands when a sample is surgically removed, stained, and observed under a microscope.

16. Alice Domurat Dreger, *Hermaphrodites and the Medical Invention of Sex* (Cambridge: Harvard University Press, 1998).

17. Hugh Hampton Young, *Genital Abnormalities, Hermaphroditism, and Related Adrenal Diseases* (Baltimore: Williams and Wilkins, 1937), xxxix–xl.

18. Young, "Genital Abnormalities," 139–42.

19. Howard W. Jones, Jr., and William Wallace Scott, *Hermaphroditism, Genital Anomalies and Related Endocrine Disorders* (Baltimore: Williams and Wilkins, 1958), 269.

20. John Money, Joan G. Hampson, and John L. Hampson, "An Examination of Some Basic Sexual Concepts: The Evidence of Human Hermaphroditism," *Bulletin of the Johns Hopkins Hospital* 97, no. 4 (1955): 301–19; John Money, Joan G. Hampson, and John L. Hampson, "Hermaphroditism: Recommendations Concerning Assignment of Sex, Change of Sex, and Psychologic Management," *Bulletin of Johns Hopkins Hospital* 97, no. 4 (1955): 284–300; John Money, *Venuses Penuses: Sexology, Sexosophy, and Exigency Theory* (Buffalo: Prometheus Publishers, 1986).

21. Robert M. Blizzard, "Lawson Wilkins," in *Wilkins the Diagnosis and Treatment of Endocrine Disorders in Childhood and Adolescence,* 4th ed., ed. Michael S. Kappy, Robert M. Blizzard, and Claude J. Migeon (Springfield: Charles C Thomas, 1994), xiii.

22. Suzanne Kessler, "The Medical Construction of Gender: Case Management of Intersexual Infants," *Signs: Journal of Women in Culture and Society* 16, no. 1 (1990): 3–26, quotation on 7.

23. John Colapinto, *As Nature Made Him: The Boy Who Was Raised as a Girl* (New York: HarperCollins, 2000).

24. American Academy of Pediatrics Section on Endocrinology and Section on Urology Committee on Genetics, "Evalution of the Newborn"; Gerardo Izquierdo and Kenneth I. Glassberg, "Gender Assignment and Gender Identity in Patients with Ambiguous Genitalia," *Urology* 42, no. 3 (1993): 232–42; Suzanne Kessler, *Lessons from the Intersexed* (New Brunswick: Rutgers University Press, 1998); Barbara C. McGillivray, "The Newborn

with Ambiguous Genitalia," *Seminars in Perinatology* 16, no. 6 (1992): 365–68; Meyers-Seifer, "Diagnosis and Management."

25. The best source to view the dynamics of the medical reliance on prevarication is B. Diane Kemp, Sherri A. Groveman, Anonymous, H. Deni Tako, and Karl M. Irwin, "Sex, Lies and Androgen Insensitivity Syndrome," *Canadian Medical Association Journal* 154, no. 12 (1996): 1829–33, available from MACROBUTTON HtmlResAnchor <http://www.cma.ca/cmaj/vol-154/1829e.htm>. For evidence that the practice of withholding the diagnosis from intersex patients is still common, see Robert Marion, "The Curse of the Garcias," *Discover* 21, no. 1 (2000): 42–44, available from MACROBUTTON HtmlResAnchor<http://www.findarticles.com/cf 0/m1511/12_21/67185294/p1/article.jhtml>. Representative older works recommending withholding the diagnosis include Tom Mazur, "Ambiguous Genitalia: Detection and Counseling," *Pediatric Nursing* 9, no. 6 (1983): 417–22, 431; J. Dewhurst and D. B. Grant, "Intersex Problems," *Archives of Disease in Childhood* 59, no. 12 (1984): 1191–194; Froukje M. E. Slijper, Stenvert L. S. Drop, Jan C. Molenaar, and R. J. Scholtmeijer, "Neonates with Abnormal Genital Development Assigned the Female Sex: Parent Counseling," *Journal of Sex Education and Therapy* 20, no. 1 (1994): 9–17.

26. Claude J. Migeon, Gary D. Berkovitz, and Terry R. Brown, "Sexual Differentiation and Ambiguity," in *Wilkins the Diagnosis and Treatment of Endocrine Disorders in Childhood and Adolescence,* 4th ed., ed. Michael S. Kappy, Robert M. Blizzard, and Claude J. Migeon (Springfield: Charles C Thomas, 1994), 573–715.

27. Lalitha Raman-Wilms, Alice Lin-in Tseng, Suzanne Wighardt, Thomas R. Einarson, and Gideon Koren, "Fetal Genital Effects of First-Trimester Sex Hormone Exposure: A Meta-Analysis," *Obsterics and Gynecology* 85, no. 1 (1995): 141–48; J. Fichtner, D. Filipas, A. M. Mottrie, G. E. Voges, and R. Hohenfellner, "Analysis of Meatal Location in Five Hundred Men: Wide Variation Questions Need for Meatal Advancement in All Pediatric Anterior Hypospadias Cases," *Journal of Urology* 154, no. 2 (1995): 833–34; Melanie Blackless, Anthony Charuvastra, Amanda Derryck, Anne Fausto-Sterling, Karl Lauzanne, and Ellen Lee, "How Sexually Dimorphic Are We? Review and Synthesis," *American Journal of Human Biology* 12, no. 2 (2000): 151–66; Anne Fausto-Sterling, *Sexing the Body: Gender Politics and the Construction of Human Sexuality* (New York: Basic Books, 2000).

28. Milton T. Edgerton, "Discussion: Clitoroplasty for Clitoromegaly due to Adrenogenital Syndrome without Loss of Sensitivity," *Plastic and Reconstructive Surgery* 91, no. 5 (1993): 956.

29. Hendricks, "Is It a Boy or a Girl?" Quotation on 15.

30. Stecker, "Hypospadias Cripples."

31. Devore, "Surgical Maelstrom."

32. Robert E. Gross, Judson Randolph, and John F. Crigler, "Clitorectomy for Sexual Abnormalities: Indications and Technique," *Surgery* 59, no. 2 (1966): 300–308, quotation on 307.

33. Oesterling, "Unified Approach."

34. Kiira Triea, "The Awakening," *Hermaphrodites with Attitude* (Winter 1994–95): 1, available from <http://www.isna.org/hwa/winter94–95/winter94–95.html>; Susan Stryker, "My Words to Victor Frankenstein above the Village of Chamounix," *GLQ: A Journal of Gay and Lesbian Studies* 1, no. 3 (1994): 237–54.

35. Morgan Holmes, "Medical Politics and Cultural Imperatives: Intersexuality beyond Pathology and Erasure," master's thesis, York University, 1994.

36. Sandy Stone, "The Empire Strikes Back: A Posttranssexual Manifesto," in *Body Guards: The Cultural Politics of Gender Ambiguity,* ed. Julia Epstein and Kristina Straub (New York: Routledge, 1991).

37. Kessler, *Lessons from the Intersexed,* 53.

38. Ellen Barry, "United States of Ambiguity," *Boston Phoenix,* Nov. 22, 1996, style section, 6–8.

39. Cheryl Chase, *Hermaphrodites Speak!* thirty-minute videotape (San Francisco: Intersex Society of North America, 1997), available from <http://www.isna.org>; Kessler, *Lessons from the Intersexed;* Dreger, ed., *Intersex in the Age of Ethics;* Angier, "Intersexual Healing"; *Is It a Boy or a Girl?* directed by Phyllis Ward, Discovery Channel, March 26, 2000, available from <http://www.isna.org>; Ruth G. Davis, "Was I Meant to Be a Man?" *Cosmopolitan* 228, no. 4 (2000): 200–203.

40. Similarly, some Western feminist opponents of African genital cutting have taken it upon themselves to speak for those affected, under the assumption that they are either too ignorant or too vested in the practices to make any valid contributions (Claire C. Robertson, "Getting beyond the Ew! Factor: Rethinking U.S. Approaches to African Female Genital Cutting," chapter 2 in this volume).

41. Anne Fausto-Sterling, "The Five Sexes: Why Male and Female Are Not Enough," *The Sciences* 33, no. 2 (1993): 20–25; Anne Fausto-Sterling, *Myths of Gender: Biological Theories about Women and Men,* 2d ed. (New York: Basic Books, 1985), 134–41.

42. Kessler, "Medical Construction of Gender."

43. Alice Domurat Dreger, "The Limits of Individuality: Ritual and Sacrifice in the Lives and Medical Treatment of Conjoined Twins," *Studies in History and Philosophy of Biology and Biomedical Science* 29, no. 1 (1998): 1–29; Alice Domurat Dreger, "Doubtful Sex: The Fate of the Hermaphrodite in Victorian Medicine," *Victorian Studies* 38, no. 3 (1995): 336–70; Alice Domurat Dreger, "Hermaphrodites in Love: The Truth of the Gonads," in *Science and Homosexualities,* ed. Vernon A. Rosario (New York: Routledge, 1997), 46–66; Alice Domurat Dreger, "Doctors Containing Hermaphrodites: The Victorian Legacy," *Chrysalis: The Journal of Transgressive Gender Identities* 2, no. 5 (1997): 15–22.

44. Fausto-Sterling, *Sexing the Body;* Kessler, *Lessons from the Intersexed;* Dreger, ed., *Intersex in the Age of Ethics;* Dreger, *Hermaphrodites and the Medical Invention of Sex.*

45. Joycelyn Elders and David Chanoff, *From Sharecropper's Daughter to Surgeon General of the United States of America* (New York: William Morrow, 1996), 150–54; "Dr. Elders' Medical History," *The New Yorker,* Sept. 26, 1994, 45–46.

46. Mt. Sinai School of Medicine, Conference on Pediatric Plastic and Reconstructive Surgery, New York City, May 16, 1996.

47. Angier, "Intersexual Healing."

48. Hendricks, "Is It a Boy or a Girl?" More than one ISNA member has discovered that the surgeons who operated on them did so at no charge. A 1994 wire service news article (Tom Majeski, "Surgery Changes Russian Child's Sex," *San Jose Mercury News,* July 25, 1994, A11) relates how a Moscow family, driven to thoughts of murder-suicide by their one-year-old son Misha's anatomy, searched high and low until they connected with an American pediatric urologist. The urologist operated for free, the hospital donated its services,

and an airline footed the expenses for a round trip to St. Paul for the entire family. Doctors removed Misha's penis, testis, and ovary and instructed the family to rename him and to move. The family plans never to reveal any part of the story to relatives or to their now-daughter Masha. The medical establishment's fascination with its power to change sex and its drive to rescue parents from intersex children are so strong that intervention can be delivered across national borders and without regard to the commercial model that ordinarily governs U.S. medical services.

49. The first exception was urologist Justine Schober, who, after watching a videotape made at the 1996 ISNA retreat and receiving other input from various intersex groups, suggested in a new textbook on pediatric surgery that although technology has advanced to the point that "our needs [as surgeons] and the needs of parents to have a presentable child can be satisfied," it is time to acknowledge that there are problems that "we as surgeons, despite the most technically perfect surgeries, cannot address." She then called for a thorough reevaluation of the protocols surrounding medical management of intersexuality: "Surgery makes parents and doctors comfortable, but counseling makes people comfortable too, and is not irreversible." Justine M. Schober, "Feminizing Genitoplasty for Intersex," in *Pediatric Surgery and Urology: Long Term Outcomes,* ed. M. D. Stringer et al. (London: W. B. Saunders, 1998), 549–58. By early 2001, there was finally growing acknowledgment within the medical community that all is not well. Surgeon Ian Aaronson, in forming a "North American Task Force on Intersex" in 2000, acknowledged that "long-term outcome data [on intersex genital surgeries] is very sparse and selective, and this puts surgeons on tenuous ethical grounds." The July 2000 issue of the American Academy of Pediatrics' journal *Pediatrics* carried an article that called for a moratorium on pediatric genital surgeries: Chanika Phornphutkul, Anne Fausto-Sterling, and Philip A. Gruppuso, "Gender Self-Reassignment in an XY Adolescent Female Born with Ambiguous Genitalia," *Pediatrics* 106, no. 1 (2000): 135–37. Unfortunately, it also carried an announcement of a newly adopted policy of the academy calling for continued pediatric genital surgeries as standard practice (American Academy of Pediatrics Section on Endocrinology and Section on Urology Committee on Genetics, "Evaluation of the Newborn").

50. Patricia Schroeder, "Female Genital Mutilation," *New England Journal of Medicine* 331, no. 11 (1994): 739–40; Nahid Toubia, "Female Circumcision as a Public Health Issue," *New England Journal of Medicine* 331, no. 11 (1994): 712–16.

51. Isabelle R. Gunning, "Female Genital Surgeries: Eradication Measures at the Western Local Level—A Cautionary Tale" (chapter 4 in this volume).

52. Dugger, "New Law Bans Genital Cutting."

53. Fran P. Hosken, *The Hosken Report: Genital and Sexual Mutilation of Females,* 4th rev. ed. (Lexington: Women's International Network News, 1994).

54. Robin Morgan and Gloria Steinem, "The International Crime of Genital Mutilation," *Ms.* 8, no. 9 (1980): 65–67, 98, quotation on 65.

55. Mariella Furrer, "Ritual Agony," *Life* 20, no. 1 (1997): 38–39.

56. Robertson, "Getting beyond the Ew! Factor"; see also Pulitzer Prize Board, *Feature Photography: Stephanie Welsh* (1996), available from MACROBUTTON HtmlResAnchor <http://www.pulitzer.org/year/1996/feature-photography/>.

57. Linda Burstyn, "Female Circumcision Comes to America," *Atlantic Monthly* 276, no. 4 (1995): 28–35, quotation on 31.

58. Martha C. Nussbaum, *Sex and Social Justice* (New York: Oxford University Press, 1999), 122–23.

59. One wishes that first-world critics of African genital cutting would do their homework. It is easy (and free) to perform an Internet search of the National Library of Medicine's database of medical publications. Searching for "clitoris" and "surgery" and then eliminating references to cancer, transsexuals, animals, and bladder exstrophy produced 196 citations in April 2000. Of these, 33 relate to folk genital cutting practices, while 125 relate to genital surgery for transforming intersex genitals into normative female ones. Many of the titles should draw immediate feminist suspicion: "The Surgical Management of the Enlarged Clitoris," "Surgical Technique for Clitoral Reduction," "A New and Simplified Method for Concealing the Hypertrophied Clitoris," "Clitoridectomy or Plastic Reduction of the Clitoris in the Adrenogenital Syndrome," "Operative Reduction of the Enlarged Clitoris," "Technique of Vaginoplasty and Clitoridectomy in the Adrenogenital Syndrome," "A Simple Technic for Shortening the Clitoris without Amputation," and "Clitorectomy for Sexual Abnormalities: Indications and Technique." Nearly all the articles on folk genital cutting use condemnatory language, while those on intersex genital surgeries all represent it as therapeutic.

60. Susan Jahoda, "Theatres of Madness," in *Deviant Bodies: Critical Perspectives on Difference in Science and Popular Culture,* ed. Jennifer Terry and Jacqueline Urla (Bloomington: Indiana University Press, 1995), 273; Letter to the Editor, *Ms.* 8, no. 10 (1980): 12.

61. Patricia, Farnes and Ruth Hubbard, Letter to the Editor, *Ms.* 8, no. 10 (1980): 9–10.

62. Compare Seble Dawit and Salem Mekuria, "The West Just Doesn't Get It," *New York Times,* Dec. 7, 1993, A27.

63. Butler, *Gender Trouble,* 8.

64. Kessler, "Medical Construction of Gender," 25.

Appendix:
Advocacy Organizations Opposed
to Female Genital Cutting

The following is a list of organizations that work to eradicate female genital cutting. Although it is not an exhaustive list (some organizations either did not respond or provided incomplete responses to our survey), it does provide an indication of the kinds of organizations operating in different parts of the world. It may also provide opportunities for supporting efforts to eradicate female genital cutting.

Babiker Badri Scientific Association for Women Studies (BBSAWS)
P.O. Box 167 ARDA
Omdurman,
Sudan
Tel.: 53363 54409
Fax: 249 11 564401
(Sumaiya El-Tayeb, executive director)

British Medical Association
BMA House
Tavistock Square
London WC1H 9JP,
England
Tel.: 44(0)20 7388 8296
Fax: 44(0)20 7383 6911
Web-site: info.northtrans@bma.org.uk
For issues around FGC, contact:
Medical Ethics Department
Tel.: 44(0)20 7383 6286
Fax: 44(0)20 7383 6233
E-mail: ETHICS@bma.org.uk

(Gillian Romano-Critchley, executive officer, medical ethics; E. M. Armstrong, secretary)
Among other things, this organization provides ethical and medico-legal advice to doctors caring for women who are, or are likely to become, victims of female genital mutilation.

Commission pour L'Abolition des Mutilations Sexuelles
6 Place Saint-Germain-des-Prés
75006 Paris,
France
Tel.: (33) 1 45 49 0400
Fax: (33) 1 45 49 16 71
E-mail 112111@club-internet.fr
(Linda Weil-Curiel, lawyer)
Spreads information on FGM (via leaflets, posters, video, and meetings) and takes part in trials of parents and/or excisors.

Egyptian Society for the Care of Children and Prevention of Traditional Practices Harmful to Women and Children (ENC)
25 Kadri St.
Sayeda
Zeinab
Cairo, Egypt
Tel.: (20–3) 362 0467
Fax: (20–3) 363 1613
(Mrs. Aziza Kaamel/Dr. Mohamed El-Tobgui)

FORWARD Foundation for Women's Health, Research and Development
6th Floor, 50 Eastbourne Terrace
London W2 6LX,
England
Tel.: 44(0)20 7725 2606
Fax: 44(0)20 7725 2796
E-mail: forward@dircon.co.uk
Web-site: www.forward.dircon.co.uk
(Faith Mwangi-Powell, director; Naana Otoo-Oyortey, chair)

Inter-African Committee on Traditional Practices Affecting the Health of Women and Children
Inter-African Committee
c/o Economic Commission for Africa/ACW
P.O. Box 3001
Addis Ababa,

Ethiopia
Tel.: 25 11/5172 00, 515793
Fax: 25 11/514682
Liaison Office:
Inter-African Committee
147 rue du Lausanne
Ch-1202 Geneva,
Switzerland
Tel.: 41 22/731 24 20 *or* 732 08 21
Fax: 41 22/738 18 23
E-mail: cominter@prolink.ch
(Berhane Ras-Work, president of liaison office; Elizabeth Alabi, senior program officer, headquarters)
Twenty-six national committees (affiliates) in Africa.

International Confederation of Midwives
Eisenhowerlaan 138
2517 KN The Hague,
The Netherlands
Tel.: 31 70 3060520
E-mail: 100702.2405@compuserve.com *or* Intlmidwives@compuserve.com

International Planned Parenthood Federation
IPF, Regent's College, Inner Circle
Regent's Park
London NW1 4NS,
England
Tel.: 44(0)20 7487 7900
Fax: 44(0)20 7487 7950
E-mail: info@ippf.org
Web-site: www.ippf.org
(Ingar Brueggemann, director general; Pramilla Senanayake, head of the Global Advocacy Division, which is in charge of the work on FGM)
Contact sheet available for *Roundtable on Eradicating Female Genital Mutilation at the Community Level: Overcoming Constraints with Culturally-Sensitive Approaches*

Intersex Society of North America (ISNA)
P.O. Box 301
Petaluma, CA 94953
Tel.: 707–283–0036
Fax: 707–283–0030
E-mail: info@isna.org
Web-site: www.isna.org

(Cheryl Chase, director)
ISNA works to create a world free of unwanted genital surgery for people born with
atypical sex anatomy.

London Black Women's Health Action Project (LBWHAP)
Cornwall Avenue Community Centre
1 Cornwall Ave.
London E2 OHW,
England
Tel: 44(0)18 1980 3503

National Organization of Circumcision Information Resource Centers (NOCIRC)
P.O. Box 2512
San Anselmo, CA 94979–2512
Tel.: 415 488 9883
Fax: 415 488 9660
E-mail: nocirc@concentric.net
Web-site: www.nocirc.org
(Marilyn Fayre Milos, RN, director)

Population Action International
1120 19th St. NW Suite 550
Washington, D.C. 20036
Tel.: 202 659 1833
Fax: 202 293 1795
E-mail: tlb@popact.org
(Amy Coen, president; contact Terri Bartlett, vice president for public policy at stra-
tegic initiatives)

Population, Development and Reproductive Health
Norman Shaw South, Room 301
Victoria Embankment
London SW1A 2H2,
England
Tel.: 44(0)17 1219 2492
E-mail: trudydavies@easynet.co.uk

RAINBO (Research Action and Information Network for the Bodily Integrity of
Women)
Web-site: www.rainbo.org
In the United States:
915 Broadway, Suite 1603
New York, NY 10010–7108

Tel.: 212 477 3318
Fax: 212 447 4154
E-mail: info@rainbo.org
In U.K.:
59 Bravington Road
London W9 3AA,
England
Tel.: 44(0)18 1968 5573
Fax: 44(0)18 1958 5573
E-mail: RAINBOuk@aol.com
In Burkina Faso:
01 BP 515
Ouagadougou 01,
Burkina Faso
Tel.: 226 30 79 15
Fax: 226 31 67 37
In Egypt:
18 Mourad El Sherei St.
Nouzha, Santa Fatima
Heliopolis,
Cairo, Egypt
Tel.: 202 243 2589
Fax: 202 431 0213
(Nahid Toubia, M.D., RAINBO president; board of trustees: Abdullahi An Na'im, Jose
Barzelatto, Rev. Joseph Ben-David, C. Valerie Dabady, Lynn P. Freedman, Ayesha
Imam, Afa Mahfouz, Jeffrey Mecaskey, and Sadig Rasheed)

Royal College of Midwives
15 Mansfield St.
London W1M 0BE,
England
Tel.: 44(0)20 7312 3535
Fax: 44(0)20 7312 3536
E-mail: info@rcm.org.uk
Web-site: www.rcm.org.uk

Royal College of Nursing of the United Kingdom (RCN)
RCN Headquarters
20 Cavendish Square
London W1M 0AB,
England
Tel.: 44(0)17 1409 3333
Fax: 44(0)17 1647 3435

E-mail: rcn.institute@rcn.org.uk
Web-site: www.rcn.org.uk
(Christine Hancock, general secretary)

Socialstyrelsen
The National Board of Health and Welfare
106 30 Stockholm,
Sweden
Tel.: 46 8 555 530 00
Fax: 46 8 555 532 52
E-mail: socialstyrelsen@sos.se
(Annika Eriksson, director/administrator; project manager for the board's work on violence against women, including FGM)

Sudan National Committee for Eradication of Harmful Practices (SNTCP)

Women's International Network News (WIN)
187 Grant St.
Lexington, MA 02420
Tel.: 617–862–9431
Fax: 781–862–1734
(Fran Hosken, editor)
A quarterly journal reporting on women and development since 1975, WIN News campaigns against FGM in the section on Female Genital and Sexual Mutilation. WIN developed the Universal Childbirth Picture Books, with additions to prevent excision and infibulation. More than fifty thousand have been distributed throughout Africa in English, French, Arabic, and Somali.

Suggested Reading and Films

Books and Articles

Abdalla, Raqiya. *Sisters in Affliction: Circumcision and Infibulation of Women in Africa.* London: Zed Press, 1982.

Ahmed, Leila. *Women and Gender in Islam: Roots of a Historical Debate.* New Haven: Yale University Press, 1992.

Babatunde, Emmanuel D. *Women's Rights versus Women's Rites: A Study of Circumcision among the Ketu Yoruba of South Western Nigeria.* Lawrenceville, N.J.: Africa World Press, 1998.

Barker-Benfield, Ben. "Sexual Surgery in Late Nineteenth Century America." *International Journal of Health Services* 5, no. 2 (1975): 279–98.

"Beijing Declaration and the Platform for Action of the Fourth World Conference on Women" (A/CONF.177/20, 17 Oct. 1995). In *The United Nations and the Advancement of Women, 1945–1996.* Rev. ed. New York: Department of Public Information, United Nations, 1996.

Berkey, Jonathan P. "Circumcision Circumscribed: Female Excision and Cultural Accommodation in the Medieval Near East." *International Journal of Middle Eastern Studies* 28, no. 1 (1996): 19–38.

Boddy, Janice. "Womb as Oasis: The Symbolic Context of Pharaonic Circumcision in Rural Northern Sudan." *American Ethnologist* 9, no. 4 (1982): 682–98.

Boulware-Miller, Kay. "Female Circumcision: Challenge to the Practice as a Human Rights Violation." *Harvard Women's Law Journal* 8 (1988): 155–77.

Chase, Cheryl. "Hermaphrodites with Attitude: Mapping the Emergence of Intersex Political Activism." *GLQ: A Journal of Gay and Lesbian Studies* 4, no. 2 (1998): 189–211.

"Colloquium: Bridging Society, Culture, and Law: The Issue of Female Circumcision." *Case Western Reserve Law Review* 47, no. 2 (1997): special issue.

Crenshaw, Kimberlé et al., eds. *Critical Race Theory: The Key Writings That Formed the Movement.* New York: New Press, 1995.

Daly, Mary. "African Genital Mutilation: The Unspeakable Atrocities." In Daly, *Gyn/Ecology: The Metaethics of Radical Feminism*. Boston: Beacon Press, 1978.

Dawit, Seble, and Salem Mekuria. "The West Just Doesn't Get It." *New York Times*, Dec. 7, 1993, A27.

Dorkenoo, Efua. *Cutting the Rose: Female Genital Mutilation, the Practice and Its Prevention*. London: Minority Rights Group, 1994.

Dreger, Alice Domurat. *Hermaphrodites and the Medical Invention of Sex*. Cambridge: Harvard University Press, 1998.

———. *Intersex in the Age of Ethics*. Hagerstown, Md.: University Publishing Group, 1999.

El Saadawi, Nawal. *The Hidden Face of Eve: Women in the Arab World*. Trans. and ed. by Sherif Hetata. London: Zed Press, 1980.

Fausto-Sterling, Anne. "The Five Sexes: Why Male and Female Are Not Enough." *The Sciences* 33, no. 2 (1993): 20–25.

———. *Sexing the Body: Gender Politics and the Construction of Sexuality*. New York: Basic Books, 2000.

Gordon, Daniel. "Female Circumcision and Genital Operations in Egypt and the Sudan: A Dilemma for Medical Anthropology." *Medical Anthropology Quarterly* 5, no. 1 (1991): 3–14.

Gruenbaum, Ellen. "Women's Rights and Cultural Self-Determination in the Female Genital Mutilation Controversy." *American Anthropology Newsletter*, May 1995, 14–15.

Gunning, Isabelle R. "Arrogant Perception, World Traveling and Multicultural Feminism: The Case of Female Genital Surgeries." *Columbia Human Rights Law Review* 23, no. 2 (1992): 189–248.

Hammond, Tim. "Long-Term Consequences of Neonatal Circumcision." In *Sexual Mutilations: A Human Tragedy*, ed. George C. Denniston and Marilyn Fayre Milos, 125–29. New York: Plenum Press, 1997.

Hayes, Rose Oldfield. "Female Genital Mutilation, Fertility Control, Women's Roles and the Patrilineage in Modern Sudan: A Functional Analysis." *American Ethnologist* 62, no. 4 (1975): 617–33.

Hicks, Esther. *Infibulation: Female Mutilation in Islamic Northeastern Africa*. Rev. ed. New Brunswick: Transaction Publishers, 1996.

Hosken, Fran P. *The Hosken Report: Genital and Sexual Mutilation of Females*. 4th rev. ed. Lexington, Mass.: Women's International Network News, 1994.

James, Stanlie. "Challenging Patriarchal Privilege through the Development of International Human Rights." *Women's Studies International Forum* 17, no. 6 (1994): 563–78.

Kassindja, Fauziya. *Do They Hear You When You Cry?* New York: Delacorte Press, 1998.

Kenyatta, Jomo. *Facing Mount Kenya: The Tribal Life of the Gikuyu*. 1938. Reprint. New York: Vintage, 1965.

Kessler, Suzanne. "The Medical Construction of Gender: Case Management of Intersexual Infants." *Signs: Journal of Women in Culture and Society* 16, no. 1 (1990): 3–26.

Koso-Thomas, Olayinka. *The Circumcision of Women: A Strategy for Eradication*. London: Zed Press, 1985.

Kouba, Leonard J., and Judith Muasher. "Female Circumcision in Africa: An Overview." *African Studies Review* 28, no. 1 (1985): 95–100.

Laqueur, Thomas. *Making Sex: Body and Gender from the Greeks to Freud.* Cambridge: Harvard University Press, 1990.

Lewis, Hope. "Between *Irua* and 'Female Genital Mutilation': Feminist Human Rights Discourse and the Cultural Divide." *Harvard Human Rights Journal* 8 (1995): 39–61.

Lightfoot-Klein, Hanny. *Prisoners of Ritual: An Odyssey into Female Genital Circumcision in Africa.* New York: Haworth Press, 1989.

Lyons, Harriet. "Anthropologists, Moralities and Relativities: the Problem of Genital Mutilations." *Canadian Review of Sociology and Anthropology* 18, no. 4 (1981): 499–518.

Morgan, Robin, and Gloria Steinem. "The International Crime of Genital Mutilation." In Steinem, *Outrageous Acts and Everyday Rebellions,* 330–40. New York: Holt, Rinehart and Winston, 1983.

Report from the Seminar on Female Genital Mutilation, Copenhagen, May 29, 1995. Copenhagen: Danida, 1995.

Robertson, Claire C. "Grassroots in Kenya: Women, Genital Mutilation and Collective Action, 1920–1990." *Signs: Journal of Women in Culture and Society* 21, no. 2 (1996): 615–42.

Sanderson, Lillian Passmore. *Female Genital Mutilation: Excision and Infibulation, A Bibliography.* London: Anti-Slavery Society for the Protection of Human Rights, 1986.

———. *Against the Mutilation of Women: The Struggle to End Unnecessary Suffering.* London: Ithaca Press, 1981.

Schroeder, Patricia. "Female Genital Mutilation." *New England Journal of Medicine* 331, no. 11 (1994): 739–40.

Slack, Alison T. "Female Circumcision: A Critical Appraisal." *Human Rights Quarterly* 10, no. 4 (1988): 438–87.

Smith, Robyn Cerny. "Female Circumcision: Bringing Women's Perspectives into the International Debate." *Southern California Law Review* 65, no. 5 (1992): 2449–504.

Thiam, Awa. *Speak Out, Black Sisters: Feminism and Oppression in Black Africa.* Trans. Dorothy S. Blair. Dover, N.H.: Pluto Press, 1986.

Thomas, Lynn. "'Ngaitana (I will circumcise myself)': The Gender and Generational Politics of the 1956 Ban on Clitoridectomy in Meru, Kenya." *Gender and History* 8, no. 3 (1996): 338–63.

Toubia, Nahid. "Female Circumcision as a Public Health Issue." *New England Journal of Medicine* 331, no. 11 (1994): 712–16.

The Vienna Declaration and Programme of Action (A/CONF.157/24 13 Oct. 1993). New York: United Nations, 1993.

Warsame, Aamina, Sadiya Ahmed, and Aud Talle. *Social and Cultural Aspects of Female Circumcision and Infibulation.* Mogadishu, Somalia/Stockholm, Sweden: Collaborative Report of the Somali Academy of Sciences and Arts and Swedish Agency for Research Cooperation, 1985.

Wing, Adrian, ed. *Critical Race Feminism: A Reader.* New York: New York University Press, 1997.

Winter, Bronwyn. "Women, the Law and Cultural Relativism in France: The Case of Excision." *Signs: Journal of Women in Culture and Society* 19, no. 4 (1994): 939–74.

Films

Fire Eyes Female Circumcision. Soraya Mire. New York: Filmakers Library, 1994. Sixty minutes; best used with another selection here.

Femmes aux yeux ouverts (Women with open eyes). Anne-Laure Folly. San Francisco: California Newsreel, 1994. Fifty-two minutes; English subtitles.

In the Name of God: Changing Attitudes towards Mutilation. Leyla Assas-Tengroth. New York: Filmakers Library, 1997. Twenty-nine minutes.

Rites. Penny Dedman. New York: Filmakers Library, 1991. Fifty-two minutes.

Contributors

CHERYL CHASE is the founder and director of the Intersex Society of North America (ISNA), the largest, most visible association of intersexed persons in the world. She directed and produced *Hermaphrodites Speak!* the first documentary conveying the voices and experiences of intersexed people. Her articles have appeared in a wide variety of popular and scholarly publications. In 1999 she was author of an amicus brief for the Constitutional Court of Colombia, a document that was key to the court's decision to limit genital surgeries on intersex infants. In 2000, ISNA received the Felipa da Souza Award from the International Gay and Lesbian Human Rights Commission.

ISABELLE GUNNING is a professor of law at the Southwestern University School of Law in Los Angeles. She teaches on international human rights, women and the law, immigration law, alternative dispute resolution, and evidence, as well as clinical or skills-oriented classes. Her research interests have been primarily in the areas of international and transnational law, with a critical focus on women of color. Her community activities include working with immigrant and refugee women, many from African nations, who now live in the United States.

STANLIE M. JAMES, associate professor of Afro-American studies and women's studies at the University of Wisconsin-Madison, is chair of the Afro-American studies department. She has completed a four-year term as director of the university's Women's Studies Research Center and is also affiliated with its African Studies Program. With Abena Busia, she coedited *Theorizing Black Feminisms: The Visionary Pragmatism of Black Women.* James's articles have appeared in *Signs, Women's Studies International Forum, Women in Pol-*

itics, Africa Today, and the *Journal of African Policy Studies.* Her areas of interest include black feminisms and women's international human rights.

CLAIRE C. ROBERTSON is associate professor of history and women's studies at The Ohio State University and adjunct professor of African studies at Indiana University. She has published five books, including *Trouble Showed the Way: Women, Men, and Trade in the Nairobi Area, 1890–1990* and *Sharing the Same Bowl: A Socioeconomic History of Women in Accra, Ghana,* which won the Herskovits Prize of the African Studies Association in 1985. Most recently, '*We Only Come Here to Struggle': Stories from Berida's Life* appeared along with *Second Face,* a companion videotape. It is the life history of Berida Ndambuki, a Nairobi market woman and coauthor of the volume. Claire Robertson has also published numerous articles and is working on the oral history of Saint Lucia in the Eastern Caribbean.

CHRISTINE WALLEY is assistant professor of anthropology at the Massachusetts Institute of Technology. She is at work on a book that examines social conflict over the environment and development in Tanzania as local, national, and international actors participate in the establishment of that country's first national marine park. She is also an associate producer on a documentary, *Containment: Three-Mile Island Twenty Years after the Accident.*

Index

ABC, 17, 35; *Day One,* 35; *World News To-night,* 18
Abdalla, Raqiya, 60
adrenal disorder, 131
adrenogenital syndrome, 151
"Advancing Luna—and Ida B. Wells" (Walker), 93
Africa: images of, 60ff
African immigrants: to U.S. and Europe, 17, 18, 29, 34
African Queen (film), 59
African Studies Association, 36
"African Women in the Diaspora and the Problem of Female Mutilation" (Dawit), 6
Against the Mutilation of Women (Sanderson), 65
age-sets, 30
Ahmed, Leila, 39, 41
Ahmed, Sadiya, 60
Akamba (people), 62
Algeria, 39–40
All Things Considered (National Public Radio), 18, 105–7
ambiguous genitals, 131–32
American Academy of Pediatrics, 117, 139
Amistad (film), 60
anomaly of sex differentiation, 130
anthropology, 18–19, 26, 32, 34, 46, 56
arrogant perception, 89–90, 93–94, 116
"Arrogant Perception, World Traveling, and Multicultural Feminism: The Case of Female Genital Surgeries" (Gunning), 94
asylum (case law on), 58, 67, 74–77

Babatunde, Emmanuel, 10, 66
Barker-Benfield, Ben, 94
Beijing Declaration and the Platform of Action, 96
Beloved (film), 60
Berkey, Jonathan P., 93, 100–103
Bettelheim, Bruno, 82n3
binary oppositions: first world and third world, 37–38
black feminisms, 103
Boddy, Janice, 27–29
Boulware-Miller, Kay, 69
bridewealth, 75
Brothers, Joyce, 79
Bukusu (people), 22, 26, 31
Burt, James C., 107
Butler, Judith, 44, 145

California Immigrant Women's Health Act, 119
Canada, 76–77
Chatterjee, Partha, 41
Chelala, Cesar, 78
Chicago Tribune, 78
Christianity, 23, 27
circumcision, 20; female, 57, 67, 69, 76; male, 73–74, 117

clitoral hypertrophy, 127, 132, 142
clitoridectomy, 1, 2, 6, 7, 10–15, 17, 19, 20, 21, 26, 30, 36, 38, 40, 46, 58, 62, 66, 72, 89, 98, 143; in first world, 145
clitoris, 20; size of, 127, 130
clitoroplasty, 132
CNN, 37, 58, 68, 82n7
colonial feminism, 39
colonialism, 30–31, 34, 38–39, 41, 43, 46; European, 59, 72–73
The Color Purple (film), 87
Commaret, Prosecutor, 72, 82n6
"communities of resistance," 104
cosmetic surgeries, 70
Coulibaly family, 72–73
Cromer, Lord, 39
"crying the knife," 30
"cultural defense" arguments, 42
cultural relativism, 1, 5, 19, 32, 43, 56–57
culture, 18–19, 32, 35, 43, 46
"culture is not torture," 35

Daly, Mary, 33, 34, 60, 62–63
Darod (people) of Somalia, 95
Dateline NBC, 18
Dawit, Seble, 6, 37, 43–44, 81
Dey, Lynda, 6
Diara, Kerthio, 106
Dii (people) of Cameroon, 97–99
Diop, Aminata, 88
Dirie, Waris, 74, 85n40
"Discourse of the Veil at the Turn of Two Centuries" (Ahmed), 89
Dogon (people), 29
Dorkenoo, Efua, 44, 54, 60, 66, 107
Dowayos (people), 98
Dreger, Alice, 138, 141
Dugger, Celia, 36, 67–68, 78, 85nn43, 45
Dunn, Kevin, 59
Durkheim, Emile, 82n3

Edgerton, Milton, 131
Egypt, 19, 40, 58, 68, 78, 80, 100
El Dareer, Asma, 60
Elders, Joycelyn, 139
El Saadawi, Nawal, 33, 90–91, 108
England, 40, 44
Ethiopia, 57
Ethiopia National Committee against Circumcision, 108
ethnocentrism, 90, 126
excision, 10, 19, 26, 89; Islam and, 101

Facing Mount Kenya (Kenyatta), 71, 91
Farnes, Patricia, 144
Fausto-Sterling, Anne, 138–39, 141
female circumcision (*sunna*), 7, 10–12, 14, 17, 19, 20, 44, 85, 88, 96, 98, 118, 119, 140
"Female Circumcision: Bringing Women's Perspectives into the International Debate" (Smith), 95
female fertility, 130
female genital cutting, 5, 6–8, 10, 12, 13, 89; contextualization of, 55, 73, 80; criminalization of, 71–74; eradication efforts toward, 61–62, 64, 78; health consequences, 36; reactions to, 54; representations of, 59–81; use of term, 54
female genital mutilation (FGM), 5, 7, 18–19, 20, 44, 55, 57, 63, 66, 88, 96, 114, 118, 119, 140
female genital operations, 7, 17–30, 44, 89; co-optation of, 45–46; feminist confrontations and, 33–38, 40, 46; third-world women and, 33–38; Western feminist response to, 32–33, 36–38, 40, 43, 45–46
female genital surgeries, 7, 12, 13, 89, 114, 117
female pseudo excision, 99
female sexuality, 145
feminine: as condition of lack, 131
feminism, 57, 60–69, 145
feminist criticism of science, 138
feminist positions, 18, 24, 33–35
feminizing pediatric genital surgery, 132
Fire Eyes: Female Circumcision (film), 107–8
fistulas, 108
foot-binding, 39, 90
Forward International, 142
France, 17, 29, 35–39, 46, 71–73, 83n12
Freud, Sigmund, 25, 82n3
Frye, Marily, 89
Fullerton, Elizabeth, 78
Functionalism, 56

Gambia, 65
Gates, Henry Louis, 37
gay civil rights, 135
Gearhart, John P., 139–40
gender boundaries, 126
genital ambiguity, 129, 131, 132, 136, 139, 144, 145
genital manipulation, 96
genital surgeries, 94
Goffman, Erving, 25, 27, 29–31
Goldschmidt, Walter, 26, 27, 29–31
Goodman, Ellen, 141

Gunning, Isabelle, 69, 83n10, 89, 93–94, 108
Gyn/Ecology (Daly), 62–63

hadiths, 100–101
Hardin, Blaine, 67
Hartsock, Nancy, 95
Hasche, Tilman, 36
Hayes, Rose Oldfield, 27–28
Hermaphrodites with Attitude, 139
hermaphroditism. *See* intersexuality
Hicks, Esther, 57, 61
historical transformation of circumcision
    practices, 31–33
Hofriyat (Sudanese village), 28–29, 32
Holmes, Morgan, 135
Hosken, Fran, 2, 34, 35, 60–64, 70, 83n11, 141
The Hosken Report on Genital Mutilation, 2,
    60–61
Howard, Rhoda, 69
Hubbard, Ruth, 144
human rights, 69–77
hypospadias, 129, 133

identity politics, 44–45
Igbo (people), 75
India, 39, 41
infibulation, 1, 2, 5, 6, 8, 12, 13, 17, 19, 20, 27,
    28, 30, 37, 38, 46, 57, 58, 61, 64, 70, 89. *See
    also* pharaonic circumcision
initiation rites, 22–24
insider/outsider debates, 21
Inter-Africa Committee, 88
International Human Rights, 90
Intersex Genital Mutilation (IGM), 140
Intersex Society of North America (ISNA),
    136–37
intersexuality, 128
*In the Name of God: Helping Circumcised
    Women* (film), 107–8
irua ceremony, 95
Islam, 10, 19, 27

Jahoda, Susan, 143–44
jesting relationship, 98–99
John/Joan case, 130
Johns Hopkins University, 129
Joshi, Rama, 39
journalism, 58

Kandiyoti, Deniz, 40
Kassamali, Noor J., 84n33
Kassindja, Fauziya, 17, 35–37, 45, 67–69, 74, 142

Kaudjhis-Offoumou, Francoise, 56
Keita, Soko Aramata, 71–73
Kelson, Gregory, 75, 85n44
Kenya, 19–20, 22, 20–32, 39–41, 61, 64, 68, 71,
    78, 85n45
Kenyatta, Jomo, 41, 71, 91, 98–99
Kessler, Suzanne, 129, 137–39, 145
Khartoum Conference (1979), 62
Kikuyu (Gikuyu) people, 11, 40–42, 62, 65,
    71, 85n36
kinship, relation to, 28
Koptiuch, Kristin, 42
Koso-Thomas, Olayinka, 60, 91, 108

labia majora, 1, 20
labia minora, 1, 20
Lancaster, John, 78
Lantier, Jacques, 70
Law to Ban Female Genital Mutilation
    (U.S.), 127–28
Law and Order (television show), 73–74
Lengila, Seita, 68
lesbians and lesbianism, 77, 134
Levi-Strauss, Claude, 12, 15
Lewis, Hope, 69
Liddle, Joanna, 39
Lightfoot-Klein, Hanny, 29, 60, 63–64, 91
Lyons, Harriet, 56, 82nn3–4

Maendeleo ya Wanawake (Kenyan women's
    organization), 40, 104
male circumcision, 10
male/female dimorphism, 128
Mali, 19
Malinowski, Bronislaw, 41
Mani, Lata, 39, 41, 42
Mauritania, 69, 78
Mayo, Katherine, 39
media representations, 17, 128, 140
medical intervention, 145
medicalized clitoral surgery (U.S.), 141, 143,
    144
medical records, 133
medical taxonomy, 129
Meillassoux, Claude, 73
Mekuria, Salem, 43–44, 81
Melching, Molly, 78, 105–6
micro aggressions, 122
micropenis, 132
Mire, Soraya, 107
missionaries, 61–62
Mohanty, Chandra, 104

Moi, President Daniel, 24
Money, John, 129–30
Montagu, Ashley, 82n3
Morgan, Robin, 32, 142, 144
Mother India (Mayo), 39
Mugo, Micere Githae, 93
Muller, Jean-Claude, 93, 97–99
mutilation, 107
Muuya, Leah, 105

nationalism: and female genital surgeries, 39–41
National Organization of Women, 33–34, 44
"the natural," 128
Nazis, 73
New York Times, 17, 36, 43–44, 62, 67, 78
Ng'ang'a, Lorna, 65
Nigeria, 17, 19, 36, 62, 65, 71, 85n36
non-governmental organizations (NGOs), 80–81
normalizing surgery, 129
Ntanira na Mugumbo (Circumcision through Words program), 104–5
Nussbuam, Martha, 143

Obiora, L. Amede, 69
objectivity: of intersex people, 138
Oluloro, Lydia, 17, 36, 45, 74–77
oppositional agency, 108
orgasm, 133
Out of Africa (film), 59

pain, 21
Pala-Okeyo, Achola, 46
Palmer, Parker, 7
Parmar, Pratibha, 6, 17, 35, 43, 64–66, 83n21
patriarchy, 62, 71–72
Paulme, Denise, 82n4
pediatric genital surgeries, 7, 10, 12, 13, 131
penis size, 127, 130
perspicacious integrity, 90, 109
Peyrot, Maurice, 72
pharaonic circumcision, 8
Pollis, Adamantia, 69
polygyny, 61, 65, 75, 84n24
Posnansky, Merrick, 85n43
Possessing the Secret of Joy (Walker), 17, 38, 43, 64, 87, 93, 97, 103
Prisoners of Ritual: An Odyssey into Female Genital Circumcision in Africa (Lightfoot-Klein), 63–64

Program for Appropriate Technology in Health (PATH), 104–5
Prohibition of Female Genital Mutilation Act, 141
pseudo-hermaphroditism, 129
psychosocial emergency, 130
psychotherapy, 134, 137

racism, 58
Randolph, Judson, 132
Ras-Work, Berhane, 107
reconstructive surgery, 127, 129, 131
relativism, 56–57, 71
Report on Human Rights in Nigeria (U.S. State Department), 75
representations: of female genital surgeries, 36–40
Rites (film), 107
Roots (film), 60
Rosenthal, A. M., 36, 62, 67

Saadawi, Nawal El, 33
Sabaot (people), 22, 27–29, 31
Sacramento Bee, 78
Sande (women's society), 11
Sanderson, Lillian, 65
San Francisco Chronicle, 78
Sankofa (film), 60
sati (widow-burning), 38
Saurel, Renee, 83n17
Sawyer, Forrest, 35
Schlussel, Richard, 139
Schroeder, Pat, 58, 86n45, 141
Schwab, Peter, 69
science, 143
Scotland, Church of, 40
Sebei (people), 26–27, 29
Secret and Sacred (video), 105
Senegal, 65, 66, 78, 80, 105–6
sex: assignment, 131, 137; determination, 128, 133; differences, 130
sexual consequences, 25, 28
sexual control, 27, 29–31
sexual dysfunction, 134
"Sexual Surgeries in Late Nineteenth Century America" (Barker-Benfield), 94
Sierra Leone, 11, 73
Slack, Alison, 69, 70
slavery, 59–60
Smith, Robyn Cerny, 69–71, 93, 95, 97
social construction of gender, 128

Social Darwinism, 56, 66
Somalia, 57
Spreitzer, Heike, 142
Stamp, Patricia, 89
Steinem, Gloria, 32–33, 142, 144
stigma, 130
Strathern, Marilyn, 18
structural functionalism, 56–57
Sudan, 27–29, 56–57
suicide, 134
sunna (medical procedure), 20, 38
Sunni schools of law, 100–101
surgery: reconstructive, 132
symbolism, 45

Tarzan, the Ape Man (film), 59
Thiam, Awa, 60, 65, 81
the three Rs, 5, 73
Time, 17
Togo, 17, 19, 35–36, 67
Tolstan (breaking through) Program, 106, 108–9
torture (female genital), 19, 20, 37, 119
Toubia, Nahid, 29, 60, 81n2
transgender political movement, 127, 135
tribe: use of term, 59, 72–73
"true sex," 129–31
Turner's Syndrome Society, 137–38
Turner, Victor, 26, 27, 95

Uganda, 26
United Nations: Convention on the Elimination of All Forms of Discrimination against Women, 96; Decade for Women, 33; World Conference on Women (Beijing), 96, 119; World Conference on Women (Copenhagen), 33, 82n2; World Conference on Women (Nairobi), 64, 67
United States, 54, 76–81, 86n49; genital cutting in, 126, 127; media in, 59–81, 126

Van Gennep, Arnold, 26
veiling, 38, 41, 90
Verdier, Raymond, 72
Victorian feminists, 29, 42
Vienna Declaration and Programme of Action, 96
violence against women, 75–77
virginity, 27
Vogue, 58

Walker, Alice, 6, 15, 17, 33, 34, 35, 38, 43, 44, 64–65, 83n21, 87–89, 90–93, 103, 107, 162–63, 165–66, 172–73, 192, 199, 200
Walley, Christine, 62, 64, 69
Walt, Vivienne, 78
Wambui Otieno case, 41–42
Warrior Marks (Walker and Parmar), 17, 33, 35, 43, 64–66, 88, 93
Warsame, Aamina, 60
Washington Post, 17, 67, 78
Weil-Curiel, Linda, 35
Welsh, Stephanie, 68, 85n45
Western feminism, 145–46
Western images of clitoridectomy, 142–43
Western medical community, 146
West: genital surgeries in, 33
Wilkins, Lawson, 129
Winter, Bronwyn, 34
Women's Caucus African Studies Association, 2, 5, 6, 36
Women's Caucus Position Paper, 2, 5, 6, 36
Women's International Network News, 2, 90
women's studies, 57
World Health Organization Technical Report, 96
world traveling, 108

Young, Hugh Hampton, 129

The University of Illinois Press
is a founding member of the
Association of American University Presses.

Composed in 10.5/13 Adobe Minion
by Celia Shapland
for the University of Illinois Press
Manufactured by Thomson-Shore, Inc.

University of Illinois Press
1325 South Oak Street
Champaign, IL 61820-6903
www.press.uillinois.edu